Solution-Focused Therapy

Brief Therapies Series

Series Editor: Stephen Palmer
Associate Editor: Gladeana McMahon

Focusing on brief and time-limited therapies, this series of books is aimed at students, beginning and experienced counsellors, therapists and other members of the helping professions who need to know more about working with the specific skills, theories and practices involved in this demanding but vital area of their work.

Books in the series:
Solution-Focused Therapy
Bill O'Connell

A Psychodynamic Approach to Brief
Counselling and Psychotherapy
Gertrud Mander

Brief Cognitive Behaviour Therapy
Berni Curwen, Stephen Palmer and Peter Ruddell

Solution-Focused Groupwork
John Sharry

Brief NLP Therapy
Ian McDermott and Wendy Jogo

Transactional Analysis Approaches to Brief Therapy
Keith Tudor

Handbook of
Solution-Focused Therapy

edited by
Bill O'Connell
and
Stephen Palmer

Los Angeles | London | New Delhi
Singapore | Washington DC

For Mum and Dad, for all they taught me, and for my sister Maureen, and brothers Maurice and Bob, with love and thanks.

Bill O'Connell

For Kate, Kevin and their future. All my love.

Stephen Palmer

Contents

The Editors   ix

The Contributors   xi

Acknowledgements   xv

1   Introduction to the Solution-Focused Approach   1
    Bill O'Connell

2   Research in Solution-Focused Brief Therapy   12
    Alasdair J. Macdonald

3   Solution-Focused Groupwork   25
    Pat Hoskisson

4   Solution-Focused Practice with Families   38
    Guy Shennan

5   Solution-Focused Parent Training   48
    John Sharry

6   Solution-Focused Couples Therapy   61
    Chris Iveson

7   Solution-Focused Therapy and Mental Health   74
    Tom Dodd

8   The Solution-Focused Approach in Higher Education   84
    Nigel White

9   Solution-Focused Therapy in Schools   95
    Harvey Ratner

10 Solution-Focused Practice in Social Work   106
    John Wheeler

11 Using Solution-Focused Therapy with Women   118
    Jane Lethem

12   A Solution-Focused Approach to Sexual Trauma   129
     Melissa Darmody

13   Solution-Focused Therapy and Substance Misuse   138
     Paul Hanton

14   A Solution-Focused Approach to 'Psychosis'   146
     Dave Hawkes

15   Solution-Focused Reflecting Teams   156
     Harry Norman

16   The Future for SFT   168
     Bill O'Connell

Appendix One: Solution-Focused Agencies   173

Index   174

The Editors

Bill O'Connell is a Senior Lecturer in Counselling at the University of Birmingham where he is a tutor on the MA in Solution-Focused Brief Therapy. He is also a Director of Focus on Solutions, a training and consultancy agency specialising in the solution-focused approach. He has been a counsellor, trainer and supervisor for over twenty years and is a Registered Counsellor and Fellow of the British Association for Counselling and Psychotherapy. He has trained many hundreds of people in the solution-focused approach. He has contributed chapters on solution-focused therapy to *Introduction to Counselling and Psychotherapy* (Sage, 2000) and *Counselling – the BACP Reader* (Sage, 2001), as well as articles on the approach. He is the author of *Solution-Focused Therapy* (Sage, 1998) and *Solution-Focused Stress Counselling* (Continuum, 2001).

Professor Stephen Palmer is Director of the Centre for Stress Management, London and the Centre for Coaching, London. He is Honorary Professor of Psychology at City University, and Visiting Professor of Work Based Learning and Stress Management at the National Centre for Work Based Learning Partnerships, Middlesex University. He is Honorary President of the Association for Coaching, Honorary Vice-President and Fellow of both the Institute of Health Promotion and Education and the International Stress Management Association (UK) and Chair of the Association for Rational Emotive Behaviour Therapy. He is a Fellow of the British Association for Counselling and Psychotherapy. He has written or edited over 25 books and at least 100 articles and chapters for books. He edits a number of book series including Stress Counselling (Continuum) and Brief Therapies (Sage). He is Editor of the *International Journal of Health Promotion and Education*, Co-editor of the *Rational Emotive Behaviour Therapist*, and Associate Editor of *Psychology and Psychotherapy: theory, research and practice*. He is a chartered psychologist (counselling and health) and a UKCP-registered psychotherapist (CBT and REBT). In May 2000 he received the Annual Counselling Psychology Award from the British Psychological Society, Division of Counselling Psychology, for his 'outstanding professional and scientific contribution to counselling psychology in Britain'. He is a regular broadcaster.

The Contributors

Dr Melissa Darmody formerly worked at a rape crisis centre in Dublin. She now works full time in private practice. She is a member of the Dublin Brief Therapy Group. She co-authored *Becoming a Solution Detective: a strengths-based guide to brief therapy* (BT Press, 2002).

Tom Dodd has been a registered mental health nurse since 1991 and has experience of developing and delivering assertive outreach services in the statutory and non-statutory sectors. He is editorial adviser and reviewer for *Mental Health Practice* and is the Chairman and clinical supervisor to the REST team, a rural non-statutory mental health service provider in the West Midlands. He is the Deputy Director of Programmes at the National Institute for Mental Health in England. He has spoken extensively in this country and abroad on issues related to Assertive Outreach and severe mental illness.

Paul Hanton has worked in drug and alcohol services in London and South Yorkshire for the last eleven years and is currently the Joint Commissioning Manager for Substance Misuse Treatment across health and social care in Barnsley, South Yorkshire. He is in his research year of the MA in SFT at Birmingham University. Paul has been a member of DrugScope Young People's Good Practice Unit Advisory Group, and chaired the Northern Young People's Drug Workers' Forum.

Dave Hawkes trained as a registered mental nurse and went on to complete training in systemic therapy at the Kensington Consultation Centre in London. He trained in Milwaukee, USA in 1992 with Steve de Shazer. On his return he adapted the model to an adult mental health caseload and was awarded the Queens' Nursing Institute Award in 1993 for his solution-focused work in the NHS. He is the primary author of *Solution Focused Therapy: a handbook for health care professionals* (Butterworth-Heinemann, 1998). He completed his MA in Mental Health in 2000 and is a lectuer in Mental Health at Anglia Polytechnic University.

Pat Hoskisson is a counsellor in primary care with extensive experience of running groups in mental health settings. She started running solution-focused groups while working as part of a community mental health team. Now, in addition to group work and one-to-one counselling, she is involved with training other mental health workers in the solution-focused approach.

Chris Iveson is a founder member of the Brief Therapy Practice and has used the solution-focused approach extensively in his work with couples. He is a member of the Institute of Family Therapy and the author of *Whose Life? Working with Older People* (2001) and co-author of *Problem to Solution* (1999). Both are published by BT Press.

Jane Lethem is a member of the Brief Therapy Practice in London and author of *Moved to Tears, Moved to Action: solution focused brief therapy with women and children* (BT Press, 1994). She works as a consultant clinical psychologist at Parkside Clinic in London.

Dr Alasdair Macdonald is an honorary consultant psychiatrist. He is a leading member of the Research Group of the European Brief Therapy Association. He has published widely, including papers in solution-focused therapy. He currently works as a freelance trainer and management consultant in the solution-focused model.

Harry Norman has provided intensive skill-building courses in solution-focused brief therapy and solutions coaching at work for organisations such as Bristol University, National Health Trusts and Relate. He has also applied solution-focused thinking to team building and development and to action-learning sets in mental health and business. He has a degree in applied psychology, is a UKCP-accredited psychotherapist and has advanced certification in NLP. He has had articles published in *Rapport, NLP World* and *Context*.

Harvey Ratner is a founder member of the Brief Therapy Practice in London. In addition to his training, supervision and therapy activities, he is a counsellor in a secondary school. He has written several articles and chapters on solution-focused brief therapy, and is co-author of *Problem to Solution* (BT Press, 1999). He is a qualified family therapist and is registered with UKCP.

Dr John Sharry is a principal social worker based in the Department of Child and Family Psychiatry at the Mater Misericordiae Hospital in Dublin. He is also a member of the Dublin Brief Therapy Group which organises conferences and provides training in brief therapy models. He is the author of *Solution-Focused Groupwork* (2001) published by Sage and co-author of *Becoming a Solution Detective: a strengths-based guide to brief therapy* (2002) published by BT Press.

Guy Shennan is a UK social worker and freelance trainer/consultant in solution-focused practice. He first started using a solution-focused approach whilst doing statutory social work with children and families. Having set up and run an early intervention service for families within a child welfare charity for the past four years, Guy has recently returned to statutory social work. He has also written about involving service users in the assessment of student social workers, and systemic practice in child protection.

John Wheeler is a social worker with twenty years' experience of working with children and families in a child mental health setting. He has an MA in family therapy, an Advanced Award in Social Work and is a UKCP-registered systemic psychotherapist, and has published a number of articles on solution-focused therapy. He has provided training in the approach to many professional groups over the past seven years.

Nigel White has worked as a counsellor in higher education and in general practice for over ten years. He is a trained cognitive analytic therapist and uses solution-focused therapy with 90 per cent of his clients.

Acknowledgements

As ever, my biggest thanks go to my family for their unstinting encouragement and support. In particular I would like to thank my wife Moira who, despite a very difficult two years as she bravely fought the consequences of an accident, has always been there to keep me going with good ideas, delicious meals, cups of tea and lots of love! Thank you also to my daughters Donnamarie, Joanne and Katrina who always make me feel proud to be an author and their Dad. Thanks to Cynthia and John for their generosity and kindness. Many thanks to all my colleagues at Birmingham University Selly Oak, and especially to Janet for putting up with me over the past eight years (happy retirement, Janet!), to Maureen for her support and humour, to Maggie for her countless kindnesses over the years and to Marian for her help with the manuscript. Thanks to Gerry for his friendship and conversations about books, spirituality and golf. Thanks are due to Alison Poyner of Sage, for her patience in waiting for this manuscript. I am also indebted to my co-editor Stephen Palmer for encouraging me to write about solution-focused work. Finally, thank you to the many students, clients and workshop participants over the years for all they have taught me about life and therapy.

Bill O'Connell

I would like to say how rewarding it has been working on the *Handbook of Solution-Focused Therapy* (SFT). It has been an excellent continuing professional development programme, reading and editing this book. Thanks to all our authors for their support on this project. I never realised when I met Bill O'Connell six years ago that we would end up editing the UK's first SFT handbook. Thanks Bill.

Stephen Palmer

1

Introduction to the Solution-Focused Approach

Bill O'Connell

This book describes how a wide range of professionals in many different settings use a solution-focused approach to their work. They report that the approach energises and motivates them as much as it does their clients. For some it saved them from burnout.

The client groups they work with include:

- patients with psychotic symptoms;
- families subject to child abuse investigations;
- young people abusing drugs and alcohol;
- women suffering from the consequences of sexual assaults and rape;
- parents learning to care for their children;
- couples in conflict;
- pupils in trouble in schools.

Many of the contributors describe how, to their surprise, clients who had been written off by the system moved forward in their lives, once there was a shift from problem exploration to solution construction. Clients and helpers found renewed hope and optimism when they held conversations about strengths, qualities, transferable solutions and preferences for the future. Faced with evidence that their work was making a difference, helpers experienced a new sense of purpose and value.

This chapter describes the key ideas of a relatively new model for helping people known as the solution-focused approach. It is not just a way of doing therapy. The ideas, attitudes, values and interventions can be adapted to a wide range of settings and client groups. In recent times I personally have taught the method to groups as diverse as careers officers; parent support helpers; drug workers; teaching assistants and trade union shop stewards. Anyone who uses interpersonal skills to help their 'clients' to solve problems will find solution-focused interventions useful additions to their repertoire. In the light of this, I use the term 'helpers' in this chapter as it encompasses a range of people who 'help others'.

Origins

There is some disagreement over the origins of the solution-focused approach. There is always a history to ideas and it is not always possible or even desirable to identify a single founder. Historical influences certainly include the work of Alfred Adler, Milton Erickson, John Weakland and his colleagues at the Mental Research Institute in California. Key developers of the method include Bill O'Hanlon, Steve de Shazer and Insoo Kim Berg. De Shazer and his colleagues (1986) observed that their clients were able to make changes in their lives following extended conversations with the therapist about their preferred futures. These conversations began to outweigh any attention to discussion about the problems. As they explored solutions there was apparently less and less need to understand the causes of the problem itself. They discovered that solutions could be evoked from clients by the use of future-oriented questions. This led them to develop standard interventions to be used whatever the nature of the problem. These included: finding exceptions to the problem; getting the client to 'do something different'; the use of scaling; the miracle question; the taking of one small step and the giving of therapeutic compliments.

Definition

> The Solution Focused approach builds upon clients' resources. It aims to help clients achieve their preferred outcomes by evoking and co-constructing solutions to their problems. (O'Connell, 2001, p. 1)

The helper attends to clients' favoured futures rather than to their problem-laden histories. Instead of analysing problems they co-construct solutions. They set out to clarify what the clients want to happen in their lives and to seek strategies to bring this about. The solution-focused emphasis is on what the clients are doing that is right; on what works; on what the past has taught them; on their strengths and on what they can already do. Although the approach is called 'solution focused' this does not imply that there is a solution to every problem in life, but it does suggest that there are ways in which clients can be empowered to manage their problems better. Berg and De Jong (1986) describe solutions as 'changes in perceptions, patterns of interacting and living, and meanings that are constructed within the client's frame of references' (p. 377).

There is a powerful sense of a close and collaborative working partnership in which the helper conveys respect to a competent, resourceful problem solver. It seeks to help clients to solve problems for themselves, but not by themselves. It requires a more positive and egalitarian stance from the helper than the conventional 'expert' position. 'Expertism' is often claimed at the expense of the client's expertise. One of the reported benefits of a more respectful working relationship is that practitioners value and like their clients more! They see the client as a problem solver rather than as someone who is 'damaged', 'ill', 'inadequate' or 'dysfunctional'.

Solution-focused helpers are curious about the theories or explanations clients hold about their problems. Some of these explanations can compound the problem, particularly those which define the problem as:

- stable – 'You won't change me, that's the way I am.'
- permanent – 'I've always been like this.'
- internal – 'I've a depressive personality.'
- global – 'I'm like this with everyone.' (McLellan-Buchanan and Seligman, 1995)

Client explanations can be part of the problem or part of the solution. When they are part of the problem they may need to be examined or deconstructed in ways which make them less of a force against change. For example, clients who believe their problems are entirely due to chemical imbalances or genetic inheritance are less likely to see themselves as having the power to change. Some clients need help to find evidence to contradict the oppressive theory they hold about themselves. To do this they need to be open to new learning about themselves. As clients begin to focus more on 'what works' or what helps them, they can begin to discard unhelpful attitudes and behaviours. Their problems occupy less space as they become more interested in their solutions. With some clients, the helper hardly needs to discuss the problems because the client quickly engages in solution talk. But other clients need time to explore problems 'in depth' before feeling able to engage in solution talk. The helper needs to respect this and allow the client therapeutic space, otherwise the alliance will collapse. As the helper listens attentively, he or she encourages the client to find a rationale for the problems that make change more attainable. These tend to be explanations that imply that the problem is:

- unstable – 'So you want to get back to the way you used to be.'
- occasion-specific – 'You feel anxious in certain situations.'
- external – 'Depression gets hold of you sometimes and it's hard to fight it off.'
- transient – 'So it lasts for about a day and then somehow it passes.'

Clients may hold negative and destructive ideas about their problems as a result of the socialisation they have experienced at the hands of professionals. Professional diagnosis and assessment can contribute towards a definition of 'the problem' that makes it more difficult to solve. An example of this is the *Diagnostic Manual* used in the USA. White and Epston (1990, p. 58), the narrative therapists, juxtapose change-oriented descriptions with many of the diagnostic categories employed. For example:

Diagnostic Manual	v.	Reframe
Avoidant Personality Disorder		Likes to be alone
Dissociative Disorder		Uses a left-over coping skill
Bipolar Disorder		Overly moody

Reframing these heavy medical terms makes the problem more solvable. The obsession with pathological labels leads to a dismissal of the strengths of clients and their unique 'problem' experiences. In a strong consumer culture however, the public is less willing to accept uncritically the 'world view' propagated by professionals, many of whom are overworked, tired and under-resourced.

Professionals, in turn, are slowly beginning to realise that the client or the patient may actually have something worthwhile to contribute to the healing or recovery process. Many professionals are required to carry out assessments which are so weighted towards problems and deficits that they lose sight of the fact that everyone is a problem solver just from the fact that they have survived the numerous challenges life has thrown at them!

Helpers are also curious about their clients' ideas on how change does or will take place. Respecting the client's view about change increases the potential for co-operation. Clients' attitudes towards their future and their capacity to influence their destiny will vary according to cultures and individual life experiences. Most people are more interested in their future than in their past. One of the strengths of the solution-focused approach is the way the helper stays respectfully close to what the client wants. The helper stimulates clients to develop powerful visualisations of their desired future and invites them to experience aspects of it. Clients are facilitated to talk their way into a better future. Throughout the process the worker needs to be aware of his or her own personal beliefs, biases and prejudices in order to respect the client's frame of reference.

To respect and privilege the client's own ideas (local knowledge) contrasts with theories of helping which see the helper as the expert who generates the only valid theory (universal knowledge). Local knowledge is often more useful and accessible than universal knowledge. When I play my tee shot at the fifth hole on my local golf course, I know I need to aim twelve yards to the right of the flag at the grassy bank which gathers the ball and rolls it down to the flag at the right speed. If I play a visitor to the course, even if he or she is a better golfer (not too difficult to find in my case), I have a significant advantage. No textbook knowledge gives that kind of edge! Similarly clients have access to knowledge about themselves and their social environment that no helpers could have, no matter how skilled they were. Yet many professionals ignore or dismiss clients' ideas, expecting them to be irrelevant or unhelpful. Solution-focused helpers believe that clients have a repertoire of personal stories about themselves which are potentially more powerful and helpful than those advanced by 'experts'. Labels bestowed by other professions are treated with caution and even scepticism.

Alternative stories about clients' strengths, qualities, solutions and unique strategies have often gone unheard and invalidated because of their source. In the face of professional ignorance and contempt clients can learn to doubt their own wisdom. The solution-focused position is that clients already have a 'shadow' or alternative story about themselves which foregrounds times when they overcame their difficulties; times when they demonstrated courage, perseverance, imagination, generosity, self-discipline and many other qualities. These stories are themselves embryonic solutions. They embody the knowledge and skills clients need to overcome their difficulties. They portray a different person from the one who feels inadequate, pathetic, helpless and blamed.

Stories need to fit well enough for clients to recognise themselves. If the new story co-authored between the client and the helper is too fanciful or obscure, the client will reject it and possibly the helper as well. This should not happen if the client is the principal author.

Language

Therapists and others using therapeutic skills only have language as an instrument of change. How they shape verbal interactions influences how clients perceive their situation. In most types of therapy the worker adopts a structuralist view of language which sees meaning 'behind' the words the client uses. The task of the therapist is to dig deep behind the presenting issues to locate the 'real' cause of the person's problem. The solution-focused approach takes a poststructuralist position which emphasises that versions of the 'truth' about people are not objective discoveries, but are socially negotiated between people, within the parameters currently in place in any given culture. As Hawkes et al. (1998) state, 'Meaning can be decided upon by those present according to fit and usefulness rather than interpretation or "facts"' (p. 117). Diagnostic labels such as depression, anorexia or substance misuse are constructed by the professionals who control the language territory. The solution-focused approach challenges this power by deliberately using language to:

- obtain descriptions of people's unique experiences rather than definitive formulations of them;
- suspend assumptions about the client;
- elicit the choices clients have in how they frame their situation;
- talk about the problem as in a constant state of change;
- affirm the unspoken or understated story about exceptions and competence;
- amplify solution talk;
- validate the expertise of the client;
- illuminate the client's preferred future.

Solution-focused helpers believe in minimal intervention in clients' lives. They see the therapeutic task as raising clients' awareness of the constructive solutions already in their lives and to help them find ways to expand upon them. In short, helpers trust clients as they tread lightly through their lives, always being aware that they are guests in someone else's private space.

In order to maintain focus the helper has a range of techniques which are employed at a pace that fits the client. These form the basic structure of a session (see Figure 1.1).

Interventions

In this section I will describe the key solution-focused interventions. These are used in a creative and client-centred way. This is not therapy by numbers, but a skilled crafting in which the sequence and mix of interventions will vary. If the

> Problem-free talk
>
> Pre-session change
>
> Goal setting
>
> Exception seeking
>
> Competence seeking
>
> The miracle question
>
> Scaling
>
> Between-session work

Figure 1.1   *Structure of a session*

helper is skilful he or she will be flexible to the needs of the client and be willing to adapt the model to fit the situation.

Techniques are inseparable from the relationship between helper and client. Technical competence is secondary to the quality of 'presence for' that the client experiences from the worker. The helper empathically acknowledges the concerns and feelings of the client and develops rapport through a warm, positive, accepting relationship in which the client can feel safe, understood and respected. This experience is in itself potentially transforming.

Problem-free talk
In a sense most of a solution-focused session consists of problem-free talk, but there are also times, usually at the beginning of a session, when the helper engages the client in a discussion completely unrelated to the problem. They may briefly explore the client's preferred leisure pursuits for example. Problem-free talk conveys the message that there is more to this person than the problem and can also reveal potentially transferable strategies, beliefs, values and skills.

Pre-session change
There is a core solution-focused belief that clients are already engaged in constructive action when they seek help. Some of these actions are positively helpful and others are preventing the situation from getting worse. Where practicable, clients are asked when they make an appointment to notice any changes that take place between then and the first session. Where that is not possible, the helper in the first session listens for evidence of what the client has already done that works for him or her. This could be a behaviour or an attitude or an emotion. The client gets instant (but not hyped-up) credit from the worker for their prior experience and learning, setting the tone for what is to follow. Any compliments need to be

delivered in a non-patronising manner. By acknowledging pre-session change. the helper underlines that the client, not the helper, is the agent for change.

- How will you know that coming here has been worthwhile for you?
- What are your best hopes for this session?
- How long do you think it will take before things get better?
- How do you think coming here might help you?
- How will you know when things are getting better?
- What will be the first sign for you?
- What is your main concern?
- Where do you want to start?
- If you were able to make some changes soon, which would be most helpful to you?

Figure 1.2   *Negotiating the client's agenda*

Goal setting

Figure 1.2 shows how the focus is clearly on the client's preferred outcomes. The questions emphasise the direction and purpose of the work. It is entirely at the service of the client. It is designed to help them get to where they want to go. The questions imply that this is a joint enterprise and that both parties have a distinct contribution to make. The language chosen reinforces the message that clients have choices and that they have the power to shape their future.

As the work progresses, continuity with the client's agenda is maintained through a process of regular evaluation and review.

Exception seeking

The client is likely to bring an account of how 'the problem' is affecting his or her life. While listening and acknowledging the difficulties, the solution-focused helper listens for times when the problem is not present, or is being managed better. This includes searching for transferable solutions from other parts of the client's life or past. There are always exceptions waiting to be found. If clients experience difficulties 40 per cent of the time then it follows they are problem free for 60 per cent of the time! What is happening during those times? What are they doing that is helpful? How did they do it? Could they do it again?

Competence seeking

Helpers encourage clients to find and acknowledge their own resources, strengths and qualities. Since clients are often blamed, criticised and judged, their sense of competence is often buried. They have lost confidence in themselves and forgotten what they do well. The solution-focused philosophy is to 'light a candle, instead of cursing the darkness'. So the worker is always looking for opportunities to feed back to clients what they are doing right. The use of 'how' questions invites. clients to think about what it took for them to carry out a constructive action.

- How did you manage to do that?
- How did you know it was a good idea to try that?
- How did you know it was a good time to do that?
- How did you learn that?
- How did you start?
- How did you keep that going?

'How' questions are usually a lot more productive than 'why' questions. The latter invite clients to justify their behaviour often to the 'expert', whereas 'how' questions invite conversations about a client's constructive strategies. They imply credit and recognition for their strengths.

Following on from the above questions the helper may ask questions such as these.

- What did you learn from that?
- What does that say about you?
- Has that changed your opinion about yourself?
- Were you surprised you did that?
- What did other people think about that?

The miracle question

The miracle question is a central intervention in the solution-focused repertoire. It helps clients to identify existing solutions and resources and to elicit realistic goals for themselves. It invites clients to use their imagination to describe in some detail what their lives will be like when the problem no longer dominates or controls it.

The question (although he maintains he never asks it the same way!) was designed by Steve de Shazer (1988). The standard version is:

> Imagine when you go to sleep one night, a miracle happens and the problems we've been talking about disappear. As you were asleep, you did not know that a miracle had happened. When you wake up what will be the first signs for you that a miracle has happened?

This imaginary format helps the client to overcome negative thinking. It can be adapted in different ways to suit clients. For those who want to avoid the word 'miracle', it can be asked as: 'You come back from holiday and find that the situation has changed for the better, what will be the first signs for you that something amazing has happened?' The worker helps the client to develop answers to the miracle question by active listening, prompting, empathising and questioning for more and more descriptions of life after the miracle. If it is effective, exceptions (small miracles), will be unearthed and the client will also come to realise that he or she does not need to wait for a miracle for some of these changes to come about. The miracle question is not a fantasy question about a perfect day or a perfect life. It is a 'wonderful' (Hanton, 2002) question which bypasses problem talk and enables the person to describe the kind of life they want to lead. In my experience, it is a remarkably effective intervention. Many clients make some part of the miracle happen in the ensuing weeks.

Scaling

Scaling can be used at any point in a session, but often supplements the miracle question. Normally the helper uses a scale of zero to ten, with ten representing 'no problem' and zero representing the worst the problem has been, or perhaps how the client felt before contacting the helper. The purpose of scaling is to help clients set small identifiable goals; measure progress and establish priorities for action. Scaling questions can also assess client motivation and confidence. Scaling is a practical tool which a client can use between sessions. The use of numbers is purely arbitrary: only the client knows what they really mean. It is amazing how much one can achieve using this simple technique. It fits clients who find talking difficult. It contains the problem and gives clients a sense of ownership and control. It is easy to practise between sessions.

Between-session work

Towards the end of each session, the helper will have arranged with the client to take a short break to think about what has been said in the session. Traditionally, this break was an opportunity for the helper to compose 'the message' – a form of feedback to the clients which complimented them on what they were doing that was helpful, followed by an agreed task for them to do before the next session. In some settings helpers actually leave the room for a few minutes to do this, but where that is not feasible a short pause is needed for the helper to consult his or her notes and compose a short message for the client.

The feedback consists of:

- a compliment or compliments about how the client has participated in the session today and the helper's feelings about that;
- a short summary of what the client is already doing that is helpful;
- a bridging statement linking the client's actions with the stated goal or goals;
- a discussion about what the client might be considering doing in the next week or two in terms of dealing with the problem. Any suggestion made by the helper is linked clearly to what the client has already disclosed. It is most common to encourage the client to

  (a) keep doing what is working
  (b) stop doing what isn't working
  (c) do something different.

Where clients have struggled to answer questions, they might be given a 'notice task' where they look out for particular events in their lives. For example – times when they handled the problem better; times when someone did something they liked or times when they achieved something they wanted. This perceptual shift will hopefully lead to action at a later stage.

The helper is not a task giver who knows what the client should do. Clients should be fully involved in the feedback process. Their summaries of what was helpful and what they might do next are more important than those of the worker.

Guidelines

There are a number of axioms which act as useful guidelines for the worker.

If it isn't broken don't fix it
The model is careful to detach the person from the problem. The thinking behind this is that there is a lot more to the person than the 'problem'. There are areas of their lives that do not need to change, which are best left as they are. Unlike some therapies, the solution-focused way is not to look for 'underlying' issues or see the presenting problem as only the tip of the iceberg. The helper does not go in search of problems.

He or she works to the client's stated agenda – which may of course change in the course of the work.

Small change can lead to bigger changes
Change is inevitable. It is not possible to put life on hold. Everything is in a state of flux. If we change some aspect of our life then it is likely to have repercussions on other parts of our eco-system. Big problems do not always require big solutions. There is rarely one solution to a problem. When enough small pieces of the solution jigsaw are in place, then the client will report that the problem has less force, that he or she is managing it better. The experience of making changes can restore the person's sense of agency and choice and make further changes likely.

If it's working keep doing it
There is a basic assumption that clients have constructive strategies in their repertoire. Even in the most problematic situation, the client is doing some things 'right', although not enough of them to solve the problem. The helper encourages the client to 'keep doing what works for you'. Recognition of helpful strategies builds confidence in clients and prepares them for other more challenging new behaviour.

If it's not working stop doing it
The helper encourages clients to do something different to break the perceived cycle of failure. If clients can identify 'failed solutions' then abandoning them creates a therapeutic space for successful solutions to emerge. What might appear as a solution to begin with, for example using alcohol to relieve stress and tension, can become a failed solution when it gets out of control. Recognising when a behaviour has moved from a solution to become part of the problem is a useful place to start. The occasion when the client stops doing what isn't working is an important experiential learning event. Repeating solutions we know do not work may be a human thing to do, but it is not a very clever one.

Keep therapy as simple as possible
There is a danger that the beliefs of the helper, particularly if they demand a search for hidden explanations and unconscious factors, will complicate and

prolong the relationship. Most practitioners' training has encouraged them to focus on and expand problem talk. This can easily lead to an over-elaboration of the problem to the exclusion of solution talk.

Summary

This chapter has introduced the reader to some of the key ideas in solution-focused work. It is a future-oriented, competence-based, strategic-focused approach which shows great respect and trust for the clients' own strengths and strategies. It seeks to work within the client's frame of reference and co-operate in the achievement of the client's goals.

References

Berg, I.K. and De Jong, P. (1986) Solution building conversations: co-constructing a sense of competence with clients. *Families in Society: The Journal of Contemporary Human Services*, June, pp. 376–391.

de Shazer, S. (1988) *Clues: investigating solutions in brief therapy*. New York: W.W. Norton.

de Shazer, S., Berg, I.K., Lipchik, E., Nunnaly, E., Molnar, A., Gingerich, W. and Weiner-Davis, M. (1986) Brief Therapy: focused solution development. *Family Process*, 25, pp. 207–221.

Hanton, P. (2002) Personal communication.

Hawkes, D., Marsh, T.I. and Wilgosh, R. (1998) *Solution Focused Therapy: a handbook for health care professionals*. Oxford: Butterworth-Heinemann.

McLellan-Buchanan, G. and Seligman, M.E.P. (eds) (1995), *Explanatory Style*. Hillsdale, NJ: Lawrence Erlbaum Associates.

O'Connell, B. (2001) *Solution-Focused Stress Counselling*. London: Continuum.

White, M. and Epston, D. (1990) *Narrative Means to Therapeutic Ends*. New York: W.W. Norton.

2

Research in Solution-Focused Brief Therapy

Alasdair J. Macdonald

This chapter will provide an overview of published research into solution-focused brief therapy (SFBT), with discussion of key research issues and comments on methodology. Future lines of enquiry are considered. The author is a consultant psychiatrist in the United Kingdom who has published on outcomes in SFBT and in psychodynamic psychotherapy.

From the outset the development of solution-focused brief therapy by the Milwaukee team was research-based, in the sense of being driven by feedback from clients as to which elements of therapy were effective in increasing goal attainment. This differs from many styles of therapy in which therapy methods have been derived from theoretical postulates about human behaviour and how to influence it. However, scientific validation of any therapy must rely on formal evaluation.

One problem is to decide which evaluation studies should be included. For outcome studies my own criteria are that they should have been published in a durable form following peer review and that they should include some form of post-therapy follow-up data. Many psychotherapy studies record outcomes at the end of therapy, at which time there may be 'honeymoon effects' for both therapist and client. Also, unless their organisation insists, few therapists will discharge a client at a time when things are going badly. At the time of writing there are over 400 published documents on SFBT, of which 32 fit my criteria for outcome studies. Nine of these are comparison studies.

Eisengart and Gingerich (1999) choose different criteria. For them, outcome studies must formally reference solution-focused brief therapy in the text and include some form of comparison. However, they will accept case-control studies in which there is no separate comparison population and studies in which outcome is measured at the time of discharge from therapy. They do not see peer review as a necessary condition for inclusion and they include studies such as doctoral dissertations which are not easily accessible to the general reader. Using these criteria they identify 15 outcome studies. Eleven of these studies are also on the Macdonald list. Eight comparison studies are in both lists.

SFBT process research

Detailed information is now available for most major forms of psychotherapy. Whatever model is studied, it has been identified that central issues for effective therapy include client–therapist collaboration in a therapeutic alliance with an emphasis on clear goals. The techniques used only account for 15 per cent of the effects, the remainder being external and client factors 40 per cent, therapeutic relationship 30 per cent and hope/placebo factors 15 per cent (Asay and Lambert, 1999). The therapist must keep the focus on life problems and core relationships. A clear model of therapy technique and the existence of manuals for therapy both improve outcomes, perhaps through effects on the therapist rather than the client. Post-session interviewing (see below) often suggests that clients are not aware of technical aspects of therapy which the therapist regards as central. Clients expect therapy to be brief. The research material leading to these conclusions is well reviewed in Garfield and Bergin (1994) and Hubble, Duncan and Miller (1999). SFBT fits these criteria.

McKeel has updated his 1996 publication about process research on his website (1999). He concludes that solution-focused talk increases changes and the completing of therapy. Pre-treatment changes are common and premature termination is less common if the therapists talk about the pre-treatment changes (Allgood et al., 1995; Johnson et al., 1998). The miracle question leads to goal setting and optimistic attitudes. Exceptions and scaling questions are often used and lead to more talk on these topics. Clients value the SFBT emphasis on strengths, compliments and 'what works' and the atmosphere of the therapy session (Metcalf et al., 1996).

McKeel agrees that the SFBT model must be confirmed as having been followed appropriately during the therapy. He asks if only comparison studies should be acceptable as outcome research? If so, are no-treatment comparison groups necessary, valid or ethical? He proposes 'dismantling' studies in which one or more elements of therapy are different between the groups studied, or where therapist characteristics are different between the groups. The outcome measures will thus identify features which are necessary or sufficient for treatment success. Another option is to study two groups both of which receive routine treatment for their condition but where one group receives SFBT in addition. He comments that multiple measures are important in presenting SFBT to various potential consumers. Therapists may be convinced by certain measures while third-party payers, relatives or clients themselves may value different measures. Objective measures are acceptable to the scientific community and are helpful in comparing different treatment approaches.

McKeel's colleagues at Bowie Child and Family Services routinely ask clients before each session: What was useful about your last session? What changes have you made since? What can you and the therapist do today to help towards your goals? How can therapy better meet your needs? In the long term they intend to analyse responses to these questions to identify categories which will lead to a more precise focus for therapy and therapists.

The use of a similar post-therapy enquiry is reported in Shilts, Rambo and Hernandez (1997). They found the clients' replies useful and now regard this post-therapy enquiry as part of their therapy practice, because they can modify subsequent sessions in the light of the clients' reactions.

The Lonnen team in Sweden hired a researcher from another style of brief therapy to interview clients after therapy was completed. The responses were supportive of the SFBT approach. However, clients did not recall techniques such as the miracle question, which we as therapists regard as essential. (This work is available on the European Brief Therapy Association (EBTA) website at www.ebta.nu.)

Beyebach and his colleagues at the Universidad Pontifica in Salamanca have carried out a number of detailed and rigorous studies on brief therapy (1996, 1997, 2000). They have used objective measures, translating them into Spanish and revalidating them where necessary. The Salamanca team found 'Internal locus of control' in clients to be positively linked with compliance with tasks and with a threefold increase in successful outcomes for therapy. However, task compliance was not directly associated with good outcomes. Useful pre-treatment changes were reported more often by clients with belief in their own efficacy and with internal locus of control. Such pre-treatment changes were associated with a fourfold increase in successful outcomes. Clients who expected themselves to be successful had clear goals and were seeking to make changes in their situations. Clear goals predicted a twofold increase in success. The team suggest that therapy might be modified according to locus of control and expectancy measures to build on these associations.

Their 1997 data show that exchanges between therapist and client reflecting neither 'one-up' nor 'one-down' relating were associated with continuing to attend therapy. This confirms findings from studies of other brief therapies (Koss and Shiang, 1994). Competitive symmetrical escalation between therapist and client was associated with dropout from therapy Responses fitting the client's last statement were more common in cases with a good outcome. The pattern of communication between therapist and client changes after a break is taken. Outcomes suffered when the therapist sought to control the pattern of the whole session.

The well-known paper by Adams, Piercy and Jurich (1991) describes three groups of 20 families each. One group received the Formula First Session Task (FFST) and a solution-focused session 2 followed by problem-focused therapy; one group the FFST and problem-focused therapy thereafter; the third group received a problem-focused task and then problem-focused therapy. The FFST is 'Between now and the next time we meet, I would like you to observe, so that you can describe it to me, what happens in your (family, life, marriage, relationship) that you want to continue to have happen.' Compliance, clarity of goals and improvement in problem were better in FFST groups at session 2 but outcomes were equal for all at session 10.

The comparison study by Littrell et al. (1995) was between 61 students allocated to one of three conditions; 19 problem focus and task, 20 problem focus only, 22 solution focus and task. One therapy session was given to all groups. Sixty-nine per cent were better at six-week follow-up in each group but in SFBT the sessions were shorter.

Working with a rural community in Dumfries, Scotland, Macdonald's team made a trial of proceeding directly to therapy questions with all new attenders for six months without asking for any information about 'the problem'. Our outcome results for this group (in terms of goal achievement at one-year follow-up) were the same as for our overall population. However, the comments about the therapy experience were more critical, such as, 'The team had their own agenda', 'We got better but the team were not interested'. We saw this as a failure to join appropriately with the attenders. We returned to spending a few minutes defining the problem in terms of name, frequency and duration before proceeding. Critical feedback then diminished while outcomes remained the same.

In summary, SFBT process research is beginning to show us which elements of therapy are effective and for which clients. The outline which emerges is similar to that now being discerned in studies of other psychotherapies. The important difference for SFBT is that many non-essential elements within therapy have already been discarded.

SFBT outcomes – comparison studies

The only randomised controlled trial of SFBT published so far is by Lindforss and Magnusson (1997). They took their sample from those entering a Swedish prison for recurrent offenders. The base condition was therefore being an imprisoned recurrent offender and the dependent variable was the addition of SFBT. In the pilot study prisoners were allocated in turn to experimental or control conditions before being offered therapy. The experimental study was randomised more precisely because both experimental and control groups were made up of prisoners who had already agreed to have treatment if offered it. The prisoners made their own choice of problem for therapy. The therapists were independent of the prison administration. Reoffending rates formed the follow-up measure.

In the pilot study 14/21 (66 per cent) experimental and 19/21 (90 per cent) controls reoffended at 20 months. In the main study with 30 experimental and 29 controls over a 16 month follow-up, 18 (60 per cent) reoffended in the experimental group and 25 (86 per cent) in the control group. There were more drug offences and more total offences in controls. Prisoners averaged five treatment sessions. There were no significant demographic differences between the groups. Lindforss and Magnusson estimate that 2.7 million Swedish crowns were saved (nominally) by reduced reoffending.

The study is elegant and statistically significant. It is of interest that prisoners saw themselves as 'born unlucky' and therefore did not object if they found themselves allocated to the control condition. It is also interesting that in spite of the extensive provision made in Sweden to separate children and young people from bad living conditions, all the prisoners had retained active and recent contact with family members. Many of the families formed valuable resources for the prisoners in developing solutions to their problems.

Lambert et al. (1998) reported a treatment comparison study using the OQ–45, a self-report questionnaire from the USA devised specifically to measure changes resulting from psychotherapy. It measures symptoms, relationships and social functioning. Twenty-two cases treated with SFBT (from the full series of 38 cases published in Johnson and Shaha (1996)) were compared with 45 who received psychodynamic psychotherapy at a university public mental health centre. Both methods achieved 46 per cent recovery; SFBT by the third session and the mental health centre by the 26th session. The SFBT therapist was an experienced therapist in private practice; the university therapists were a more diverse group. The clients were from separate populations who were included in what were essentially two separate outcome studies. There is no information on whether therapy gains were sustained.

A precise study by Cockburn, Thomas and Cockburn in 1997 compared two approaches to rehabilitation following orthopaedic treatment for injuries. Twenty-five experimental clients were offered six SFBT sessions while 23 controls received the standard rehabilitation package. When reviewed after 60 days 68 per cent of the experimental group had returned to work within seven days compared with 4 per cent of controls.

LaFountain and Garner (1996) published a comparison study between 27 SFBT counsellors who saw 176 students and a control group of 30 non-SFBT counsellors who saw 135 students. The experimental students improved significantly on three of eight measures compared with the controls. Eighty-one per cent of the experimental group achieved their goals but no data are given for the control students. There was less exhaustion and depersonalisation in SFBT counsellors after one year compared with the non-SFBT counsellors.

A paper by Triantafillou (1997) reports that four sessions of SFBT-based supervision were provided for the staff of an adolescent residential unit. The staff's clients were compared with those of other staff who received 'standard' supervision. At 16 weeks' follow-up, the 5 clients of the SFBT group had 66 per cent less incidents and less medication use. The 7 clients in the control group had 10 per cent less incidents; the use of medication had increased.

In Newcastle upon Tyne (UK) a social worker in a public child and family clinic, John Wheeler (1995) carried out a three-month follow-up of 34 (traced) SFBT referrals and 39 (traced) routine referrals. In the SFBT group 23 (68 per cent) were satisfied versus 17 (44 per cent) of the routine care group. Other clinic resources were required by 4 (12 per cent) of the SFBT clients versus 12 (31 per cent) of the routine care group.

A study by Zimmerman et al. (1996) used standard measures to assess change in 30 clients who received 6 SFBT sessions directed at managing adolescent offspring successfully. Twelve controls received no therapy. (They received the same treatment package once the study was over.) There was improvement for the treated group on the Parenting Skills Inventory but no change on Family Strengths Assessment. The authors suggested that the latter may not be a suitable instrument for this type of study. With another set of co-workers Zimmerman

(Zimmerman et al., 1997) carried out couples group therapy using SFBT. Six groups were held at weekly intervals. There were 23 experimental clients and 13 controls. Outcomes were similar for both groups on the Marital Status Inventory but clients in the experimental group improved on the Dyadic Adjustment Scale.

SFBT outcomes – effectiveness studies

Seligman (1995) makes a valuable distinction between efficacy studies: 'this treatment works' and effectiveness studies: 'this treatment helped'. He was commenting on the Consumer Reports (1995) retrospective study which obtained self-report data from 2,900 therapy clients (albeit only 13 per cent of the sampled population). The study found that psychotherapy works, but that there was no link between problem type and which therapy helped; that clients who make active choices about therapy do better; and that exercising choice and control are beneficial for clients but will hamper randomised trials. In Seligman's view most comparison studies are efficacy studies, while naturalistic studies are generally trials of effectiveness. He suggests that effectiveness studies are more relevant to therapists than 'gold standard' controlled trials in rigid experimental conditions. The studies described below are naturalistic 'effectiveness' evaluations.

Mental health

Not surprisingly, there are a number of studies on the use of SFBT in mental health settings. Most of these are with outpatient populations. Authors report that the diagnosis or type of problem is not correlated significantly with outcome. There is little information provided in the published work about the actual diagnoses allocated. Either information on past health and treatment is not available in the settings where research occurs or it is not routinely collected by SFBT therapists, following their view that the road leading to the problem is not relevant to the question of how to solve it.

The Salamanca group have published extensively in Spanish on outcomes in SFBT. For example, Beyebach et al. (1996) followed up 39 mental health outpatients. Eighty per cent achieved their goals after an average of five sessions with a mean of 33 minutes per sessions. Agreeing concrete goals and taking note of pre-treatment change were significantly associated with good outcomes.

A telephone follow-up study was reported by the same group in 1991 (Pérez Grande). Eighty-one of 97 cases were traced 6–35 months after therapy was finished. One quarter of the cases were children and therapy lasted an average of five sessions. At the end of therapy 71 per cent reported improvement but 12 per cent reported relapse at follow-up. Other problems had improved by the time of follow-up in 38 per cent of cases. More clients dropped out of therapy if the problem was longstanding.

Another Spanish publication (Beyebach et al., 2000) reports a similar telephone follow-up of 83 cases, about a year after therapy. Eighty-two per cent were satisfied with the effect of their therapy. Therapy required an average of 4.7 sessions and outcomes did not differ between trainees and expert therapists. There was a better outcome for 'individual' problems such as anxiety, depression or addictions than for relationship conflicts. This is the first time that any study of SFBT has shown a difference in outcome on the basis of problem type.

A number of follow-up studies come from the Brief Family Therapy Center in Milwaukee, USA. De Shazer (1985) carried out a telephone enquiry six months after discharge. Twenty-three (82 per cent) had improved; 25 had solved other problems. An average of five sessions was required. De Shazer (1991) reported a further study of 29 cases. Twenty-three (80 per cent) reported that they had either resolved their original difficulty, or made significant progress towards resolving it. At 18 months the success rate was 86 per cent; 67 per cent reported other improvements also. An average of 4.6 sessions was required. Those who attended for more than four sessions were more likely to achieve their goals.

DeJong and Hopwood in Milwaukee (1996) published a telephone follow-up of 141 cases at eight months (on average) after discharge. Fifty per cent were under 19 years old and 93 per cent were under 45 years old; clients received an average of 2.9 sessions. Goals were achieved by 45 per cent, and 32 per cent made some progress towards their goals. There were equal outcomes by age, gender, race and economic status. An immediate post-therapy measure of change in scaling scores for 136 subjects was collected: 25 per cent made significant progress; 49 per cent moderate progress; and 26 per cent no progress (Berg and DeJong, 1996). The latter findings suggest that progress continues after therapy attendance has ceased. Lee (1997) reports a six-month telephone follow-up of 59 North American families using independent raters. Improvement was described by 64.9 per cent (goal achieved 54.4 per cent; part of goal achieved 10.5 per cent). On average 5.5 sessions were needed. The same researcher has other studies in preparation using validated measures.

In the United Kingdom the first published data came from the Brief Therapy Practice in London. George, Iveson and Ratner (1999) carried out a telephone follow-up six months after the end of therapy. Forty-one of the 62 traced were satisfied with the results of therapy.

Two studies from Macdonald and colleagues in the UK have been published (1994, 1997). In the first study a goal achievement questionnaire was completed by 41 cases and/or their family doctors one year after therapy had ceased. An average of 3.7 sessions had been required. Twenty-nine clients (70 per cent) had improved. Those with problems lasting more than three years did less well. That there was an equal benefit for all socio-economic classes was an important finding which contrasts with other approaches to psychotherapy. The second study used the same design and reached 36 clients successfully. Twenty-three (64 per cent) had improved; other problems had also been solved in 10 who had a good outcome and in two cases who had not achieved their main goal. An average of 3.4 sessions were used. Again there were similar outcomes for all socio-economic classes; longstanding problems did less well.

In the Macdonald studies 77 were traced out of 83 seen. The diagnoses resembled those seen at routine psychiatric outpatient clinics in the UK except that acute psychotic episodes were referred elsewhere. Relatively few drug and alcohol problems were seen because a separate specialist service existed.

There are no detailed studies of SFBT in mental health inpatient units. However Vaughn and her colleagues describe changes in practice in their Denver, Colorado psychiatric hospital (1996). Prior to the introduction of SFBT throughout the treatment programme 688 cases had an average length of stay of 20.2 days; after SFBT was introduced the length of stay for a subsequent 675 cases fell to an average of 6.6 days. Some patients began their stay in the locked ward area. The nursing staff involved are said to experience greater satisfaction in their relationships with clients and with other healthcare systems since the change to SFBT (Vaughn et al., 1995).

In a short but intriguing paper from the USA Eakes et al. (1997) studied experimental and control groups each made up of five clients with chronic schizophrenia and their families. The study differed from traditional SFBT practice in that a reflecting team was present and the miracle question was not asked. In the data comparison, for the experimental group the Family Environment Scale showed significant increase in 'expressiveness' and 'active-recreational orientation', and a decrease in 'incongruence'. Controls showed a significant increase in 'moral-religious emphasis'.

Children

In Germany Burr (1993) published the results from 55 children and young people seen at a children's clinic. They were followed up 6–12 months after treatment finished. Thirty-four were traced of whom 26 (77 per cent) were improved. Four sessions was the average; new problems were reported by four cases who had improved and four who had not. In a USA counselling study, Cruz and Littrell (1998) reviewed 16 high school students two weeks after two sessions of therapy. Ten had achieved 54.7 per cent of their various goals. Another study by Thompson and Littrell (2000) used a similar design with 12 students. Ten of the 12 had achieved 100 per cent of their goals two weeks later.

Franklin et al. (2001) investigated seven cases in detail (from a total of 19). Objective measures were collected for one month prior to therapy as a baseline and then repeated during therapy (an average of seven sessions). There was some improvement in all over the course of therapy and four of five were better when reviewed one month after therapy ended.

Franklin and her co-workers (1997) conducted a pilot study of three children to see if scales linked to specific behaviours established with the clients at the first interview ('self-anchored') could be used retrospectively and prospectively to record changes. The results were encouraging and are being pursued.

Alcohol

The specialist alcohol service in Bruges, Belgium has used solution-focused therapy for over ten years. The programme consists of inpatient treatment to a maximum of three weeks and then outpatient care, largely carried out by nursing staff. Dr Luc Isebaert and Sylvie Vuysse will shortly be publishing a formal follow-up study from the Bruges clinic. The design is a telephone follow-up of 131 alcoholics (including information from a relative) four years after an episode of inpatient care. The preliminary results show that 100 (76 per cent) were stable and that 9 had died of alcohol-related causes. More details will be needed to verify the significance of these results. So far it appears that the only relevant variable was therapy. Again in this study all socio-economic classes did equally well. However, the results must be seen in context: it is well established that 25 per cent of problem drinkers will resolve their problems without treatment and that a further 25 per cent will benefit from any treatment at all.

Violence

The Plumas County Mental Health Center in California has remarkable results with its domestic violence programme. The court gives offenders the choice of gaol or attendance at the programme, for which they must pay. The treatment is a standard package of six SFBT groups run by two therapists. Their results are collated by an independent researcher (Lee et al., 1997). In one (Sciotto, California) study of 117 clients treated between 1993 and 1997 the package was completed by 88 offenders. Only 7 per cent (6) had reoffended by 1997. In the second (Plumas, California) study carried out between 1994 and 1996, 34 clients completed seven of eight standard sessions; 3 per cent (1) had reoffended by the end of the study period. (Not yet published: 17 per cent had reoffended at follow-up after six years.) These results and those of Lindforss and Magnusson (1997; see above) are important because offenders often fail to respond to traditional psychotherapies.

Future developments

Insoo Kim Berg and Peter De Jong from Milwaukee are conducting a study of the helping relationship within child protection services in Michigan. They are using a modification of the Helping Resources Inventory, completed by both clients and workers. Karin Wallgren and Caroline Klingenstierna of Sweden are carrying out a randomised controlled study of SFBT as a tool to encourage return to work in those with long-term disability. They are using a group approach with controls receiving the same treatment package but after a period on a waiting list.

Melissa Darmody (Dublin, Ireland; darmody@tinet.ie) has a large project in progress with several experienced teams in the UK. Clients' goals and the Coping Resources Inventory (CRI) score are recorded initially. The CRI is a US-designed

60-item self-report measure looking at strengths and resources. Comments from therapist and client about the sessions and another CRI score are collected at the fourth or last session, whichever comes first. The CRI is repeated three months after therapy has ended. A number of management consultants apply SFBT concepts in their work with businesses. The approach fits well with the key values of modern corporate management, including management by objectives, using scarce resources appropriately and minimising the need for outside expertise.

The European Brief Therapy Association research project team has agreed with Steve de Shazer and the Brief Family Therapy Center that SFBT as defined for editorial purposes in research publications must include: goals; exceptions; pre-treatment changes; clients' resources; the miracle question; scaling; compliments and tasks. Return visits must begin with 'What is better?' or a similar question.

Many therapists are not natural researchers, having different skills and interests. This hampers all psychotherapy research and makes it difficult to establish the differences and similarities between different types of psychological treatments. As a step towards resolving these difficulties the international research group within the European Brief Therapy Association has developed a manual of SFBT for research purposes. Supervisors will be able to confirm that the manual is being followed correctly during the therapy. A project is under way matching client scaling against standard measures: Global Assessment of Functioning/Global Assessment of Relational Functioning (designed for use with *DSM*–IV diagnostic schemes); and the OQ-45 (see above). The measures will be completed at the start of therapy and at standard intervals thereafter. A standard goal achievement questionnaire and the objective measures will be repeated one year after leaving treatment. The study hopes to show whether SFBT is effective for problems as defined by *DSM*–IV and whether scaling is a valid measure of outcome in comparison with existing objective measures. Details and the manual are available on the SFBT and EBTA websites (www.enabling.org/ia/sft and www.ebta.nu). Data collection is now in progress.

The proposal is that a quasi-experimental design of this type can bring in results from many clients quickly, reducing problems associated with validity and avoiding the ethical issues raised by no-treatment groups. One team may choose to use the design for 50 + cases or many therapists may treat 2–3 each with central data processing. The European Brief Therapy Association may oversee the central processing of data. Instructions and a project outline pack have been prepared for interested parties. The same study design could be used in other psychotherapies with appropriate oversight of treatment conditions, thus allowing valid comparisons between different therapies and their effect for different diagnostic groups.

Conclusion

SFBT is becoming recognised as a realistic and practical approach to many problems in mental health and elsewhere. The model is cost-efficient and training is straightforward. There is evidence for the benefits of clinical supervision in

SFBT. There is an increasing body of published work which supports the SFBT model. Outcome and process studies on SFBT are in progress in many parts of the world. The total amount of available research knowledge compares favourably with that of many other psychological therapies. Further research may help to reduce the number of clients who do not benefit from the SFBT approach.

SFBT therapists seem to fare better than therapists who use other methods. Some SFBT therapists say there is a 'secret society of skilled clients' who make surprising and rapid changes with a minimum of therapist help. 'Burnout' among SFBT therapists may be less, thus preserving valuable resources for the community. Cost-efficiency considerations along with social and technological changes may make therapy by telephone or via the Internet the preferred approach for the future. SFBT and SFBT-based supervision is well suited to such developments. There is a promising future for SFBT and its talented clients.

References

Adams, J.F., Piercy, F.P. and Jurich, J.A. (1991) Effects of solution-focused therapy's 'formula first session task' on compliance and outcome in family therapy. *Journal of Marital and Family Therapy*, 17: 277–290.

Allgood, S.M., Parham, K.B., Salts, C.J. and Smith, T.A. (1995) The association between pretreatment change and unplanned termination in family therapy. *American Journal of Family Therapy*, 23: 195–202.

Asay, T.P. and Lambert, M.J. (1999) The empirical case for the common factors in therapy: quantitative findings. In M.A. Hubble, B.L. Duncan and S.D. Miller (eds), *The Heart and Soul of Change: what works in therapy*. Washington, DC: American Psychological Association.

Berg, I.K. and DeJong, P. (1996) Solution-building conversations: co-constructing a sense of competence with clients. *Families in Society*, 376–391. (briefftc@aol.com)

Beyebach, M. and Carranza, V.E. (1997) Therapeutic interaction and dropout: measuring relational communication in solution-focused therapy. *Journal of Family Therapy*, 19: 173–212. (mark.beyebach@upsa.es)

Beyebach, M., Morejon, A.R., Palenzuela, D.L. and Rodriguez-Arias, J.L. (1996) Research on the process of solution-focused brief therapy. In S.D. Miller, M.A. Hubble and B.L. Duncan (eds), *Handbook of Solution-Focused Brief Therapy* (pp. 299–334). San Francisco: Jossey-Bass.

Beyebach, M., Rodriguez Sanchez, M.S., Arribas de Miguel, J., Herrero de Vega, M., Hernandez, C. and Rodriguez Morejon, A. (2000) Outcome of solution-focused therapy at a university family therapy center. *Journal of Systemic Therapies*, 19: 116–128.

Bowie Youth and Family Services (1999) Client Feedback Form.

Burr, W. (1993) Evaluation der Anwendung losungsorientierter Kurztherapie in einer kinder- und jugendpsychiatischen Praxis (Evaluation of the use of brief therapy in a practice for children and adolescents). *Familiendynamik*, 18: 11–21. (German: abstract in English). (wburr@t-online.de)

Cockburn, J.T., Thomas, F.N. and Cockburn, O.J. (1997) Solution-focused therapy and psychosocial adjustment to orthopedic rehabilitation in a work hardening program. *Journal of Occupational Rehabilitation*, 7: 97–106. (fthomas@dfw.net)

Consumer Reports (1995) *Mental Health: does therapy help?* 734–739.

Cruz, J. and Littrell, J.M. (1998) Brief counseling with Hispanic American college students. *Journal of Multicultural Counseling and Development*, 26: 227–238. (jlittrel@iastate.edu)

DeJong, P. and Hopwood, L.E. (1996) Outcome research on treatment conducted at the Brief Family Therapy Center 1992–1993. In S.D. Miller, M.A. Hubble and B.L. Duncan (eds), *Handbook of Solution-Focused Brief Therapy* (pp. 272–298). San Francisco: Jossey-Bass. (djon@calvin.edu)

de Shazer, S. (1985) *Keys to Solutions in Brief Therapy*. New York: W.W. Norton. (brieffic@aol.com) de Shazer, S. (1991) *Putting Differences to Work* (pp. 161–162). New York: W.W. Norton.

Eakes, G., Walsh, S., Markowski, M., Cain, H. and Swanson, M. (1997) Family-centred brief solution-focused therapy with chronic schizophrenia: a pilot study. *Journal of Family Therapy*, 19: 145–158.

Eisengart, S. and Gingerich, W. (1999) *Solution-focused brief therapy: a review of the outcome research*. (http://members.tripod.com/wjg45/SFBT/research.htm)

Franklin, C., Corcoran, J., Nowicki, J. and Streeter, C.L. (1997) Using client self-anchored scales to measure outcomes in solution-focused therapy. *Journal of Systemic Therapies*, 16: 246–273.

Franklin, C., Biever, J.L., Moore, K.C., Clemons, D. and Scamardo, M. (2001) The effectiveness of solution-focused therapy with children in a school setting. *Research on Social Work Practice*, 11: 411–434. (cfranklin@mail.utexas.edu)

Garfield, A.E. and Bergin, S.L. (eds) (1994) *Handbook of Psychotherapy and Behaviour Change* (4th edn). New York: Wiley.

George, E., Iveson, C. and Ratner, H. (1999) *Problem to Solution* (2nd edn). London: Brief Therapy Press. (brief3@aol.com)

Hubble, M.A., Duncan, B.L. and Miller, S.D. (1999) *The Heart and Soul of Change: What works in therapy*. Washington, DC: American Psychological Association.

Isebaert, L. and Vuysse, S. (in preparation) (luc.isebaert@skynet.be)

Johnson, L.D., and Shaha, S. (1996) Improving quality in psychotherapy. *Psychotherapy*, 33: 225–236. (ljohnson@inconnect.com)

Johnson, L.N., Nelson, T.S., and Allgood, S.M. (1998). Noticing pretreatment change and therapeutic outcome: An initial study. *American Journal of Family Therapy*, 26: 159–168.

Koss, M.P. and Shiang, J. (1994) Research on brief therapy. In: A.E. Garfield and S.L. Bergin (eds), and *Handbook of Psychotherapy and Behaviour Change* (4th edn). New York: Wiley.

LaFountain, R.M. and Garner, N.E. (1996) Solution-focused counselling groups: the results are in. *Journal for Specialists in Group Work*, 21: 128–143.

Lambert. M.J., Okiishi, J.C., Finch, A.E. and Johnson, L.D. (1998) Outcome assessment: from conceptualization to implementation. *Professional Psychology: Research and Practice*, 29: 63–70.

Lee, M.Y. (1997) A study of solution-focused brief family therapy: outcomes and issues. *American Journal of Family Therapy*, 25: 3–17. (lee.355@postbox.acs.ohio-state.edu)

Lee, M.Y., Greene, G.J., Uken, A., Sebold, J. and Rheinsheld, J. (1997) Solution-focused brief group treatment: a viable modality for domestic violence offenders? *Journal of Collaborative Therapies*, 4: 10–17. (pcmhs@psln.com)

Lindforss, L. and Magnusson, D. (1997) Solution-focused therapy in prison. *Contemporary Family Therapy*, 19: 89–104. (lotta.lindforss@mbox200.se; dan.magnusson@brottsforebygganderadet.se)

Littrell, J.M., Malia, J.A. and Vanderwood, M. (1995) Single-sessions brief counseling in a high school. *Journal of Counseling and Development*, 73: 451–458.

Macdonald, A.J. (1994) Brief therapy in adult psychiatry. *Journal of Family Therapy*, 16: 415–426. (ajmacdon@psychsft.freeserve.co.uk)

Macdonald, A.J. (1997) Brief therapy in adult psychiatry: further outcomes. *Journal of Family Therapy*, 19: 213–222.

McKeel, A.J. (1996) A clinician's guide to research on solution-focused therapy. In S.D. Miller, M.A. Hubble and B.L. Duncan (eds), *Handbook of Solution-Focused Brief Therapy* (pp. 251–271). San Francisco: Jossey-Bass.

McKeel, A.J. (1999) A selected review of research of solution-focused brief therapy. (No paper publication – original version available at http://www.enabling.org/ia/sft)

Metcalf, L., Thomas, F.N., Duncan, B.L., Miller, S.D. and Hubble, M.A. (1996) What works in solution-focused brief therapy. In S.D. Miller, M.A. Hubble and B.L. Duncan (eds), *Handbook of Solution-Focused Brief Therapy* (pp. 335–349). San Francisco: Jossey-Bass.

Pérez Grande, M.D. (1991) Evaluacion de resultados en terapia sistemica breve (Outcome research in brief systemic therapy). *Cuadernos de Terapia Familiar*, 18: 93–110. (Spanish)

Seligman, M.E.P. (1995) The effectiveness of psychotherapy. The Consumer Reports study. *American Psychologist*, 50: 965–974. (http://www.apa.org/journals/seligman.html)

Shilts, L., Rambo, A. and Hernandez, L. (1997) Clients helping therapists find solutions to their therapy. *Contemporary Family Therapy*, 19: 117–132.

Thompson, R. and Littrell, J.M. (2000) Brief counseling with learning disabled students. *The School Counselor*, 2: 60–67.

Triantafillou, N. (1997) A solution-focused approach to mental health supervision. *Journal of Systemic Therapies*, 16: 305–328. (nickt@interlynx.net)

Vaughn, K., Webster, D.C., Orahood, S. and Young, B.C. (1995) Brief inpatient psychiatric treatment: finding solutions. *Issues in Mental Health Nursing*, 16: 519–531.

Vaughn, K., Young, B.C., Webster, D.C. and Thomas, M.R. (1996) A continuum-of-care model for inpatient psychiatric treatment. In S.D. Miller, M.A. Hubble and B.L. Duncan (eds), *Handbook of Solution-Focused Brief Therapy* (pp. 99–127). San Francisco: Jossey–Bass.

Wheeler, J. (1995) Believing in miracles: the implications and possibilities of using solution-focused therapy in a child mental health setting. *ACPP Reviews and Newsletter*, 17: 255–261. (John@jwheeler.freeserve.co.uk)

Zimmerman, T.S., Jacobsen, R.B., MacIntyre, M. and Watson, C. (1996) Solution-focused parenting groups: an empirical study. *Journal of Systemic Therapies*, 15: 12–25. (lindsay@picasso.colostate.edu)

Zimmerman, T.S., Prest, L.A. and Wetzel, B.E. (1997) Solution-focused couples therapy groups: an empirical study. *Journal of Family Therapy*, 19: 125–144.

3

Solution-Focused Groupwork

Pat Hoskisson

I am employed as a counsellor in a psychology and counselling department working within a multidisciplinary primary care mental health team. Other team members are community psychiatric nurses (CPNs), psychologists and counsellors. All referrals to the team are patients of either general practitioners or psychiatrists. Following assessment by CPNs, clients are allocated to the service best able to meet their needs.

Clients referred for counselling have either:

(a) life event adjustment difficulties accompanied by excessive or abnormal psychological disturbance, which include:

- self-image and identity issues;
- bereavement, including abnormal grief reaction and unresolved grief;
- trauma;
- the need to cope with injury or illness;
- developmental or life crises;
- loss of relationship, employment, health, etc.;

or
(b)

- mild to moderate depression;
- anxiety;
- self-esteem or anger problems where a focal difficulty can be identified;

or
(c) relationship difficulties including:

- family issues;
- sexual relationship problems;
- sexual identity issues.

Clients with moderate to severe anxiety, depression, post-traumatic stress disorder, obsessive-compulsive disorder and eating disorders are generally referred to psychologists. However if these difficulties are of a less severe nature or are identified once counselling has begun, the clients usually remain with the counsellor.

All clients receive one to one therapy by psychologists or counsellors before being offered referral to a solution-focused group.

Why run solution-focused groups?

Usefulness to the service

- As a unit within the National Health Service, employers have a vested interest in providing best value for money, so having a brief yet effective intervention has to be cost effective.
- Brief therapy has increased in importance as a way of coping with the high volume of referrals.
- The group utilises the skills and expertise of therapists working within the team.

Usefulness to clients

- One to one work can lead clients to the point where they see the usefulness of attending a group with a specific focus.
- Clients no longer feel alone. Meeting others experiencing similar difficulties is a major factor in consumer satisfaction.
- They have the opportunity to witness and confirm each other's successes and strengths in contrast to problems and failures.
- It is an opportunity for clients to learn from each other and gain a different perspective.
- The choice and variety of solutions is multiplied.
- Having a shift to a solution-focused (SF) perspective can be helpful if the client has got stuck in a problem-focused mode.
- The solution-focused group can be a forum for clients to discover untapped skills.

Usefulness to the SF therapist
It provides an opportunity:

- to develop expertise in a chosen field that fits well with the needs of the department;
- to develop SF groups and to collect evidence of effective practice;
- to contribute to the evidence base for using SF groupwork in a mental health setting;
- to collaborate with a co-worker and obtain feedback.

As a result of the psychological trauma caused by their problems, clients often suffer from low self-esteem, assertiveness difficulties, acute anxiety states and panic attacks. Assertiveness groups, which aim to increase clients' self-esteem and help them to develop strategies for coping with anxiety, have proved to be a valuable resource.

Developing solution-focused group practice

Using solution-focused therapy (SFT) in one to one counselling and experiencing the rapid measurable change in both outlook and behaviour of clients encouraged me to introduce it into the cognitive behavioural groups I was running. Increasing my own job satisfaction was also a motive as I had witnessed positive changes in individual clients. It is exciting both for the clients and for the therapist to discover what they can do when they have spent much of their lives being only too aware of what they can't do.

In moving away from the directive/teacher/learning model used in cognitive-behavioural therapy it took me some time and the completion of a few groups before I established a sound SF framework. The leader's role is very different since it is primarily to facilitate the discovery of what works for group members both individually and jointly. There were few precedents in the literature about SF groupwork so I had to be creative, make my own mistakes and work out my own rules. There is no single way to do SF therapy and I would add that there is no single way to run a SF group. Running SF groups does however require the same basic organisation and decision making as for running any group (Nelson-Jones, 1995).

Composition of the group

Experience has shown that a closed group of six to ten members of a single gender, run for two hours once a week for six to eight weeks, with a review session four to eight weeks later, provides the best format for positive change for my client group. Clients have usually entered the service with multiple and often complex problems and have received individual therapy before being introduced to or offered a group setting. Solution-focused theory suggests that the nature of the client's problem is of secondary importance, so group members do not have to have the same problem. However, clients need to be willing to address a focal issue which is open to change and can be shared with other members of the group.

Pre-first session processes

When a new group is being formed colleagues are sent an outline of the proposed group agenda. They discuss this with those clients who they think would benefit from attending and, if they agree, they are referred and sent additional information. It is explained that the group is an opportunity to explore new and different ways of dealing with their difficulties. Expectations are not raised too much as this would impose pressure on both client and therapist. At the same time it is made clear that a certain amount of commitment will be required. We give the client the opportunity to meet with the facilitators prior to the start date. The benefits of this are:

- individuals can make enquiries and express any concerns regarding attending the group;
- clients have the benefit of meeting a friendly face to link up with at session 1;
- they familiarise themselves with the venue and explore the journey to get there;
- practical difficulties such as poor hearing, eyesight or inability to read can be disclosed in a safe environment and such information is very important to the facilitator;
- a clear outline of the purpose of the group is given;
- anxieties around client self-disclosure are allayed and boundaries set (clients are not expected to tell their whole life story but any specific information that fits in with identified shared issues would be welcome);
- they are reassured that all those attending have a shared problem/difficulty;
- using SF techniques throughout the interview introduces the theme of change;
- the added advantage to the leader/facilitator of the group is that clients are initiated into SF thinking before the group meets for the first time.

Clients are asked if they have belonged to a therapy group before and, if so, what was the best part of it for them? If anxieties stem from previous group experiences, SF questions about how they coped with the situation and what they would like to be different in this group allow both clients and therapist to start finding out what works for them. The suggestion that before the first session it would be useful for them to look at a time when they didn't have the specific problem or to notice times when the problem either doesn't happen, happens less often or isn't present at all, sets the scene and facilitates movement in the first session as well as accelerating the rate of change. It would be easy to move into extended therapy at this stage but keeping the interview short (20 minutes) allows it to be focused. Some of the material arising from this preparatory work may be shared by the client at the first and subsequent sessions.

Aims and objectives

The aims and objectives of each session form a constructive platform for what will become a client-led agenda. Information obtained in the meetings and from the client and co-worker feedback helps to establish areas of need. The aim of the course is to give clients an experience which widens their ability to recognise their competencies and shows them how to use their competencies to best advantage.

Typical outline of aims and objectives

Session 1

Aims: To bond/unite the group; establish ground rules and explore why we are here.
Objectives: To agree clear expectations (goals) and how the group will run.

Session 2

Aims: To explore types of assertive behaviour using the clients' own experiences and to establish their competencies.

Objectives: Each member to identify forms of assertive behaviour they use. What works and what does not? (Where? When? How?)

Session 3

Aims: To explore rights and responsibilities in being assertive and how to avoid aggressive behaviour and negative script writing. (Timing and clear communication?)

Objectives: Each member to identify exceptions to problematic assertiveness behaviours and to choose a personal situation they would like to change.

Session 4

Aims: To explore appropriate and inappropriate anger responses.

Objectives: Members to identify their own responses to anger and to explore how to avoid inappropriate angry responses and be comfortable with their own feelings and especially with appropriate anger.

Session 5

Aims: To expand on strategies suggested by the group.

Objectives: Members to identify the choices they have and the strategies that work for them. (An ongoing theme.)

Session 6

Aims: To reinforce positive learning experiences.

Objectives: To enable group members to identify some of their strengths; build on learned positive experiences and to set simple achievable goals. (A continuous process throughout the course.)

Session 7

Content and format flexible dependent on what has happened in previous sessions. Group ending.

First session

The first session is in many ways the most important. It is crucial to make the group feel safe. We normalise clients' apprehension and stress their achievement in coming to the group. We use solution-focused coping questions to explore how they came through similar situations in the past. The negotiations about ground rules such as starting on time; breaks; respect and the need for 'no gossip outside the group', ease tension and help the group to feel together and safe. Contracting about attendance is done at the end of this session to allow clients the opportunity to become familiar with the process and comfortable with the group. To ground, unite and focus the group they are reminded that they have a current specific common difficulty, even though they may all have life experiences that are different. At this stage contributions from members about how they want their life to be different will help to define the problem and allow the facilitator to guide participants towards the aims and objectives of the group. Realistic personal goals are very important, as achievements, however small, are necessary to improve self-esteem. Although goals may differ, the group will come to see that they share the same need to change.

Reciting the adage, 'If you always do what you've always done you will always get what you've always got' is an eye opener for them. 'What do you think this means for you?' usually brings the desired responses, 'We need to change something, do something different, stop doing what we are doing now, it's us that have to change.' A copy is pinned on the wall at every session and they take great delight in pointing at it when they realise that it applies to them. 'So if you always do it and it doesn't work what do you need to do?' 'CHANGE!'

Participants come to the group used to and expecting negative responses from others. They often put themselves down and feel frightened they will make 'mistakes'. Using questions that allow them to externalise the 'problem' removes this threat to some extent because it is not possible to have a right or a wrong answer. Putting psychological distance between the person and the problem also helps to protect clients from too much risk taking before they are ready for it.

'Do you know anyone who is assertive? How do they behave? What are they like? Do you want to be like them or different?' 'How will life be different for you when you are able to be more assertive?' Brainstorming and using a flip chart is entirely compatible with the model and is useful to highlight specific needs and expectations. All members tend, at this stage, to focus on feelings, and a list of goals such as being more relaxed, less guilty, happier, liking oneself more, etc., produces lots of head nodding and sharing. Changing the focus to: 'When you are feeling a bit better, (more assertive) what will you be able to do that is different?' often brings blank faces. This is a useful spot to introduce a version of the miracle question or the 'future video'.

'Picture yourself doing some of the things you would like to be doing but are not able to do now. What do you see?'

(In future sessions this can be revisited to re-evaluate changes that have already taken place, including any changes in expectations. The whole group can be involved in feeding back to individuals what they have noticed is different.)

Exploring expectations at an early stage enables group members to think about what they really want. The facilitator can then help them to focus on the possible and changeable. This leads to the establishing of specific realistic goals for each member.

(In the second session, Jane saw herself living away from home. She explored what she would need to do first and the whole group encouraged her to look at what she felt she had already achieved and any past experiences that would be useful to help her. As a result smaller targets were set in place.)

We use an exercise in which members form pairs and encourage each other to share what they are good at. They discover personal competencies and a realisation that some situations which others find difficult are not a problem for them. What they perceive as ordinary and routine is seen by others as a real achievement. Responses such as 'I couldn't do that' and, 'How on earth do you manage it?' reinforce their positive achievements and strengths. Giving and receiving feedback about this gives them an experience of praise. With the facilitator's help no one is allowed to 'fail'. At some stage during the first session, reference must be made to the 'notice' task given at the pre-session meeting. 'Has anyone noticed a time when the situation has been less difficult, when you may have been coping a bit better?' 'In what kind of situation are you a little more assertive (less stressed, worried, anxious)?' Given space to explore these situations both individuals and the group build up a repertoire of better experiences and why they have occurred.

Encouragement to share stories about what has worked for them generates solutions. What has worked for one may not work for others but members can see and adapt solutions. It can be difficult if a solution put forward by one member is dismissed by another who claims to have tried it without success. There is no one solution for a problem or for a person. There is no 'one size fits all' solution for the whole group but there are skeleton solutions which fit many problems and can be used to great effect. Addressing the 'successful' person and encouraging him or her to explore how the solution worked can elicit these. The facilitator may then ask the person who felt the solution had not worked for him or her: 'How was the situation different?' 'If you were to try again what would you do differently?' 'What else would be useful for us to explore that would help you?' This encourages the development of unique personal strategies. Using the term 'us' is collaborative while at the same time 'you' confirms the importance of the individual.

It is very helpful to have a co-worker observe and note expressed needs, as well as strengths and changes both in the group and in individual members. In a group setting these can be missed. The co-worker helps keep the therapist on a positive track while being aware of individual and group problems. It is empowering for group members to give positive feedback to individual members and the group as a whole about their strengths, skills and resources. It enables them to see that they are not as helpless as they had previously thought. Even those who have said very little or nothing at all can be given some constructive feedback. 'I notice that you have been listening very attentively and seem to be agreeing with quite a lot that you have heard' is a positive statement and affirms their involvement. Shy or withdrawn participants are taking part just by being there and sharing how difficult it is. The discovery that they are not alone helps them to relax and eventually this can lead them to be more themselves and this in turn can result in more active involvement. Exclusion from groups on the grounds that a client is shy or withdrawn is not an option I would consider.

We introduce the idea of the group members doing tasks between sessions by asking questions such as the following.

- What will you take from this session that you might like to try?
- Is there something simple that you might try to accomplish?
- Could you break the task into smaller parts?
- What could you do that might help?
- How will you recognise if anything is different as a result of your efforts?

Members may adopt tasks designed by other group members. For example: 'When Mary went to the shop she chose a quiet day and only went for one thing. I think that would be better for me too.' A scaling exercise is a useful tool for both members and facilitator to evaluate the session. Each person is able to measure changes, both in feelings and achievements, and is given the opportunity to reflect on what they would like to try. The facilitator is able to focus on what clients want and to monitor what is effective as well as identifying areas of difficulty.

Session 2 and beyond

We refer to between-session tasks at the start of each meeting.

> 'Some of you may not have had the opportunity to carry out the tasks you set yourselves but it would be useful to hear of any changes that have happened over the past week.'

The group is able to celebrate successful strategies and to explore how these new-found skills can be transferred to other situations. We also explore any difficulties people may have experienced in order to discover which elements of the strategy worked and what could be modified on future occasions.

Partly due to their initial low self-esteem and, on occasions, high expectations, individuals often do not remember or give themselves credit for the successful parts of their strategies. Many of them are used to putting others before themselves and are good at looking for others' successes but not their own. It is interesting to hear participants using solution-focused questions on each other. As the group makes progress the facilitator can step back and take more of a caretaker role.

We have a gap of four to eight weeks between the final session and a follow-up session. The final meeting before the break is used to summarise what they have discovered about themselves and what is beginning to work for them. Flip charts from the first session, their own personal scaling charts and video pictures are useful tools for this. They are encouraged to identify further realistic goals and strategies. The gap is to give them the opportunity to experiment with what works for them. They are encouraged to use scaling to monitor their progress.

The follow-up session highlights all levels of change and achievement and reinforces strengths and abilities. Fears of relapse are explored and normalised and, using contributions from the whole group, strategies are developed to help them recognise obstacles and how to overcome them. Often the group will decide to continue to meet in some other place so it is useful for them to explore how they will use their experience in the group to support and encourage others.

Culture, race and gender

Since our culture and belief systems are the filters that help us interpret the world it is a challenge for groups whose members come from disparate cultures to find common goals or solutions. The solution-focused emphasis on developing client-centred skills unique to the client's social environment enables cross-cultural sensitivities to be respected and affirmed. Individual members have the opportunity to teach the others their way of interpreting their world and to demonstrate their solution-creating processes. These solutions may turn out to be quite unique or be common to a number of people in the group. It is important that the time and space given to this sharing of cultural values is done fairly otherwise one group or individual may feel resentful that another person is being given a privileged place. Sharing out different aspects of the cultural storytelling and engaging the whole group in further exploration helps to make it more of a group experience. Culture can be part of the problem and part of the solution. At times it has been necessary to recognise how cultural values or practices inhibit movement towards personal change. A realistic view of cultural influences helps in the setting of realistic goals. Groups of mixed race and culture have been run with positive outcomes when everyone has matching central issues and a common language.

In the early days I discovered that male/female mixed groups were not so beneficial to participants. This was mainly due to the disparity of numbers between the sexes and the safety issues of many referred females who did not feel secure enough to risk change with its accompanying vulnerability in a mixed group. The brevity of solution-focused work often made it very difficult to tackle this issue satisfactorily. The consensus among our clients is that they prefer single sex groups.

SFT and cognitive-behavioural therapy (CBT)

The SF group approach, unlike the cognitive-behavioural one we previously used, does not delve into the causes of negative behaviours. However, searching for and testing solutions can help to throw light on how maladaptive behavioural and cognitive patterns occurred in the past. The contrast between constructive and helpful behaviours can reveal the faulty thinking which led to previous destructive behaviours. CBT is described as 'Individual therapy done in a group' (Alladin, 1988) and although the same can be said for SF groups, interaction and sharing is actively encouraged.

In our experience, group members find it less threatening to explore solutions than to examine possible faults in thinking which led to problem behaviour. By sharing what they are able to do they come to recognise that at least some of their ways of thinking and acting work well for them. In one of our exercises we divide into pairs with the brief to discover what is positive about the other person. When the results are reported back in the large group the experience of constructive feedback helps to shift negative self-perceptions. Hearing and making positive observations about each other can help to correct distorted impressions and assumptions.

SF groupwork is discovery orientated right from the beginning. We use the resources of each individual and the group as a collective whole to construct personal styles and strategies which work for people. We use written material (often recommended by the clients), charts, handouts and book references to back up experiential learning.

One of the biggest advantages of any group is that it overcomes social isolation. Members begin to realise that they are not the only one having feelings of anxiety or depression. This felt experience can reduce the sense of stigma or exclusion. Feeling that one is being silly or stupid or pathetic can be normalised as understandable in the circumstances. Difficulties and expectations are invariably expressed as feelings in the first instance. 'I feel anxious all the time.' 'I want to feel more relaxed.' While acknowledging feelings, the facilitator invites participants to picture what they would be doing when they felt less anxious or more relaxed. Clients sometimes think that they can change their feelings directly without reference to the behaviours which accompany them. Exploring better times also serves to generate some of the feelings that change could bring. Negative feelings are also recognised. With clients who rarely report positive feelings it may be that the group can only explore the person's coping strategies: 'Feeling the way you do, how do you get by? What do you do that helps even though you feel low?' 'How do you stop feeling worse?' People usually see their feelings as the measure of their success. When they report they are feeling better it is important to link it to the behavioural evidence. 'I'm feeling much better. I'm feeling more in control,' would be followed up by asking, 'What is happening which makes you feel you are more in control? What are the signs for you that you are feeling better? What have you started or stopped doing?' This amount of detail ensures that a progressive narrative begins to develop as a counter-plot to the problem-dominated one.

One of the joys of running SF groups is observing the positive changes in members' body and verbal language.

Case studies

The following is an excerpt from the third session of a group.

Carol, a group member, was looking decidedly unhappy while some of the group recounted what they had noticed worked for them since attending the last session.

Carol: [*sounding very frustrated, angry and defensive*] I decided to tackle my daughter about helping me on a Sunday. She always sits there reading the paper while I'm up to my armpits in washing and trying to get the lunch. Well it didn't work!

[*The rest of the group started being very sympathetic towards her and were in the process of affirming the selfishness of children and how helpless it could make one feel when I interjected.*]

Facilitator: It sounds as though you tried a really tough one, Carol. Have you ever had a time when you and she could talk things through?

Carol: We always used to but it's since she came back home to stay with her partner while they wait for their house to be finished that she's taken me for granted and been very snappy. I just feel tired all the time.

Jane: I remember going back to live with my mum and dad for a bit. It wasn't easy. We'd both got our own way of doing things and got on each other's nerves.

Carol: I suppose we do get on each other's nerves. It was like that when my other daughter came home from university in the holidays. We were just about getting along OK when it was time for her to go back.

Facilitator: What had happened by the end of the holiday to make it different to the beginning?

Carol: We'd got used to each other.

Facilitator: How did that happen?

Carol: I think it must just have been time. I used to get cross because she was different and I wanted her to be just the same.

Facilitator: Were you just the same?

Carol: Well I was at the beginning but I got so worn out that I stopped clearing up after her and I made her do her own washing. Well in the end she had to because I stopped doing it and she had nothing clean left to wear! [*Everyone, including Carol laughed at this point.*]

Facilitator: Does all this sound familiar?

Carol: I'm doing it again, aren't I? I know. 'If you always do!'

At this point there were many roads to go down but I chose with her permission to use Carol's situation to explore issues around normal feelings and feelings invoked by negative scriptwriting. It was also useful to reflect on how past negative to positive experiences can give us useful information to deal with similar situations.

This excerpt also illustrates not only how members of the group could side-track and start negative discourse, but also how their personal reflection could trigger additional insight into solutions.

The following is an extract from a session that could have gone horribly wrong. In spite of the initial meeting and the first session being all about establishing clear, attainable goals somehow we had not got through to Kate.

At the third session Kate was developing a habit of rejecting ideas and this was worrying as it had the potential to undermine the group and demoralise individuals. The facilitator decided to tackle it head on.

Facilitator: Something seems to be bothering you, Kate.

Kate: It's all very well changing these little things but what about the big ones? You know, the really important ones?

Facilitator: Such as?

Kate: Well, I want to get back to work as well as start feeling better.

Facilitator: On a scale of nought to ten where do you need to be regarding feeling better before you start looking at getting back to work?

Kate: A six or a seven.

Facilitator: Where are you now?

Kate: About a four.

Facilitator: Where were you when you first came?

Kate: [*with a wry grin*] About zero.

Facilitator: What has helped move you to a four since the first session?

Kate: Finding that I can mix and talk to people and that I am not on my own.

Facilitator: Anything else?

Kate: Well I suppose that me and the children are getting on better and I'm not being so ratty. They are helping round the house too.

Facilitator: What else?

Karen: [*butting in*]   I've noticed that you are talking more. When you first came you were sitting sideways on and hardly said anything.

Kate: I didn't think that I had anything to say or that anyone would be interested.

Facilitator: And now?

Kate: Well I know I can talk and that you listen.

Yvonne: You told me that the children are taking more notice of what you say too.

Kate: But it's still not getting me back to work!

Facilitator: OK, let's have a recap. In two weeks you have found that you can mix in a group, you can talk and be listened to and people are interested, the children are helping round the house and you are less ratty. Your eventual goal is to reach a six or seven on the feeling better scale in order to get back to work. At present you are a four but are feeling anxious and stressed. If you weren't feeling like this would it make a difference?

Kate: I guess it would. I've been off work for so long and I thought that it would prove to everyone that I was better so I've been pressurising myself. I do feel better but I need other people to see I am. [*After a pause she continued*] I haven't been noticing whether they have or not, but now we've talked about it I think they must have.

Facilitator: Some of the changes you have described show a knock-on effect, don't they? Could you notice some of these between now and when we next meet together?

Kate agreed that it would be a useful exercise over the following week. When we next met not only did she come up with her own discoveries, she was able to relate conversations with her family (another change) in which they had confirmed a positive change in her. Nobody else was pressurising her to return to work, so she was more relaxed and prepared to tackle smaller but related changes. We can do our best to modify clients' expectations but there are often hidden agendas which block reception to anything that falls short of their own firmly fixed goals. We were fortunate that Kate was able to rationalise hers.

No matter how well we prepare the ground for a group there will always be unforeseen issues. We cannot ignore them, because they will not go away! Experience has shown that addressing problems as soon as they are identified allows the group to move on.

Personal reflections

Supplementing my one to one practice with running solution-focused groups has been an invigorating personal learning experience. The variety of experience, knowledge, skills and learning styles (Honey and Mumford, 1992) which people bring to the group makes it both challenging and awe inspiring. Although CBT groups were effective they generated less involvement by the members.

Feedback from groups and other workers suggests that the SFT groups are proving popular. Most clients attend the whole course and feel (and show through scaling) that it has helped them begin to change. The main question for me is, how long do these changes last? Long-term follow-ups do not take place but one group, reviewed after six months, showed that half the members were continuing the process of change and a quarter could see that they were maintaining their previous position. The remainder admitted to being bogged down by new life events which they felt had set them back. Scaling records and reviewing their personal 'video pictures' proved valuable in highlighting changes in relation to initial expectations, commitment and hopefulness and allowed them to normalise their current position.

The composition of groups and even the time of year bring challenges. Spring groups are thirsting for change, summer groups seem to settle quickly but groups run in the winter are more demanding. This may say more about the therapist than the group members! There are times when groups are not functioning well that the therapist has to adopt the solution-focused maxim of 'doing something different'. Running the groups feels like being a privileged guest witnessing the birth of small miracles in people's lives!

References

Alladin, W. (1988) Cognitive behavioural group therapy. In M. Aveline and W. Dryden (eds), *Group Therapy in Britain*. Buckingham: Open University Press.

Honey, P. and Mumford, A. (1992) *A Manual of Learning Styles*. Maidenhead: Peter Honey.

Nelson-Jones, R. (1995) Group counselling. In R. Nelson-Jones, *Theory and Practice of Counselling*. London: Cassell.

4

Solution-Focused Practice with Families

Guy Shennan

In some ways it may seem odd to find a specialist chapter in a book about solution-focused brief therapy devoted to its application with families, given that the approach arose from within the family therapy tradition (de Shazer, 1991; Cade and O'Hanlon, 1993). However, the rapid growth of the approach in recent years appears to have been accompanied by a distancing from its family therapy roots, to the extent that recently trained solution-focused practitioners may not even be aware of the model's origins. The tendency of training courses and basic texts to introduce the model as it is used with individuals has contributed to this, even where texts have included sections on work with families (Berg, 1991; Lethem, 1994; DeJong and Berg, 2001; George et al., 1999).

In the earlier days of the approach, this lack of attention to its applications with families would have been less significant, as most of its practitioners themselves came from a family therapy background. This was clearly the case in the United Kingdom given the crucial developmental role played by the Brief Therapy Practice (George et al., 1999), whose original members were all qualified family therapists. 'Doing it' with families was just a 'natural' thing to do, and no particular attention had to be paid to how this actually differed from doing it with individuals. The clearest statement of this position is found in de Shazer, 1988 (p. 151), where he compared four case examples which he claims were essentially alike even though one was with a family of four, one with a couple, and the other two with individuals. They were alike 'because all four clients describe exceptions', and 'number of individuals is not a complicating factor'. Yet when I first sat down in front of a family, fresh from my solution-focused training, the number of individuals present did indeed seem to be a complicating factor.

So in the best traditions of solution-focused brief therapy, the focus of this chapter is a pragmatic one. It contains an attempt to suggest, in a very small way, some answers to the question, 'What do you do when you want to do solution-focused work and you are with a family?' The suggestions offered are based on attempts made over several years to use a solution-focused approach with families, firstly within a Social Services children and families team,[1] and more recently within a therapeutic service offered to families by a child welfare voluntary agency.[2] It is not argued that these services provide a blueprint which can necessarily be applied wholesale to other contexts, but rather that our experiences can add to the pool of practice wisdom from which practitioners can draw.

Convening

Before we can consider what to do when in a room with a family, we need to consider how it is that a family arrives there in the first place. Reacting against the traditional focus on psychotherapy with individuals, family therapists were keen to see the whole family, and devised a number of strategies for ensuring the attendance at sessions of various family members (Burnham, 1986). The solution-focused approach followed the brief therapy strand within family therapy in challenging this notion. The principle that change in one part of a system leads to changes in the system as a whole (Watzlawick et al., 1974) caused de Shazer and his colleagues (1986, p. 210) to be puzzled by the idea 'that "family therapy" means that the therapist must meet with the whole family'.

So when should more than one person attend a session and who should decide? Convening meetings has traditionally been seen as a therapist activity, whereas following the solution-focused principle that the client is 'the expert in their own and their family's lives' (Iveson, 1996), we have handed this role over to the client. Our service is triggered by a parent wanting help, and we invite them to see us either on their own or bringing with them whoever they feel needs to attend. We find that an initial telephone contact is more useful than a letter to clarify this, and it is also helpful when parents need reassurance for their sometimes tentative ideas about who should come. As it is common both for parents to come to first sessions on their own and to come with one or more of their children, it is possible for the worker making the appointment to support the parent's ideas either way, with a comment such as, 'That makes a lot of sense – lots of parents decide to do that for the first session'.

Joining

There has been a perception that solution-focused brief therapy has not paid enough attention to the relationship between practitioner and client and attempts have recently been made to rectify this (Turnell and Lipchik, 1999). Joining with the client is now seen as a 'precondition' of the approach (Sharry et al., 2002, p. 26). How are we to join with more than one client at a time?

When a family group is present, it is likely that there will be different levels of willingness to be there. Children have often had little say about attending, and it is useful for workers not to assume that they will want to take part, but to ask their permission to ask them questions. They need to be prepared for a negative response. For example, a 13-year-old boy brought along by his mother, having been asked 'Is it OK if I ask you some questions?' shook his head. The worker[3] replied that this was perfectly OK, invited the boy to join in at any time if he wished to, and simply directed his questions to the mother. After a break, the worker's feedback included a compliment to the boy about how he had stuck to his guns even though he might have felt under some pressure to talk. The same happened in the second session and the boy was given the same compliment.

Then in the third session he started talking as soon as he arrived, agreed it would be OK if he were asked questions, and joined in throughout. He was complimented at the end of this session for knowing when would be the right time for him to talk and sticking to this.

When they have given permission to be asked questions, children can be helped by hearing themselves successfully answer some at an early stage. A useful means of achieving this is by checking basic factual details, such as how old the children are and what school they go to. If there are several children present it may be that they receive just one such question each, whereas to one child there could be a series.

The main joining activity of solution-focused work is normally described as 'problem-free talk' (George et al., 1999, p. 13), though this is a somewhat neutral label and 'strengths talk' or 'competency talk' more accurately reflects what is intended. In family sessions it can be extremely useful to have individuals comment on each other's strengths, and this can be achieved simply by asking what each person present is good at in turn. At the beginning of first sessions, children are often extremely nervous and may be expecting to receive a lot of negative attention due to their parents' view of their behaviour. It can come as a welcome surprise to them to hear their parents and siblings being invited to describe their better qualities, and this is frequently accompanied by their visibly relaxing. Another advantage of this exercise is that the family members' strengths are now present in the room and can be drawn upon to help in the work to come.

When working with a family the question of who to ask what and when frequently arises. There is a strong argument for respecting the family hierarchy, which often involves asking the parents certain questions first. This is often done when getting down to the business of finding out what is wanted from the work, and this is the subject of our next section.

What does the family want?

The bedrock of the solution-focused approach is the attention paid to what the client wants. This raises a number of questions for practitioners working with a family. Do we ask what the family as a whole hopes for? Do we check this out with each family member individually? What if their individual hopes are conflicting?

A flexible, 'both/and' position can be a useful one to hold, with the practitioner eliciting both individual and shared goals. Sometimes it will be apparent that everyone wants to head in the same direction, at others there may appear to be irreconcilable wishes. The worker can provide an opportunity for each family member's wishes to be heard, and for commonalities and differences to emerge. It is important to bear in mind that it is the family members who are themselves responsible for resolving differences or, if these are not resolvable, finding ways of living with them. The worker who tries to force through agreements and joint goals will soon find that he or she is working harder than the family and running into a brick wall.

So, how to go about constructing goals, individual and shared? A good, practical starting point is to ask each person present what their 'best hopes' are for coming. It is generally sensible not to explore each answer in detail initially, as it is useful first to gain a general impression of what each person wants, and to what extent goals are shared. Before considering the next step, let us look at a practice issue that often arises at this stage of the work.

It is not uncommon for parents to answer the question about their 'best hopes' by saying something about what they would like to take place during the sessions, and the worker needs to be careful to differentiate here between means and ends. The most common example is the request for advice about how to manage a child's behaviour. This may seem to pose a challenge to the non-directive, solution-focused worker, but it is important to bear in mind that this is not a goal in the solution-focused sense, but the means by which the parents believe that the changes they want can be achieved. Therefore the worker needs to ask questions aimed at discovering what these actual changes might be.

> *Worker:* What are your best hopes for coming here today?
> *Parent:* Well, I'm looking for some ideas on what to do with Jason.
> *Worker:* If you were to get some ideas, how would you later find out that they had been helpful?
> *Parent:* I suppose if he was to calm down a bit.

Another common example is the parental desire for a child to talk about their feelings during a session.

> *Parent:* I'm worried about James bottling everything up. I'd like him to be able to open up to you.
> *Worker:* And if James were to feel able to talk while we are here, how would you know that that had been useful?

It is usually sensible to avoid any protestations that we do not give advice, or that nine-year-old boys do not often 'open up' about their feelings in this way, by simply continuing to probe for what it is that the parents want to be different in their family's life. When these desired differences have been elicited the way has been cleared to explore the detailed effects which these differences will produce. Where the request for advice is pressed, tentative suggestions can be offered as part of the final feedback, based on any constructive actions by the parents which have been unearthed during the session.

When each person has stated his or her general hopes for the work, where better to turn than to the miracle question? There are various ways in which this can be used with a family, which include the development of a joint miracle, a series of individual miracles, or a mixture of the two. Where there is common ground in the hopes expressed, a family can be invited to paint a miracle picture together. By not looking at anyone in particular while asking the miracle question, the worker can allow the family to make its own decisions about how to begin to answer. When the various family members are encouraged to contribute, rich descriptions of a more wanted family life can unfold. These descriptions can be brought to life when individuals are asked to think about their effects on each other.

> Worker: … and when your mum came into the kitchen, what would you notice about her that would tell you that the miracle had happened?
> Lucy: She'd be smiling …
> Worker: What else?
> Lucy: … and she wouldn't be stressed out. She'd be sitting down, having a cup of tea and a cigarette.
> Worker: – and Mum? Suppose that's how you were, smiling, and having a cup of tea and a cigarette. What would you notice about Lucy?
> Mum: She'd have a big smile on her face as well. And she'd have a cup of tea too, and sit down next to me.

While a joint miracle is being created, individuals can elect to leave it at certain points where what they want differs from other family members.

> Mum: … and when he comes in from school, he'd talk to me about what he'd been doing.
> Dipak: No, I wouldn't. I'd go straight out to see my mates.
> Worker: OK, so this bit of your miracle, Mum, is different from Dipak's. So tell me what would happen for you first, then, Dipak, I'll find out what would happen after school for you.

Sometimes it is better to ask about separate miracles from the start, for example if there appears to be little common ground in the hopes initially expressed. An advantage of asking each individual to describe their own miracle is that it enables family members to hear clearly what each other wants. Unexpected results can follow. In a first session with a mother, father and two daughters, a tiny aspect of ten-year-old Sarah's miracle, unremarked on at the time, was 'eating my mum's cereal' for breakfast. A week later, the family were describing significant improvements in how they were getting on and in Sarah's behaviour in particular. Her mother, reflecting on how the improvements had occurred, said that they had not realised how the muesli had been perceived as 'hers' and the Rice Krispies as the children's, and she had since made a point of ensuring Sarah had access to all the cereals! A minor point in itself, but her mother's action may well have demonstrated to Sarah how closely she had been listening to her.

What is the family doing to get what it wants?

There are some advantages in working with more than one person when considering what is already being done that is helping. The more people involved, the more likely it is that someone has noticed progress, and will notice it between sessions. But in many ways this aspect of the work is not affected by numbers present. Each person should be given an opportunity to consider how far they have already moved towards achieving their goals, whether these are individual or shared, and to describe how they have done this. Scales are useful tools for this, with a little care needed when defining the endpoints. Ten can represent the family's miracle where this has been created jointly, or the individual's in the case of separate goals.

By asking each person to write down their point on the scale, the worker can both introduce a little playfulness and prevent people influencing each other's answers. They can then be asked to guess who has given each answer. Starting with the highest tends to help: 'Someone thinks things are at 6. What do you think that person has noticed happening in your family? Who do you think it is? Is N. usually the one who is most likely to notice positive things happening?'

There are many variations on these comparative and hierarchical questions. 'Whose scale will start to go up first? Who will be the first person to notice things improving? Who is best in your family at spotting good things happening?' There is a healthy amount of presupposition in such questions, which do not doubt that positive change will happen, only who will create or notice it first.

Another advantage of working with more than one person is that it can reduce the effects of client reluctance in taking the credit for change. For example, the mother of a ten-year-old whose behaviour has improved greatly between sessions cannot think of anything she has done to help this to happen. Her partner, however, points out that she has been consistent and firm with him, more often sticking to her guns when she has said 'no'.

There is no doubting the difficulties where there are markedly different, even mutually exclusive goals. The worker can ask the family about the possibility of these differences being resolved and agreed goals being reached. The possibility of agreement can be scaled. If there is thought to be a low possibility, how are they going to live with this? This may become almost a goal of the work in itself. Another response is simply to accept the existence of different goals and treat each person as an individual client, asking each about their own scale. Questions of resolving differences can be left unsaid, for the family to work out. Questions can also be asked about how movement on one scale will affect the scales of other family members.

Fluidity and client-directedness

As we continue to develop our practice with families we are increasingly reaching towards more fluid ways of working. We feel there is a danger in the solution-focused approach of an over-concentration on unchanging, concrete goals, which lends a mechanical quality to the work. The process can become very linear, with the worker fixing the goal in the first session, setting a course towards it, then not allowing for any deviation from this course as the sessions proceed. While being all for retaining a focus in our work, we do not feel that such a process reflects the messy nature of everyday family life. There are two ways in particular that we try to match our style of working to this messiness. Firstly, our future focus is more loosely defined than a definition of circumscribed goals and stolid pursuit of incremental steps towards them. Rather, it comprises a mixture of developing a generally forward momentum towards various, more desired ways of living, and considering possible ways of dealing with the vicissitudes that modern life throws at families. Secondly, we are open to any combination of family members coming to each session. Putting these two together we see that there can be different levels of continuity between sessions. To use a soap opera analogy, it can be either *Casualty*, with a separate storyline each week, though with the same characters and general themes, or *Coronation Street*, where the story continues between episodes. Or, like *The Bill*, it can be a mixture of the two!

Some of the fluidity results from another practice aspiration, to become maximally client-directed, in which we are supported by research which suggests that 'clients – not models – should organise the treatment process' (Duncan and Miller, 2000, p. 31). The client organises who attends, decides whether or not to have further sessions, and the subjects and themes to be discussed from session to session. We are also using the idea of the client-directed break (Sharry et al., 2001), where we invite the family to use the break to discuss any ideas for moving forward they have had themselves from the session, rather than it being for the worker alone to generate ideas in an expert fashion. This notion of client direction of the work does however raise questions in the context of working with families.

Power issues

For the clients to be directing the process requires a transfer of power from worker to client. Where there is more than one client, it is unlikely that this power will be divided up equally between them. What will tend to happen is that it will be shared out disproportionately in a way that reflects existing power balances, or rather imbalances, within the family. Solution-focused brief therapy has been criticised for its neglect of these power differences (Dermer et al., 1998), two major determinants of which are gender and age. A model which prides itself on its empowering nature needs to take care that its non-directive client-centredness is not achieved at the expense of the less powerful members of a family. During sessions we sometimes have to become directive in ensuring that each person present has a voice. We remain uneasy about one effect of our handing over the role of organising attendance at meetings to the client. In practice this client is usually the mother, and we find ourselves working with mothers and children, fathers being noticeable by their absence. More comfortable with a proactive role, mainstream family therapists have paid greater attention to involving men in their work (Dienhart, 2001; Walters et al., 2001).

I would suggest that this is one outcome of solution-focused brief therapy, in its purest form, seeking to have no other agenda than helping the client present in the therapy room to achieve his or her goals. The danger is that the therapy takes place in a hermetically sealed bubble, free from the necessity of engagement with the messy, real world outside.

The Smith family

In the case of the Smith family, the real world was constantly making its presence felt in the work which took place in the clinic setting. Jane Smith had contacted the Early Response Project due to difficulties with the behaviour of her 12-year-old daughter, Katie. This was set against the background of a dispute which was being brought before the court between Jane and Katie's father over Jane's plans to move to France. Jane decided to bring the whole family to the first meeting, Katie and her other two children, Becky, 13 and Nathan, 6, her partner Tony and his 13-year-old daughter, Lisa. The worker,[4] aware that Katie in particular may have been expecting a hard time, was keen to begin with 'competency talk'.

> Worker: ... Well, I don't know much about you. Let's see, who should we start with, what about oldest first? What's Becky good at?
> Jane: She's good at lots of things, she's good at helping me round the house.
> Worker: Really? I bet you're pleased about that. What else is Becky good at? [It emerges that Becky has a good singing voice, Lisa is doing well at school, especially at French, and is good at tidying her room!]
> Worker: That's great. OK, what about Katie, what is Katie good at?
> Jane: Well, she's good at cooking, making cakes and things like that. She likes to help out in the kitchen.
> Worker: It sounds like you've got some children who are pretty helpful around the house here. You've got them well trained! Have they always been so helpful?
> Jane: Yes, since they've been old enough to, they've always done their share, well most of the time anyway.

Katie's thoughtfulness was also mentioned, as when she had recently made her Mum a cup of tea, having overheard her say how tired she was. A positive note had been struck before getting down to business.

> Worker: OK. Right, I'd like to ask you each a different type of question now. Can I start with you, Jane? I'm wondering, what are your best hopes from coming here?
> Jane: Best hopes? I'd just like some sort of normality back in our lives again, that's all. Everyone's falling out with each other, and I've just about had enough of it. I'd like a little bit of stability in the family.
> Worker: How about you, Tony, what are your best hopes for this?
> Tony: Just the same as Jane really. If we just had a nice, steady family, with not so much arguing all the time, with everyone getting along with everybody else.
> Jane: Yes, if we could just have a little bit of give and take.
> Worker: OK, if I could just check this out with the rest of you. How about starting this side and then going round? Lisa, what do you hope could happen from coming here?
> Lisa: ... ermm, just if everyone in our house could get on.
> Worker: OK, sure, makes sense. And Katie, how about you?
> Katie: I don't know what could happen.
> Worker: Well, just suppose that somehow coming here turns out to be useful to you, from your point of view. What would have to be happening so that you could think to yourself, 'Hey, it was useful going there'?
> Jane: What do you want to be different, Katie?
> Katie: For me not to be left out all the time.
> Worker: Right, OK. And if you don't get left out all the time, what would be happening?
> Katie: Becky or Lisa would do something with me.
> Worker: Um-hum.
> Katie: And Mum would talk to me when I come in from school.
> Worker: Right, I get you, ah-ha. And how about you, Becky? What needs to happen so that coming here is helpful for you?

Becky, like Katie, wanted someone else to change, in this case Katie to stop being 'horrible' to their mum. The others had voiced general hopes about the family getting on better. The worker used the miracle question to elicit a more specific description of this, and the family slowly painted a joint picture of a miracle day.

Jane: There'd be no arguments!
Worker: OK, there'd be no arguments. What would you notice happening if there were no arguments? What would be the first things you'd each notice?
Katie: Mum would be singing, and Becky would be singing.
Becky: Katie would get up in a good mood.
Worker: How would you be able to tell she was in a good mood?
Becky: She'd be smiling.
Worker: So Katie, you'd notice Becky singing and Becky, you'd see Katie smiling.
Becky: And I would go in to wake up Mum and Tony, and they would wake up straight away!
Worker: And what would you notice about them when they woke up that would tell you the miracle had happened?
Becky: They'd have big smiles on their faces!
Worker: Jane and Tony, suppose that happened, what would you notice about Becky?
Jane: She'd have brought us a cup of tea up for a start-off.
Tony: She'd be happy herself.
Worker: How would you know?
Tony: Well, she'd be smiling.
Jane: And she might be singing. She'd probably say something like 'come on you two, get a move on now, don't stay in bed all morning'.

This opening session, and the preferred version of their life together developed by the family, served as a foundation for the rest of the work. It was the only one attended by the whole family, Jane using later sessions for varying purposes. A common thread was to help Katie in her relationships with different members of the family, Becky and Tony in particular, and also with her feelings about her problematic contact with her father. Jane and Katie attended all six sessions, some on their own, and others with Becky or Tony. There were consistent themes which linked sessions together, and other issues which were tackled in individual sessions. The worker had to address the continuities and also the self-contained nature of sessions. For example, when Becky attended her second session, which was Jane and Katie's fourth, exploration of what had been better between sessions was followed up by the question: 'So, given that Becky is here today, what needs to happen for *this* session to be useful?'

This reflects the nature of everyday family life, and the ways in which families tackle difficulties themselves. It is not often that families will sit down all together and have a formal 'whole family' meeting. It is more likely that family members will talk in different combinations at different times, depending on what needs to be resolved. Life is messy, and reflecting this, the provision of help will often be messy. The days when we could categorise ourselves as working with either individuals or families are long gone. We need 'therapists who are not bounded by notions of individual or family' (Anderson, 2001, p. 358). Solution-focused practitioners, with their healthy disregard for received ideas about helping, are well suited to the task.

Notes

[1] An 'access team' in an English local authority Social Services department.
[2] The Early Response Project at Leicester Family Service Unit.
[3] Guy Shennan.
[4] Guy Shennan.

References

Anderson, H. (2001) Postmodern collaborative and person-centred therapies: what would Carl Rogers say? *Journal of Family Therapy*, 23(4): 339–360.

Berg, I.K. (1991) *Family Preservation: a brief therapy workbook*. London: BT Press.

Burnham, J. (1986) *Family Therapy: first steps towards a systemic approach*. London: Tavistock.

Cade, B. and O'Hanlon, B. (1993) *A Brief Guide to Brief Therapy*. New York: W.W. Norton.

DeJong, P. and Berg, I.K. (2001) *Interviewing for Solutions* (2nd edn). Pacific Grove: Brooks/Cole.

de Shazer, S. (1988) *Clues: investigating solutions in brief therapy*. New York: W.W. Norton.

de Shazer, S. (1991) *Putting Difference to Work*. New York: W.W. Norton.

de Shazer, S., Berg, I.K., Lipchik, E., Nunnally, E., Molnar, A., Gingerich, W. and Weiner-Davis, M. (1986) Brief therapy: focused solution development. *Family Process*, 25: 207–222.

Dermer, S., Hemesath, C. and Russell, C. (1998) A feminist critique of solution-focused therapy. *American Journal of Family Therapy*, 26(3): 239–250.

Dienhart, A. (2001) Engaging men in family therapy: does the gender of the therapist make a difference? *Journal of Family Therapy*, 23(1): 21–45.

Duncan, B. and Miller, S. (2000) *The Heroic Client: doing client-directed, outcome-informed therapy*. San Francisco: Jossey-Bass.

George, E., Iveson, C. and Ratner, H. (1999) *Problem to Solution: brief therapy with individuals and families* (2nd edn). London: BT Press.

Iveson, C. (1996) Solution-focused brief therapy: working with young people. in A. Sigston, P. Curran, A. Labram and S. Wolfendale (eds), *Psychology in Practice: with young people, families and schools*. London: Fulton.

Lethem, J. (1994) *Moved to Tears, Moved to Action: solution-focused brief therapy with women and children*. London: BT Press.

Sharry, J. Madden, B., Darmody, M. and Miller, S. (2001) Giving our clients the break: applications of client-directed, outcome-informed clinical work. *Journal of Systemic Therapies*, 20(3): 68–76.

Sharry, J., Madden, B. and Darmody, M. (2002) *Becoming a Solution Detective: a strengths-based guide to brief therapy*. London: BT Press.

Turnell, A. and Lipchik, E. (1999) The role of empathy in brief therapy: the overlooked but vital context. *Australian and New Zealand Journal of Family Therapy*, 20(4): 177–182.

Walters, J., Tasker, F. and Bichard, S. (2001) Too busy? Fathers' attendance for family appointments. *Journal of Family Therapy*, 23(1): 3–20.

Watzlawick, P., Weakland, J. and Fisch, R. (1974) *Change: principles of problem formation and problem resolution*. New York: W.W. Norton.

5

Solution-Focused Parent Training

John Sharry

Parents managing behavioural problems in their children have traditionally been offered behavioural parent training when they have been referred to child mental health clinics (Kazdin, 1995; Patterson et al., 1992; Webster-Stratton and Herbert, 1994). Solution-focused therapy (Berg, 1991, 1994; de Shazer, 1985, 1988, 1991; O'Connell, 1998) with its emphasis on helping clients generate their own solutions, can help this process be more collaborative. This chapter describes the Parents Plus Programme (Sharry and Fitzpatrick, 1997), a group parent training programme which teaches behaviour management techniques while drawing upon a solution-focused group process in helping parents adapt the ideas to their unique living situations.

In particular, I describe a solution-building process which encourages parents to use the techniques or 'prescribed solutions' of behavioural parent training in conjunction with their own naturally emergent solutions. Parents are encouraged both to personalise the presented techniques and ideas and to generate their own alternative solutions, depending on which better fits their unique context and living situation. In this way parents have the best of both worlds. They have access, not only to the creativity of their own solutions and those of other parents in the group, but also to solutions and ideas researched as effective within behavioural parent training.

Parent training – an overview

Children with severe behaviour problems are at serious risk of a wide range of long-term problems including school dropout, criminality, drug and alcohol abuse, and relationship difficulties (Kazdin, 1995; Offord and Bennett, 1994). Furthermore their parents and families are often under enormous stress and are isolated and under-supported (Webster-Stratton and Herbert, 1994). The prognosis is worst for young children whose behaviour problems become apparent in early childhood (Campbell, 1995). Such problems are common and account for nearly two-thirds of referrals to child mental health services.

Parent training approaches to behaviour problems, based on social learning ideas, have been extensively studied over the years and have been shown to produce effective results both in reducing children's behaviour problems, and in reducing parental stress in two-thirds of cases (Kazdin, 1997a; Webster-Stratton and Hammond, 1997). There have been three main traditions in parent training: behavioural/social learning programmes (Patterson et al., 1992), Adlerian approaches such as the STEP programme (Dinkmeyer and McKay, 1982) and humanistic/Rogerian approaches such as Parent Effectiveness Training (Gordon, 1975). Of the three traditions, behavioural parent training has been the most robustly researched as effective in clinical settings (Kazdin, 1997b).

However there are groups of families for whom the approach has been less effective or for whom the early gains are not maintained in the long term (Miller and Prinz, 1990). This is particularly the case for families who experience social problems or who are difficult to engage within formal parent training (Webster-Stratton, 1997).

In response to these obstacles new ways of enhancing the effectiveness of parent training have evolved. For example video materials have been introduced into parent training programmes to make them more accessible and appealing. This approach, pioneered by Webster-Stratton in America (Webster-Stratton, 1992) and developed in Europe (Sharry and Fitzpatrick, 1997), does not demand literacy and uses a medium familiar to parents. It has produced robust results in terms of reduced child behaviour problems and increased parental satisfaction (Sharry et al., 1995; Webster-Stratton et al., 1988).

Equally, the method of facilitation in parent training has come under increased scrutiny. The original didactic approach has been criticised for imposing solutions which are either 'resisted' by parents or which do not endure beyond the training period as they do not fit with the parents' living situation. As a result, more effective collaborative approaches have developed which focus on individual parental goals, relationship-building techniques, positive reframing and building on parents' existing knowledge (Dembo et al., 1985; Webster-Stratton and Herbert, 1994; Chamberlain and Baldwin, 1987). There continues to be a search for therapist approaches which are effective and empowering, especially with 'difficult to engage clients'. Solution-focused therapy (SFT) with its positive emphasis on the clients' strengths, skills and resources and on co-operation in the therapeutic relationship, has much to contribute in this arena.

Parents Plus Programme

The Parents Plus Programme (Sharry and Fitzpatrick, 1997) is a video-based parenting course for solving and managing discipline problems in young children aged 4–11. It uses video examples of parenting techniques, drawn mainly from the social learning/behavioural tradition and incorporates them into a solution-focused model of groupwork. The programme is divided into two sections.

1   *Encouraging children:* How to promote positive behaviour in children via positive attention, active listening, one on one play time, specific encouragement and rewards.

2   *Setting rules and handling misbehaviour:* How to set and follow through with rules, and to handle misbehaviour via ignoring, time out, logical consequences and sanctions.

The programme can be completed either individually by parents or within small groups over eight to ten sessions. Each session consists of the reviewing of video clips which illustrate a certain topic, followed by small group discussion, role-play and homework. Central to the programme is a collaborative solution-focused model of groupwork.

Parent training – principles

In behavioural parent training the focus is on the interaction between parent and child. Children, and indeed adults, behave the way they do because their behaviours are reinforced by the attention of their parents or other significant adults. Over time patterns can be set up, where children learn a certain way of behaving, expecting the same response from their parents and those around them. This can be a pro-social pattern, for example when a child learns to say please and thus gains the reward of parental approval, or an anti-social behaviour, for example where a child throws a tantrum, to get his parent to back down and give him what he wants.

In parent training, behavioural change is brought about by encouraging parents to behave differently towards their children. When the gain for misbehaviour is reduced and the reward for positive behaviour increased, negative patterns can be broken and new, positive ones allowed to emerge. A central principle is the praise–ignore formula (Forehand and McMahon, 1981; Webster-Stratton and Herbert, 1994). Parents can inadvertently reward their children's misbehaviour by giving it lots of negative attention (for example via scolding, shouting, criticising, nagging, etc.) and by ignoring and not rewarding positive behaviour – they only attend to their children when they are in trouble. In parent training they are encour-aged to turn this around, that is to go out of their way to notice and encourage examples of positive behaviour, while largely ignoring the misbehaviour they see. When parents come to parent training they are taught the skills of good positive attending and the more difficult skill of planned ignoring. They are also taught to use planned rewards with children when they behave and also how to apply sanc-tions and consequences when they do not. In this way parent training is psycho-educational. The emphasis is on teaching parents new skills and strategies, while providing them with therapeutic support to implement them at home.

Becoming solution-focused in parent training

Focus on goals

Client-centred goals are central to solution-focused therapy (Berg, 1991; de Shazer, 1991). It is essential to build with the client positive and detailed goals which are highly motivating and personal to them. Client-centred goals by themselves create the conditions for good collaboration. Often what is conceived as 'resistance' in therapeutic relationships is simply caused by the therapeutic goal being unclear, negatively formulated, or imposed upon the client. The Plumas project (Lee et al., 1997), which is a solution-focused groupwork programme for male perpetrators of domestic violence, deems it essential that on entry clients must have formulated a personal, positive goal which they want to work on during the programme. Such an approach creates the conditions for high collaboration with a client group often described as demotivated or hard to engage. It may also account for the high success of the programme – only 17 per cent recidivism at 5 year follow-up compared to 40 per cent in other traditional treatments (Adrianna Uken, personal communication 20/10/1999). Establishing client-centred goals is the driving force of solution-focused parent training, being central to preparation, treatment, review and follow-up.

Focus on strengths, skills and resources

A core dynamic in SFT is its positive orientation, focusing on the individual's strengths, skills and resources; the therapist looks for every opportunity to give positive feedback and to compliment client successes (George et al., 1990). This dynamic generalises into a group whereby the facilitators constantly identify and emphasise the strengths and resources of the individuals in the group and of the group as a whole. In solution-focused parent training the aim is to encourage parents to adopt this positive orientation towards both themselves and their children. Such an approach has resonance with the behavioural ideas of positive praise and systematic attention (Sharry, 1999).

As with client-centred goals, a focus on strengths and resources does much to create a context of collaboration, high motivation and hope for change. It requires a paradigm shift on the part of therapists. Many parents come to parent training feeling inadequate and blamed and often the deficit-based assumptions of traditional parent training (such as the view that these parents need to learn new skills, thus implying that they are to blame for their children's problems) can inadvertently reinforce this. However by considering these parents differently, for example as dedicated parents who have made the committed step of coming to a parenting course, and to conceive of parent training in solution-focused terms, for example as a way of enhancing and building upon the many skills parents already have, a new positive and motivating context can be established.

In addition, rather than simply pathologising the many parents who drop out of parent training or who never access it in the first place, we can view these parents in a strengths-based context. For example we can work hard to discover their real goals: perhaps they are seeking something different to parent training (perhaps support for themselves via education) or perhaps they would prefer to meet in local community settings rather than in a stigmatised mental health clinic or perhaps they would prefer interventions which include their children and/or extended family. From this perspective the onus is on professionals to find new and effective methods of reaching and meeting the needs of these parents.

A combined model

A central belief in SFT is that clients have most or all of the resources and strengths they need to solve their problems (Berg, 1991; Rhodes and Ajmal, 1995). Therapy is a process of helping the client to 'remember' or to reaccess these resources, particularly by focusing on goals and recalling exceptions to the problem, which reveal these strengths and already existing means of coping. The aim is to help clients generate their own solutions to the parenting or other dilemmas they face. The therapist adopts a stance of respectful curiosity, 'interviewing the client with a constructive ear' (Lipchik, 1988), encouraging him/her to build up a detailed solution picture.

While the behavioural model prescribes a set of 'tried and tested' techniques to parents, SFT does not prescribe a 'best solution', but simply helps the client build their own preferred solutions which uniquely apply to their situation. While the two positions may appear to be in contradiction, even diametrically opposed, it is unhelpful to conceive of either one or the other as the superior approach. Both have a validity, and in many respects there is common ground between them (for example both emphasise the power of positive attention and cognitive reframing in creating desired change).

The practical reality is that clients come to therapy possessing *most* of the resources needed to solve their problems while also looking to learn new skills and gain new ideas and perspectives. What seems to be important is for the worker to be led by the clients and to give them the option of receiving different types of help, whether behaviour management skills, solution-focused therapy or a combination of both.

A combination is often the best approach as no single model has all the answers or applies in every situation. Even well-tested behavioural techniques such as tantrum ignoring does not work for all parents, as it may not fit with their personality style. Some parents find 'workable' solutions distinct from the prescribed one; for example some parents can talk their child out of a tantrum (while still remaining firm); others might be able to distract their child out of it; and others find ways of living with this way of acting out which minimise the distress for the family. Rather than imposing a solution which may not fit (and which may increase a sense of parental inadequacy if it fails) it is more useful to discover the parents' own preferred solution which they can more readily apply. Equally, solution-focused therapists working only with the clients' generated solutions may inadvertently withhold from clients specific techniques that might enhance and expand their own natural solutions. For example, one mother in a group was struggling to get her seven-year-old daughter to bed on time. To remedy this she had tried giving her a treat before bedtime, as a means to encourage her to go to bed. Following the video input she altered this to give the reward the following morning, thus invoking the behavioural principle that the reward should come after the desired behaviour (Forehand and Long, 1996). This proved to be a more successful approach for her. In another case a parent had developed a strategy with her son's teacher to help him behave in school. They used a copybook that described the child's behaviour during the day, good and bad. This was filled in by the teacher and reviewed by the mother with her child. The mother used to spend more time discussing the negative behaviours with her son. She followed the suggestion to focus primarily on the positive behaviours, thus utilising the parent training principle of attending to the positive first (Webster-Stratton, 1992), a principle that clearly resonates with solution-focused ideas. This new approach proved more successful for her, in achieving both her goals: better behaviour at school and an improved relationship with her son.

Solution building with parents

In the Parents Plus Programme, behavioural parenting techniques are illustrated by videos and discussed by the parents in the group. These prescribed solutions are not meant to be universally applied. What is important is that they are personalised to the parent's individual situation and that each parent picks the ideas which resonate naturally with their own personality, temperamental style and living situation. Showing the video clips provides a *starting point* for debate and facilitated discussion. This gives parents the opportunity to think through how the ideas may apply in their own situation, and to generate alternatives if they don't. This process of solution building with parents is at the heart of a successful parent training group. The ideas input from behavioural parent training are mixed with the ideas generated by parents in the group discussion with the aim of finding a solution which fits. The method of facilitation is crucial, to ensure that it is not overly didactic but that it draws on parents' strengths, skills and resources and encourages them to generate their own ideas and solutions. Listed below are a number of collaborative facilitation techniques, which can help bring this about even in a highly structured parenting course.

Predicting
Prior to illustrating a behavioural principle or technique on video, the facilitator encourages the parents to predict what will be covered, thus validating their knowledge of the topic. This can be done in two ways.

Firstly, in introducing the topic, you can make links to the parents' previous examples of successful parenting which illustrate what will be seen on video. For example, 'We are now going to look at how important it is to specifically encourage children. This is something that you raised, Alice, when you described how you helped Rob learn to make his bed. Can you tell us a bit more about what made that work?'

Secondly, the parents' views can be gained more systematically by introducing the topic via a series of preliminary questions. For example in the session on encouragement the questions could be 'How important is it to encourage children?' or 'What is the best way to encourage children?' The facilitator then listens carefully to the parents' responses, validating their ideas and suggestions and looking for links to the ideas to be covered in the video input.

Such a 'prediction' approach is strengths-based in that it gives parents a sense that their ideas, which they are already applying successfully at home, are validated by many of the 'expert' approaches to parenting. Such an understanding increases their confidence and encourages them to use the course to consolidate and enhance what they are already doing right at home. Parents' ability to find and own their expertise makes change easier, more rapid and longer term.

Reviewing

When a video clip is being reviewed parents are encouraged to share their responses, ideas and judgements, for example questions like 'What specific skills is the parent using in this scene?' or 'What is making this parent's approach effective/ ineffective in this case?' It does not matter whether parents agree or disagree with the ideas being expressed, it is more important that they have an opportunity to reflect and think about what they are seeing. The videos provide a starting point for discussion and can provoke a parent into thinking about a concept or idea and how it might apply in their life. Without the input this idea might not have occurred to them. Even if they disagree with the input, the process can help them begin to understand and think about their preferred way of doing things. This thinking, reflecting and learning is the most important process in the group discussion.

Finding fit

After a review of the ideas parents are encouraged to see how they might or might not fit with their own home situation and their specific goals for coming to the group. This can be introduced by questions like 'How might you apply this idea at home?' 'What style of encouragement would work best for you?' It is during this section that differences can be explored and valued. Disagreement or challenge to the presented 'expert' ideas at this stage is a strength. The ensuing discussion can reveal how the ideas are not perfect, and that what counts is how people fit them to their own unique style of parenting and how they adapt them to their own individual situation. There is also an opportunity at this stage to explore genuine alternatives with parents. 'So you would not like to use time out with your child at her age. What alternatives could you use when she hits out?' A brainstorm in a group can reveal many creative and genuine suggestions which parents can evaluate for themselves.

Such a discussion can provide a levelling within the group, where parents see the 'expert' ideas as not necessarily better than theirs, but on an equal footing. They can feel empowered to take, leave or adapt the ideas depending on how they help them get closer to their goals for the group.

Summarising and planning

At the end of a session parents are encouraged to review their personal goals, summarise for themselves the key learning points of the session and create a plan for the following week. While the course material may contain suggestions about homework, this space is essential for parents to adapt and personalise it to their own context. Parents can reflect on their own, or in discussion in the group, or in dialogue with the facilitator.

A case study

The following extract is taken from the first session of a community-based parenting group. The group consisted of 12 parents (10 mothers and 2 fathers), whose children were attending a mental health service and who were referred due to the behavioural problems they were experiencing. All had attended an initial preparatory interview to ensure the course met their needs and to begin the process of establishing their personal goals. The first session was divided between further continuing the goal creation process and introducing one of the central behavioural principles of the course – the praise–ignore formula. This formula suggests to parents that they can encourage positive behaviour in their children by going out of their way to notice it – literally to catch their children being good – while ignoring or withdrawing excessive attention from misbehaviour.

The following extracts were chosen to illustrate the four facilitation techniques described above. The extracts aren't 'perfect' dialogue examples, in that they include overlapping talk, interruptions and theme shifting. However, they do reflect a 'real world' group interaction and how a facilitator can work with participants to keep the group solution-focused and to help them personalise the ideas. They have been slightly edited for brevity and to make the steps clearer, and all names and personal details have been changed.

The first extract is taken from the goal negotiation at the beginning of the session, and concerns the input of several parents who describe successful approaches in their parenting which linked in with the 'praise–ignore formula' to be covered in this session. The extract starts during a group round, where each parent is asked to introduce him/herself and describe their personal goal for the course.

Predicting

Paul: I'm Paul, and I would like there to be less conflict in the house, for my son to be more positive. To be honest, things have improved since we met [*addressing course facilitator and referring to screening interview*].

Facilitator (FA):   Really, tell me what has changed. [*exploring pre-session change*]

June (Paul's partner):   He's doing better at school. Last year he had a teacher who was quite rigid and highly strung. She was always hounding him to do the right thing. So he had her hounding him in school and me hounding him at home. So between the two of us he couldn't cope. This year he has a teacher who is much calmer and it's much better.

Tina: He isn't under as much pressure. [*Tina comes in to support*]

June: Yes that's right.

FA: Isn't that really interesting, the calmer approach seemed to work better with him?

June: Yeah, he hadn't a calm approach at school and he didn't have a calm approach from me at home.

Tina: I had the same problem with my son. He was getting on badly at school with one teacher and then he was taking it out on me at home. When he changed his teacher it all got a lot better, his teacher gave him a lot more attention.

FA: So the calm approach or giving positive attention works better?

June: Yeah, we have seen this. I'm not on his back all the time, I'm more positive with him.

FA: How are you more positive with him?

June: Well I'll notice if he's good or he does something nice, rather than criticising him all the time.

FA: That's really interesting, because being more positive is what we will be looking at tonight. You are way ahead of us.

June: We have seen it work.

FA: What does anyone else think?

Alison: Like June said, I found being positive made a big difference. I used to be always noticing the bad things he was doing, telling him to do it differently.

June: It's because you are worried for them, you want them to behave well, that's why I was hounding him.

FA: So it is understandable.

[June and Alison empathetically support one another and the therapist reinforces this.]

Alison: Yeah, but like yourself, I found it didn't work.

FA: What did you find that worked for you?

Alison: Actually not looking for the bad things he was doing, and being able to pick out the little good things he was doing. The more I pick them out the more he seems to do them. Like when he comes home from school with a picture or a slightly good report, we make a big deal of it and he loves it. It helped him.

FA: So picking out the positives really works for you.

Alison: Yeah.

FA: That's exactly the point we will be covering tonight, so hold on to it.

In the above sequence the therapist has identified how two parents are already applying their version of the praise–ignore formula. By drawing attention to it, he reinforces the idea in the group, flagging it for later discussion and empowering them to learn from each other.

Reviewing

In the next sequence, the group have just been shown video input on 'catching their child being good', and in particular they have viewed a role-played scene where a father sitting with his two children at dinner noticed them sharing and specifically praised them both for this.

FA: What does anyone think of that scene? Would it work?

Alison: I do encourage my children to share.

[lots of parents begin talking in the group.]

Tina: Yeah sharing is important.

Orla: That scene might work, you would say something like that.

FA: Would you? Tell me about that, Orla. How do you mean?

Orla: Well, I would say it to them if they were sitting with me like that. If you were sitting in McDonald's and you saw them share, you might say 'Oh you are very good for doing that.'

FA: So you would tell them you were pleased.

Paul: Sometimes, children don't usually share so when you see a child sharing a sweet you praise it.

FA: Hmmh, you really go out of your way to praise it then.

Orla: Yeah you naturally praise it when you see it.

June: When our child gives us a sweet, even if we don't want it we take it and say 'and look, aren't you very generous.'

FA: Because you want to encourage them to share, you make a big deal of it?

June: Exactly.

In the next sequence the therapist goes on to review a different aspect of the same video scene, notably trying to get the parents to identify the behavioural skills of specific encouragement and praise.

FA: What way did the dad do it that made it work? [*pause*] What way did he say it exactly that made it work?

Tina: He said you're very good for sharing.

FA: Yeah that's right.

Orla: He praised both of them.

FA: Yeah he praised both of them. That is really important, he praised both of them, commented on something they were both doing. What else did he do? [*pause*] What did he say exactly?

Alison: He said one was good for sharing the juice and the other was good for saying thank you?

FA: That's exactly right. He specifically commented on what they did well, didn't he? He praised one for saying thank you and the other for sharing the juice. It's really important to let children know exactly what they did right, rather than being vague, like 'good boy'. Really describe to them what you like so they know.

June: I think saying 'good boy' only puts them under pressure. You have to tell them what it is that is good, what they did that you like.

FA: That's right. You want to make them sure they know.

* *

Finding fit

In the next sequence, the group has just been shown a further video scene on 'catching their child being good', where a parent spotted her two children playing quietly together and went over and commented on it. In this sequence the group object to the idea presented. Notice how the facilitator, by accepting and understanding this objection, validates their knowledge. He then goes on to explore with the group alternatives which fit their situation.

FA: So what does anyone think?

Jean: I thought it was very over the top. A mother wouldn't go over to praise like that.

FA: So you mightn't do it like that. What does anyone else think?

Alison: If all my children were quiet like that I would be afraid to disturb them.

[*many of the parents laugh.*]

Tina: I'd be afraid they'd run out and mess around.

Paula: If Tom [her son] was as good as that, like a little angel, like we saw on the telly, and I went in and said that to him, he would laugh at me and he'd walk into the kitchen and do something bold.

FA: [*addressing group*] So what you're saying is that if your child is doing something right or behaving well, you would be tempted not to comment on it. You would be worried about interrupting the good behaviour? [*nods in group*] That seems to be what people are saying?

[*The therapist does not impose a prescribed solution, but attempts to understand the positive basis to their objection, allowing the space for alternatives to emerge.*]

Jean: There are certain times you can do it and certain times you can't do it.

FA: When can you do it, when can you pay attention?

Jean: Well if my children were playing quietly like that I would leave them to their own devices, and wait for them to come to me and say look at this picture I'm drawing. Then I would say that's lovely or great.

FA: I see what you mean. So you would follow their lead, you would wait for a good time to give attention.

Jean: Yeah that's right I wouldn't go over and interrupt them.

FA: That's an important point, waiting for a good time to go over and catch them being good.

[*The therapist explores with this parent her own adapted solution, notably waiting for the right time to give her child positive attention.*]

Summarising and planning

FA: So you [whole group] have made some very good points. It's all about trying to find ways to adapt giving positive attention to your children, in ways that it feels comfortable and works for you and gets through to your child. How do some of you do that? How might you go out of your way to notice good behaviour?

Sandra: I've got an example. My son is a bedwetter. Sometimes you get periods, maybe a few days, where he doesn't wet or whatever. I try and tell him how pleased I am, rather than only saying something to him when he wets the bed. He wet this morning and I didn't make a big fuss of it.

FA: That's excellent, you're being understanding of him, not criticising him when he falls down, but also being really encouraging of him when he manages to keep the bed dry.

Paula: I think I would be inclined, when I have a good day with Tom, to tell him at the end of the day before he goes to bed. I'd say 'Look Tom, didn't we have a good time today, wasn't it better today?'

FA: What way would things go on a good day?

Paula: Well there would be no rows, he would come in from school in better humour.

FA: So you would be getting on better, in better humour?

Paula: Yeah.

FA: And how does he respond, when you tell him these things?

Paula: Well he loves it, he's chuffed.

FA: I see, when you have a good day you tell him at night, you store up the praise. What about anyone else?

June: I find it depends on the child. My child, who I think is younger, needs constant attention. I couldn't wait until the night.

FA: So you would be more inclined to give him positive attention throughout the day, when you spot him doing something good.

Orla: You have to be careful, some children get into their own little world when they're doing something, say drawing or playing, if you went over to them and praised them you would break their concentration.

FA: Yeah you don't want to break their concentration. How could you do that? How could you give positive attention, in a way that doesn't break their concentration. [*pause*]

Orla: Well I'd wait until a good time, say when they had finished a picture.

FA: I got you, so timing is real important.

[*pause*]

FA: So there are lots of ways of doing this. It's a good idea to give attention when you spot your children being good, but timing is important, you have to wait for a good time and to do it in a way that it will get through to them, either during or just after they do something, or at the end of a good day when you are chatting to them.

In the above sequence the therapist attempts to summarise the points made and the different conclusions drawn. Notice how each of the parents cited has taken something slightly different from the discussion and all have slightly different ways of 'catching their children being good'. These differences are encouraged and validated by the therapist.

Conclusion

In this chapter I have described how solution-focused therapy's emphasis on client goals and already existing strengths and skills has much to contribute to the field of parent training, especially in creating a collaborative approach to working with parents. In particular I have described a solution-building process, which draws upon both the prescribed solutions of behavioural parent training and the natural solutions used by the parents. The video input of the Parents Plus Programme, rather than imposing ideas, provides a starting point for discussion and debate. The ideas presented are designed to stimulate and provoke parents into personalising the suggested ideas or generating their own alternatives, which better suit their unique living situation. By solution building in this way we give parents access not only to parenting techniques researched as effective within behaviourism, but also to parenting ideas generated by themselves and other group members. Parents can improve upon and expand their own natural solutions by incorporating behavioural ideas from the course input, as well as suggestions and ideas from other parents.

This solution-building process has much to contribute to the field of education, where trainers are trying to balance didactic teaching with drawing and building on students' existing knowledge. Solution building provides a means of actively co-constructing with the students knowledge which is a synergistic mixture of 'expert' and their own 'local' input. This knowledge is more likely to be meaningful, relevant and enduring because the students were partners in its co-creation and the knowledge is more personalised and better fits their own living contexts.

References

Berg, I.K. (1991) *Family Preservation: a brief therapy workbook*. London: BT Press.

Berg, I.K. (1994) *Family-based Services : a solution-focused approach*. New York: W.W. Norton.

Campbell, S. (1995) Behaviour problems in pre-school children: a review of recent research. *Journal of Child Psychology and Psychiatry*, 36: 113–49.

Chamberlain, P. and Baldwin, D.V. (1987) Client resistance to parent training: its therapeutic management. In T.R. Kratochwill (ed.), *Advances in School Psychology* (Vol. 6). New York: Plenum.

de Shazer, S. (1985) *Keys to Solution in Brief Therapy*. New York: W.W. Norton.

de Shazer, S. (1988) *Clues: investigating solutions in brief therapy*. New York: W.W. Norton.

de Shazer, S. (1991) *Putting Difference to Work*. New York: W.W. Norton.

Dembo, M.H., Sweitzer, M. and Lauritzen, P. (1985) An evaluation of group parent education programs: behavioral, PET and Adlerian programs. *Review of Educational Research*, 55(2): 155–200.

Dinkmeyer, D. and McKay, D.G. (1982) *STEP: Systematic Training for Effective Parenting*. New York: Random House.

Forehand, R.L. and Long, N. (1996) *Parenting the Strong Willed Child*. Chicago: Contemporary Books.

Forehand, R.L. and McMahon, R.J. (1981) *Helping the Noncompliant Child: a clinician's guide to parent training*. New York: Guilford.

George, E., Iveson, C. and Ratner, H. (1990) *Problem to Solution: brief therapy with individuals and families*. London: BT Press.

Gordon, T. (1975) *PET: Parent effectiveness training*. New York: Penguin.

Kazdin, A.E. (1995) *Treatment of Antisocial Behaviour in Children and Adolescents*. Honewood, IL: Dorsey.

Kazdin, A.E. (1997a) Parent management training: evidence, outcomes and issues. *Journal of the American Academy of Child and Adolescent Psychiatry*, 36: 1349–1356.

Kazdin, A.E. (1997b) Practitioner review: psychosocial treatments for conduct disorder in children. *Journal of Child Psychology and Psychiatry*, 38: 161–178.

Lee, M., Greene, G.J., Uken, A., Sebold, J. and Rheinscheld, J. (1997) Solution-focused brief group treatment of domestic violence offenders. Paper presented at the Four in One Conference, Bruges, Belgium.

Lipchik, E. (1988) Interviewing with a constructive ear. *Dulwich Centre Newsletter*, Winter: 3–7.

Miller, G.E. and Prinz, R.J. (1990) Enhancement of social learning family interventions for childhood conduct disorder. *Psychological Bulletin*, 108(2): 291–307.

O'Connell, B. (1998) *Solution-Focused Therapy*. London: Sage.

Offord, D.R. and Bennett, K.J. (1994) Conduct disorder: long-term outcomes and intervention effectiveness. *Journal of the American Academy of Child and Adolescent Psychiatry*, 33: 1069–1078.

Patterson, G.R., Reid, J.B. and Dishion, T.J. (1992) *A Social Interactional Approach: IV. Antisocial boys*. Eugene, OR: Castilia.

Rhodes, J. and Ajmal, Y. (1995) *Solution-Focused Thinking in Schools*. London: BT Press.

Sharry, J. (1999) Towards solution groupwork. *Journal of Systemic Therapies*, 18(2): 77–91.

Sharry, J. and Fitzpatrick, C. (1997) *Parents Plus Progamme: a video-based guide to managing and solving discipline problems in children aged 4–11*. Parents Plus, c/o Mater Child Guidance Clinic, Mater Hospital, North Circular Road, Dublin 7.

Sharry, J., Connolly, L. and Fitzpatrick, C. (1995) Collaborative parent training: evaluating the Webster-Stratton video-based programme in an Irish context. *Proceedings 9th Research Study Day, Research Unit, Hospitaller Order of St John of God, Dublin*, 9: 1–8.

Webster-Stratton, C. (1992) *The Parents and Children Videotape Series: programs 1–10*. Seattle: Seth Enterprises, 1411 8th Avenue West, Seattle, WA 98119 USA.

Webster-Stratton, C. (1997) From parent training to community building. *Families in Society: The Journal of Contemporary Human Services*, Special Issue (March/April) 156–171.

Webster-Stratton, C. and Hammond, M. (1997) Treating children with early-onset conduct problems: a comparison of child and parent training interventions. *Journal of Consulting and Clinical Psychology*, 65(1): 93–109.

Webster-Stratton, C. and Herbert, M. (1994) *Troubled Families, Problem Children*. Chichester: Wiley.

Webster-Stratton, C., Kolpacoff, M. and Hollinsworth, T. (1988) Self administered videotape therapy for two families with conduct disorder: comparison with two cost-effective treatments and a control group. *Journal of Consulting and Clinical Psychology*, 56(4): 558–566.

6

Solution-Focused Couples Therapy

Chris Iveson

One would expect couples to present a serious challenge to a model of therapy that relies so much on spelling out hopes for the future. It would be logical to assume that a major cause of couple trouble is divergent hopes and if the therapist's job is to help his or her clients realise their hopes then a successful outcome is hard to envisage. John is a successful corporate executive with a series of two-year postings that he hopes will lead to a headquarters-based vice-presidency: a future that requires geographical mobility. Mary wants to settle down in one place and have the chance to make a 'real' social life. George wants more sex, Josephine wants less. Sarah wants Harry to control his temper and stop beating her, Harry says he can't help it. How does solution-focused brief therapy help these couples resolve their dilemmas?

This chapter will illustrate how solution-focused brief therapists need not concern themselves with such apparently irreconcilable differences but do better to focus on the smaller, often mundane, issues of everyday living. Such an interest, rather than ignoring the issues, helps each couple find their own and each other's resources so they are better able to resolve the problems life brings them in their own way.

Working without the problem

One of the advantages of a new model of therapy is that there is no right or wrong way to do it. Each therapist may be more or less close to some founding principles but there is room for wide divergence. This book is ample evidence of the range of interpretations of de Shazer's original 'blueprint' (de Shazer, 1988). At the Brief Therapy Practice we have been interested in developing a version of solution-focused brief therapy that attempts to remove the problem entirely from the therapist's agenda (George et al., 1999). As de Shazer (1991) points out, to remove the notion of *problem* we must also abandon the notion of *solution* since it is impossible to have the latter without the former! This is not to say that we do not listen carefully to our clients' accounts of their problems when they choose to give them: not to listen would be a sure route to failure. However, we do not ourselves seek information about the problem nor do we work towards specific solutions. Instead we are interested in generating descriptions of possible futures and descriptions of what our clients are already doing that might contribute to these possible futures becoming a reality. We might also be interested in *history* but in the history of the preferred future rather than the history of the problem. Our aim is to seek only descriptions: descriptions of what might be and descriptions of what is or has been that might contribute to a realisation of what might be. And we try, with considerable success, to avoid any attempt to seek a specific solution. Instead, when we are at our best, we trust our clients to find, and choose or not choose, their own solutions.

How we do this in practice is different case by case but in each instance the therapist will be working to the same set of principles which define his or her areas of enquiry. Later in this chapter transcripts from actual sessions with couples will illustrate the application of these principles. But first, the four areas of enquiry that guide our interviews.

1   What are the client's best hopes from our work together?
2   What will the client's everyday life be like if these hopes are fulfilled?
3   What is the client already doing or has done in the past that might in some way contribute to these hopes being realised?
4   How will the client know that another small step towards the realisation of these hopes has been made?

'Best hopes'

'What are your best hopes out of our work together?'

We have come to see this as the crucial question in our work with clients. Within its simple formula rest many of the fundamental assumptions that underlie solution-focused brief therapy. To the client come several important messages including the therapist's belief that the client's agenda is paramount, that the client has agreed to the meeting for a purpose and, perhaps most important of all, the therapist has put him or herself entirely in the hands of the client since no one else in the entire universe can answer this question. During therapy these assumptions, especially the assumption of motivation, are treated as 'truths' even though they cannot be proven. This is immensely helpful because it leads the therapist not to give up on the client. If we assume that every client has agreed to speak with us for a *purpose*, and a purpose relevant to our job, then it becomes our responsibility to find this purpose. If we don't succeed it is not because the client 'lacks motivation' but rather because we have not found the right question to elicit the motivation we 'know' to be there. Ultimately there is no way to test this assumption, no way of knowing whether it is right or wrong, but what it does is keep the therapist working and stops us blaming the client when we do not succeed.

'Hopes fulfilled'

'If a miracle happened tonight while you were asleep and you woke up tomorrow with your hopes fulfilled what would be different?'

The miracle question is one of the great 'doorways' into the client's possible future and among its many variations there are three forms that are especially useful.

The 'standard' version

As expressed above, it can be used to begin a description of the hoped-for final outcome of the therapy and this is its most common usage. Each person is invited to describe in concrete detail what life without the problems that brought him or her to therapy would look like. It might include their feelings on awakening, the way they would get up, what they would have for breakfast, the looks and conversations between them, the way they would say goodbye as they went off to work, etc. Achieving *enough* of this quality of relationship becomes the goal of therapy.

Just the beginning

Sometimes, however, our client's circumstances are such that the final outcome can only be a distant prospect. If a couple are embedded in a particularly problematic set of circumstances – for example not only relationship problems but also poverty, debt, poor housing, children in trouble, depression, drink and whatever other problems might be associated with these – a less dramatic 'miracle' might be invoked: 'Let's imagine that tonight there is a miracle and though it does not actually sort these problems out what it does do is set your life going *towards* sorting them out. What is the first thing you'll notice tomorrow that begins to tell you that you are on the way to a resolution?' In this scenario the next day is much closer to the current reality of the couple's lives but includes the ingredient of movement towards a better future:

> *Therapist:* So what do you think you'll notice as you wake up?
> *Client:* Maybe I won't feel so completely hopeless.
> *Therapist:* And if you don't feel so hopeless what will you feel?
> *Client:* Well, maybe just that somehow we might get through this.
> *Therapist:* How will Gill know that you are thinking that maybe there might be a way through this?
> *Client:* I probably wouldn't be so irritable with her.
> *Therapist:* What would you be instead?
> *Client:* I don't know. Maybe I'd just ask her about her day or something.
> *Therapist:* Would Gill like that?
> *Client:* She'd be surprised!
> *Therapist:* And would she like that?
> *Client:* Yes, I think she would. I'm sure she would!
> *Therapist:* How would you know she liked it?
> *Client:* She might say so or just ask me something.
> *Therapist:* Like?
> *Client:* Just something ordinary like what am I doing at work.

In these 'miracles' the very first steps towards a resolution are charted but what is also described is how the couple might work at their best when in a crisis.

Two for one

The third variation is one that includes another agenda in addition to the client's. This is especially useful where there are two clients each of whom needs to be treated as an individual with his or her own set of unique hopes. As always, the person being asked the question is at that moment the primary client and that person's hopes are paramount: 'Let's imagine that tonight there is a miracle and it creates exactly the kind of relationship you want with your partner in a way which is right for you and right for her. What's the first thing you'll notice tomorrow that begins to tell you the miracle has happened?' The 'right for you' is the client's agenda and the 'right for her' invites the client to consider only those preferred and hoped-for futures that honour their partner's wishes as well as their own. Given the virtually infinite range of possibilities within every relationship it is unlikely that taking into account the partner's hopes and needs will be unduly restrictive of the other person's ambitions!

Whatever the starting miracle the task of the therapist is to elicit as detailed a picture as possible of what life would be like after such a miracle. The detail serves a number of purposes. Firstly, the more concrete and mundane the description the easier it is to view as a real possibility; secondly, it creates more opportunities for the client to discover bits of the miracle that are already happening; and, thirdly, a detailed description for some clients leads to a 'visualisation' which reinforces the sense that a different way of life is possible.

In the following example Mary is describing the morning routine as John leaves for work.

> *Therapist:*   And what would tell you that your relationship with John was as you wanted it to be?
> *Mary:*   I would tell by the way he kissed me goodbye.
> *Therapist:*   What would be different?
> *Mary:*   He'd just hold me a little longer.
> *Therapist:*   Would you like that?
> *Mary:*   Yes, of course!
> *Therapist:*   How would John know you liked it?
> *Mary:*   I might even tell him I love him!
> *Therapist:*   Would he like that?
> *Mary and John:*   [*laughing*] Yes!

There is a strong sense at this point that both Mary and John have in some way 'experienced' this doorstep kiss in a way which has reminded them of their love. The interview continues.

> *Therapist:*   And after John has gone what will you notice next?
> *Mary:*   After this miracle – I wouldn't immediately start worrying about everything I hadn't done.
> *Therapist:*   So what would you do instead?
> *Mary:*   Maybe I'd have a cup of tea – actually, I did have a cup of tea yesterday morning after John had gone off to work!

With this detail Mary is able to tell herself how she will know she and John are getting on better and also discover that part of it, the hitherto unnoticed cup of tea, is already beginning to happen.

As John and Mary find their way back towards a more satisfying relationship the 'problem' becomes less insurmountable – love, when it is working, conquers most things!

What are you already doing that might help?

There are many ways to invite this information. In the earlier forms of solution-focused brief therapy the most common route was through exceptions: times the problem didn't happen. More consistent with a problem-free therapy is an interest in 'times the miracle already happens'. But the most versatile and accessible way into what the client is already doing is the scale. It is always a temptation to use the scale to generate a solution: 'What do you need to do to move up one point?' Much more useful is generating descriptions of what already exists. The more the client is aware of what he or she has already achieved, however insignificant it might seem, the more confident they are likely to be in taking another step.

George and Josephine had each described their miracles which, like all good miracles, were to do with getting on with their lives together, not just about sex. The question: 'So if you had the sexual relationship you wanted what effect would it have on the rest of your relationship?' led to a very detailed and rich description of a warm and loving couple who had found each other later in life when they had each ceased to expect such a blessing. Their love had grown from friendship and throughout their lives neither had experienced so much in common with another person. As each spoke about the other, not just their hopes but what they already had, the tension between them began to be replaced by appreciation and hope. And then their sense of humour had room to show them a way forward. Music had brought them together and was about to do so again. They were going to an open-air concert that evening, the summer finale with Tchaikovsky's *1812* complete with cannons and fireworks. As George was telling me this Josephine burst in with: 'And that's George! Pure bloody Tchaikovsky! Boom, bang, crash and a lot of smoke!' George, who loved Tchaikovsky, could do little but agree. Josephine, on the other hand, preferred the more gently undulating climb towards the peak of Mozart. When asked to scale how much Mozart she was getting she was surprised to remember several occasions when George had shown distinctive tendencies towards Mozart. Cheered by this, George rashly promised to be all Mozart in the future, to which Josephine replied with horror: 'Goodness gracious, no! I love a bit of the old boom, bang, crash sometimes!'

This was an example of solution-focused brief therapy at its best: the therapist, expert on neither music nor sex, entirely in the hands of his clients for the knowledge that would take them forward. George and Josephine left the session engaged in an erudite, if giggly, conversation about obscure musical styles.

The next small step

A common mistake in solution-focused brief therapy, especially for new practitioners, is to rush towards solutions and become over-interested in how the client is going to move forward. When the therapist becomes too interested in the client's own solutions, more valid interest may be blocked out. Exploring the next small step is important, but much less important than establishing a concrete description of the preferred future and discovering everything the client is already doing that might help bring that future about. Neither need the next small step be turned into an action plan. If it is left as a selection of possible indicators of movement to be looked out for, then the client is under no pressure to perform for the therapist. 'If you were to move from two to three what might you notice different? ... What else? ... What else? ... What else?' gives the client information about a range of possible ways forward, all of which follow directly from what they have already achieved. Mary's next small steps included receiving a phone call from John during the day and an arrangement to meet a friend for lunch. George thought he might hear himself suggest going to a concert or be humming a tune at work. As 'things that might be noticed' rather than 'things that must be done' the next small steps are ways of recognising movement *as it happens*. The more the client recognises movement the more likely he or she is to feel confident about the possibility of change.

Questions as intervention

When we began to practice solution-focused brief therapy (George et al., 1999) we thought the therapist's task was to find out the small ways the client was already doing the solution (i.e. exceptions to the problem) and then find ways to get them to do more. The information we sought out during the session was intended to guide us towards constructing the right homework task. There were many 'rules' about how to do this (de Shazer, 1984, 1988) including ways to categorise clients according to motivation (customer, complainant and visitor). We struggled with these client categories and probably turned a number of good 'customers' into not very interested 'visitors' just by treating them that way! Fortunately, as we became more adept at collecting information we began to notice that clients were using the information in their own way rather than in the ways we processed it through tasks. This led us to pay much less attention to tasks, give up altogether any categorisation of our clients or the relationship we have with them, and concentrate on the process of the interview itself. Help clients articulate their hopes, help them discover the myriad ways they are already contributing to the possible realisation of their hopes and leave the rest to them. The question has become the intervention and the answer the therapy.

Motivation

For those new to solution-focused brief therapy (and even for some old hands) the assumption of motivation is hard to adhere to. As de Shazer reported the 'death of resistance' (de Shazer, 1984) a less noticed, but more significant, event was the birth of motivation. Just as assuming that all clients are co-operative has helped create the most co-operative form of therapy ever, so the assumption of motivation has produced the most motivated clients ever. This is not such an unusual idea as it seems. We assume motivation in thousands of everyday transactions and make contract after contract without even thinking of motivation. The newsagent asks, 'Can I help you?' (meaning the same as 'What do you hope from this meeting?'). We respond, 'Could I have this paper, please?' We exchange goods for money and see it as normal. And it never even occurred to us to go to the butcher's for our newspaper! Why should we see our clients as any different? They come to us because they have some business to conduct and it is business relevant to our profession – otherwise they would go to another 'shop'. Even when we send our reluctant children to the shop the transaction still takes place, if for no other reason than to keep a wider peace. When we see clients who are instructed to attend we assume some wider, but no less significant motivation. And what more powerful motivations are there than staying out of prison, keeping the chance of an education or not losing your children or partner?

It is helpful to see this assumption of motivation as a pragmatic decision and not an act of foolish optimism. Ultimately we can never know if a person is motivated, or if apparently unmotivated behaviour is in fact the reaction of a motivated person to some behaviour of our own. Not knowing puts us in the position of being able to choose. Choosing to act *as if* all clients are motivated prevents us from giving up. If we can't see motivation it must be because we are looking in the wrong place, so we look somewhere else. Since we are doing this with a living person, he or she cannot help but respond and when therapist and client join forces in the search it is most unusual for the motivation to remain unfound.

With couples the assumption is the same: each has come motivated to achieve something for themselves as individuals and for themselves as a couple – why else would they come? The motivation may be hidden behind layers of other reasons ('She told me to', 'I didn't have any choice', 'If I didn't come she'd leave me') but if these apparently negative reasons are explored they will always lead back to the client making a decision to attend and to that decision being based on positive grounds such as, 'I don't want to lose her'.

Couples as individuals

Most work with couples involves three-way conversation, building on common areas and trying to negotiate around differences. Agreement within the room is sought. Insoo Kim Berg (Hoyt and Berg, 1998) and Eve Lipchik (Lipchik and Kubicki, 1996) are examples of therapists who are more likely to work in this way. My own preference is to treat each partner as entirely separate and if they come together I do two shorter, interwoven sessions together. Typically, I will ask each partner what he or she hopes to achieve from our work together, then ask each a miracle question based on the realisation of their own hopes. Then I will ask each of them one or more scaling questions and only in the feedback at the end might I address them as a couple, for example by commenting on their mutual commitment or ways of relating during the session.

Neither during the session nor in the feedback will I try to resolve or suggest they resolve any differences that might arise in their preferred futures or interpretations of past events. Instead, I assume that like all couples they will find their own way to resolve the resolvable and live or not live with what cannot be resolved. In working with the couple as a couple the therapist is working from the premise that a good relationship will empower and satisfy the individual. My starting point is simply the other side of the same coin: the more empowered and satisfied the individual, the better the relationships they are likely to have. This notion is especially important when the work is with only one half of the couple. Because the current evidence (de Shazer, 1988; Miller et al., 1996) shows no outcome difference related to one or both partners attending for therapy (Weiner-Davies, 1992), working with whoever comes is what the solution-focused brief therapist should do. In fact, we should have no personal view at all about who should attend, but instead trust our clients to make their own best decisions.

Harry and Sarah

Harry and Sarah were 'advised' by a court to go for marital therapy if they were serious about keeping their children. Sarah had been subjected to bouts of violence throughout their twenty years together and the authorities had been called in because of the potential 'overspill' on to their small children. The referrer was doubtful about the value of therapy since neither would have sought it or seen it as potentially helpful but they did not want to lose their children. Sarah had said that she wanted to stay with Harry but only if he refrained from violence. Harry wanted to stay with Sarah but 'couldn't help himself' when he lost his temper. Both wanted professionals out of their lives.

What follow are segments from the first two sessions in which the foundation for a different kind of relationship is laid. Fifteen months later there had been no further violence.

The work begins with the therapist asking each partner the question: 'What are your best hopes out of our work together?' Both have similar answers – they want to get on with their lives and for there to be no more violence. Such answers were to be expected in the circumstances, but are no less legitimate because of that.

> *Therapist* Sarah, let's imagine that tonight there is a miracle that resolves everything that has brought you here – you're safe, you're in the kind of relationship you want to be in and getting on with your life without interference. But because you are asleep when it happens you don't know about it. What will be different when you wake up tomorrow that begins to tell you that this miracle has happened?
>
> *Sarah*: I would be happy in the relationship without any violence, jealousy and obsessiveness. That would be in even small things like me saying 'Right, I'm going to take the children to nursery and then I'm going to do some shopping', and leave Harry to potter around in the greenhouse and he'd say: 'OK, love! Off you go – see you when I see you!' instead of 'Why? Why do you have to go without me?'
>
> *Therapist* Would that surprise you?
>
> *Sarah*: Well, it's what I'm hoping will come from this.
>
> *Therapist* OK. So how would you feel hearing that?
>
> *Sarah*: Pleased.
>
> *Therapist* How would Harry know you felt pleased?

> *Sarah*:   Because I'd be happy and he'd know. Because usually he says: 'Hmph, I want to come!' or 'Why are you going now?' or 'It doesn't take that long!' or 'Why don't you want me to come?' and I'd react with 'Oh, don't be so stupid!' and then we'd be off.
> *Therapist*:   And how would he know that you'd be happy?
> *Sarah*:   Cause I'd probably be smiling and give him a kiss and say anything I can get you while I'm out?
> *Therapist*:   Would he like that, do you think – you smiling and giving him a kiss?
> *Sarah*:   Yes, I think so.
> *Therapist*:   Do you walk to nursery with the kids?
> *Sarah*:   Yes, if it's fine!
> *Therapist*:   So what would you notice as you were walking to nursery that told you you were pleased and happy to have kissed Harry goodbye?
> *Sarah*:   Well, it would just show, wouldn't it? I'd be looking at the trees and everything rather than being all knotted up.

The dialogue continues with an equally detailed description of the walk to nursery and subsequent trip to the supermarket. One of the great versatilities of solution-focused brief therapy is that it can track any aspect of a person's life and as long as it is part of a description of a preferred future, or of what might already be contributing to that future, it will be absolutely relevant to the purpose of the therapy as defined by the client. The resolution of Sarah and Harry's marital difficulties will be found just as much in Tescos as in their living room.

> *Therapist*:   So what would you be feeling as you were doing your shopping?
> *Sarah*:   I suppose I'd be relaxed, happy to be getting on with it – just ordinary. I wouldn't have the pressure of thinking 'Oh, there's a queue!' whereas before the miracle I'd be worrying about Harry and whether he was getting agitated and what state he'd be in when I got back because that would be pressure to me. Yes – I wouldn't feel that pressure, I'd just say: 'Oh well, there's a queue but it doesn't matter!'

Being alone and relaxed in a supermarket queue is part of the total picture of living a life free of domestic violence, and the more Sarah is aware of each small piece that makes up this 'jigsaw' the more she will be able to recognise the bits already in place and make decisions about possible new pieces.

She goes on to describe how she will know the miracle is continuing when she gets home. Interestingly, her description of Harry's greeting is remarkably similar: 'Where have you been, Tescos in France?' but it would be said as a joke and they'd put the shopping away together.

Like Sarah's, much of Harry's miracle takes place outside the home. Though this would probably have happened anyway, it also helps make the miracles more 'safe'. When seeing a couple together, descriptions of what they *don't* like about each other are commonly interlaced with description of the preferred behaviour ('He wouldn't be … '; 'So if he wasn't … what would he be doing?'). When there is violence in the relationship the therapist can never know if what one person says is going to be 'provocative' to the other and lead to violence when they get home. Miracles happening outside the times the couple are together makes potentially dangerous conflict less likely.

Therapist: [*turning to Harry*] So Harry –
Harry: [*laughing*] You're not going to ask me all them questions, are you?
Therapist: – if your miracle happened …
Harry: I'd go off to work more cheerfully.
Therapist: How would you know?
Harry: Singing and all that.
Therapist: How do you get to work?
Harry: Drive, normally.
Therapist: So you'd be singing as you drove along?
Harry: Yes.
Therapist: Any particular songs?
Harry: Just anything.
Therapist: Old songs, new songs, blues songs?
Harry: '60s and '70s I suppose. [*laughing*]
Therapist: And what else? What else would tell you the miracle had happened?
Harry: I wouldn't be worrying about getting back home.
Therapist: Instead?
Harry: Just singing – not worrying!
Therapist: And what would your workmates notice?
Harry: I don't know, I just go to work to do my work, you know. I don't go to muck about or anything.
Therapist: OK. If you were happy what do you think they'd notice even if they didn't say anything?
Harry: I'd talk to them, I suppose.
Therapist: So if you heard yourself talking to them that might be a sign that things are going as you want them to go. Would they like it – you talking to them?
Harry: I don't know – we've all got our separate jobs, you know.
Therapist: OK, so you'd be getting on with your separate jobs and do you think they'd like you talking to them?
Harry: I don't know them so I can't answer that.
Therapist: What do you think?
Harry: Yes, I would imagine they might.

Harry has to think very hard to find these answers and later describes this meeting as the first he's had with a professional (and he has had many!) where he has been 'listened to'. An essential part of 'listening with questions', which is one way to describe counselling, is that each question is somehow based on the previous answer. In solution-focused brief therapy another essential part is to ask questions to which the answer is in some way affirming to the client. Harry was certainly being listened to, but the most important ears were his own and what they were hearing him say.

This first meeting continued to draw out detailed descriptions of their daily routine, both in and away from each other's company. Other 'witnesses' were called: the next door neighbour seeing Sarah arrive home and Harry in the garden asking her how she'd got on; the children seeing their parents share a joke; Harry's mother seeing him visit alone. Some time was also spent exploring what they already had going for themselves as a couple; what had kept them together over twenty years; what still reminded them of why they fell in love. Though the therapist was careful to follow the clients' goals – in this case to have a better relationship – he is not concerned that he might be encouraging Sarah to stay in a dangerous relationship. When exploring hopes and accumulating existing 'credits' the client does not lose touch with reality. Instead both Harry and Sarah are likely to be assessing the chances of achieving their best hopes and counting the 'credits' to check that it is going to be worth the effort. In their case it is. They had both described in their miracle small, achievable actions, and as they talked about what worked in their relationship already, they discovered a lot for them to hang on to. Had there not been, one or the other might have reviewed their hopes.

The second session begins with 'What's better?' and Sarah says a lot of little things that mean a lot to her and which are of great interest to the therapist. She recounts how she drove to pick Harry up from work. She is late and very anxious because Harry hates her being late and they could easily get into a big argument. When she arrived he wasn't in his usual place so she became even more worried – he'd probably gone off in a rage and that spelled disaster. Then she saw him sitting on a wall a little further down the road, having a cigarette. He waved to her, walked up to the car and got in saying what a lovely day it was. Sarah was totally amazed and asked Harry why he was in such a good mood. Harry said he'd been having a laugh with his workmates and the day had gone more quickly.

Later Harry reported a story of his own. He and Sarah were in town and he saw Sarah looking in a clothes shop window. Normally he hates her buying clothes, especially summer clothes because they might be too revealing, but on this occasion he asks her if she wants to go in. They do and Sarah tries on a summer dress (she says she did this deliberately to 'test' him). When she comes out of the changing room to show him he feels his anger rise, but then says to himself, 'No, you don't want to start that up again'. Sarah said this was a wonderful moment for her, because she could see that Harry nearly lost his temper but she also saw him control it. The fact that he did control it made her realise that their hopes for the future were not pipedreams. At the end of this story the therapist took Harry back to the moment of control.

Therapist: So what did you do instead of losing control?
Harry: I looked at her differently and then realised I fancied her!

After the third session it seems that and Harry and Sarah are beginning to enjoy a different sort of relationship – one that other professionals involved also notice. A year later the courts are satisfied that the children are no longer at risk. The couple have seen the therapist a number of times in between, but it has been more about how they deal with the 'world' rather than their own relationship, which has continued to develop.

As with so many people involved in serious and chronic problems the way forward is not only there, but partly already being lived. Sometimes therapists can contribute to it remaining unfound. How might this work have gone if the therapist held the hypothesis that the problem was fulfilling some underlying need, or that men who are violent never change, or that Sarah is a 'natural victim?' Conversations based on any of these themes are potentially blaming and even humiliating and if the client begins to believe even a fragment of such stories, then the hope for the future is likely to be much bleaker. It is more affirming and efficient to take peoples' hopes seriously and assume that they are not yet met because the people concerned have not realised they already know the way forward.

When it doesn't work

'Success' in couples therapy is not always as easy to judge as with other 'problems'. Whereas the cessation of violent behaviour is clearly a success, a couple parting may not be a 'failure'. It may in the end be 'for the best'. The problem with such a view, at least for the therapist, is that it can lead to complacency – the couple split up not because they had bad therapy but because they 'needed' to. This is one of those thorny issues that even long-term research would have difficulty resolving and so we might best judge success by whether or not the client achieves their hopes, stated at the outset.

The final example illustrates this and points up one of the dilemmas couples therapy from time to time presents to us all.

Jerry and Lisa came because they were not getting on as well as they had hoped and were at that point in their relationship where a decision about children was looming. Their hope was that our meetings would lead to an improvement in their relationship so they could stay together. The first session began in a standard fashion and Lisa's 'miracle' seemed realistic, attainable and on many occasions happening. Jerry's miracle began in the same vein but when in response to the question 'How would Lisa know you were feeling warm towards her?' he said he would kiss her feet. A look of considerable distaste showed on Lisa's face and when asked what he thought Lisa's response would be, Jerry said that after the miracle she'd let him do what he wanted. Lisa's emphatic 'No way!' presented the therapist with a dilemma – should he continue with Jerry's miracle as he would normally do or should he respond in some way to Lisa's response? He chose the latter and in effect refused to pursue a scenario which required another person to subject themselves to something they found distasteful. Jerry appeared to accept that his miracle would have to go in another direction, but the session lost its energy and the couple never returned.

The moral of this story is that not going with your client's wishes is bad for therapy but sometimes you just can't do it!

References

de Shazer, S. (1984) The death of resistance. *Family Process*, 23: 79–93.

de Shazer, S. (1988) *Clues: investigating solution in brief therapy.* New York: W.W. Norton.

de Shazer, S. (1991) *Putting Difference to Work.* New York: W.W. Norton.

de Shazer, S. (1995) *Keys to Solution in Brief Therapy.* New York: W.W. Norton.

George, E., Iveson, C. and Ratner, H. (Revised 1999). *Problem to Solution: brief therapy with individuals and families.* London: BT Press.

Hoyt, M.F. and Berg, I.K. (1998) Solution-focused couple therapy: helping clients construct self-fulfilling realities. In M.F. Hoyt (ed.), *The Handbook of Constructive Therapies*. San Francisco: Jossey-Bass.

Lipchik, E. and Kubicki, A.D. (1996) Solution-focused domestic violence views. In S.D. Miller, M.A. Hubble and B.L. Duncan (eds) (1996), *Handbook of Solution-Focused Brief Therapy*. San Francisco: Jossey-Bass.

Weiner-Davis, M. (1992) *Divorce Busting: a revolutionary and rapid programme for staying together*. New York: Simon & Schuster.

7

Solution-Focused Therapy and Mental Health

Tom Dodd

People try to find a place in the world through their systems of ideas, practices and values. This should enable a sense of community where communication takes place concerning aspects of that world, and its history. A social identity is formed, along with a social position in the wider community. It seems that the experience of many people who cope with mental illnesses is that such social positions are unattractive and isolating. How is it possible, then, for individuals with mental health problems to resist (whilst being asked to contribute to) the values of society, and become competent influences in a collective system of meaning that devalues and actively discriminates against them?

This chapter seeks to explore the context within which those who experience mental illness are located, and the values systems which impact on treatment and change. Can a solution-focused framework really make any difference?

History and construction

Common representations, most often through the media, present society with a threatening picture of violence and dangerousness associated with those experiencing or recovering from mental health difficulties (Philo et al., 1993). Throughout history, madness has been represented in imagery associated with deviance, monstrosity and fear. Indeed, the treatment of choice during the seventeenth century was based on exclusion, and actively denounced any idea of integration with the community. Individuals were dehumanised and punished for their apparent lack of *reason*, and later subjected to moral training in an attempt to maintain social order. History is peppered with the use of authoritarian and custodial frameworks, which was often economically led, with a focus on marginalisation through asylum-based care (Foucault, 1967). Society is seen to be promoting and causing mental illness (and thus endorsing asylum-based care) in at least two ways. Cochrane (1983) suggested that some people are placed in more stress-inducing situations than others, and secondly are deprived of the resources required for dealing with such stress. The institutional approach and the community approach both move towards a depersonalisation of the individual in Goffman's 'total institution' (1961). By Goffman's own argument that deperson-alisation arises from a lack of choice, community living can offer only limited choices restricted by constraints of poverty, stigma, and the increasingly distant availability of resources. So simply moving the focus to one of community base cannot ensure a better-segregated system of care.

So how does a solution-focused approach contribute to a more positive future? History leaves a testament of social exclusion and indeed it could be argued that the sense of security and support present in the institution of the asylum has been lost within the institution of the community; individuality, freedom and choice remain diffused and inaccessible for many. In answering the question, we need to examine further the reality of trying to survive the experience of illness in our society.

Perceptions of experience

Those with mental health problems remain stigmatised and devalued not only at times by their families and societies, but also sometimes by the very services that strive to help them. The framework which binds healthcare professionals has been laid brick by brick to form a wall of policy frameworks, profession-ally defined values, service limitations, academia, sociological beliefs and myths, personal attitudes and judgements about experience. Some are protect-ing factors for those we work with, but some are restrictive, concerned with risk and accountability. A number of interviews carried out by the author revealed a variation in the attitudes of carers, professional health service workers and people who receive services, when discussing those coping with mental health difficulties:

- they are unpredictable – you don't know what they are going to do;
- they don't seem to know right from wrong;
- they don't have any concept of the rules that society has laid down;
- a lot of them are childlike;
- I don't think they should have any more privileges than me;
- being an outpatient means that you are unstable, unreliable and unemployable;
- you're not respected if you've got mental health problems;
- people tend to be judged by the company that they keep.

Services may unconsciously collaborate with the myths; the notion of mainte-nance, not only in clinical status but in social position, may be the resulting out-come. The notion of recovery is far more challenging to belief systems. How can people be convinced that we believe they have reason when they find themselves with little choice or information, and token roles in the decision-making process?

In accounting for the experience of illness, those interviewed had a variety of explanations, for example:

- sometimes being struck by an illness is a punishment for misdeeds;
- people are mentally ill because they just can't cope with our society;

- a lot of mental health problems are caused by people not following their course of treatment properly;
- many so-called 'mental illnesses' are actually forms of weakness or an inability to face reality.

Such explanations begin to frame the nature and value of the interactions and interventions offered. Access to meaningful systems of care is problematic for people whose choices are restricted simply because of the label they have been given. The features implied by such markers may result in quite challenging experiences for individuals. In describing their experiences, people who had been on the receiving end of care noted:

- we often feel inferior to those around us – be they professional or lay people;
- people with mental health difficulties feel devalued by society;
- to get people to believe in you, and give you a start, is twice as difficult for people who have had a mental health problem;
- it's frustrating being mentally ill – the pain is so great you couldn't explain it to anybody; if the pain you felt was physical, you'd be spurting blood all over the place, and people would rush to help you;
- most of the time, you're quite able bodied;
- sometimes, recovery from a mental illness is not an easy option.

Clinicians are pressured and influenced by a wide number of sometimes conflicting paradigms. An awareness of how these pressures may influence clinical practice is essential in understanding the extent of the boundaries within which we form relationships.

Relationships and values

The construct of relationships can be grounded in a number of areas. The absence of basic interactions, emotions and beliefs leads to a set of experiences that seem familiar to those who experience mental health problems (Figure 7.1).

The boundaries that constrain relationships with 'professionals' are under increasing pressure, and the notion of whether there can be true friendship or advocacy promotes some debate. The fewer positive aspects that are present, the more likely the consequences are to be felt. Sometimes it's easier to recognise the negative effects in a relationship when such aspects are absent.

Serious mental illness can often involve experiences of low self-esteem, low self-worth, isolation, poor confidence, being devalued, feeling inadequate, being seen as irresponsible. The relationship seems to be an opportunity to help redress the balance in people's lives between what is useful and what is destructive. Is it possible to construct a working partnership which is formed out of respect, aspirations, inclusion and opportunity? Can such a construct exist within the para-

Positive aspects of relationships	Consequences when absent
Sincerity	Deficit
	Hypercriticism
	Self-doubt
Honesty	Injustice
	Unfairness
	Impropriety
Respect	Low self-esteem
	Low confidence
	Feeling used
Friendship	Disloyalty
	Poor self-worth
	Low regard
Acceptance	Inadequacy
	Feeling judged
	Isolation
Trust	Unreliability
	Disbelief
	Irresponsibility
Worth	Feeling devalued
	Unimportance
	Feeling without merit

Figure 7.1   *Positive relationship*

Statement	Underlying values
You're not respected if you've got mental health problems	Respect
People with mental health problems are experts in their own right	Recognising people as experts in their experiences
I need to be seen as someone who is different, not ill	People are more than an illness
If you work, you earn money. You are only seen as important if you earn a wage	Being valued for more than your financial worth
People tend to be judged by the company they keep	Inclusion
	Being seen as individuals
Everyone knows right from wrong	Being thought capable of reason
It takes a long time to know that	Aspirations
somebody is absolutely, really on your side	Beliefs
People with mental health problems don't seek help when they first become ill	Flexibility
I wonder sometimes whether people are allowed to get on with their lives	Risk management
People with mental health difficulties give little back to society	Opportunity

Figure 7.2   *Underlying values*

meters that are set in the frameworks that we work within?

People were revisited to check what the key issues were around certain statements that were made, in an attempt to construct a values set which complemented what people who experience mental health problems say they need (Figure 7.2).

These clues offer a framework for dealing with the consequences of restricted relationships, unconscious and conscious discrimination, and some of the common symptoms associated with mental illness – poor self-esteem; low self-worth; isolation; lack of confidence; feelings of inadequacy and feeling devalued. In helping explore more positive futures and address what people are asking for, a framework needs to be proactively constructed using these base materials (Figure 7.3). What does solution-focused therapy offer in these areas?

People give us clues every day about what seems to work positively for them. Perspectives on accounting for experience may be biological, spiritual, cultural, behavioural or socially constructed, depending on your philosophy, training or life experience. Multidisciplinary teams of healthcare workers can provide a range of sometimes conflicting, sometimes supportive, explanations. During my clinical experience of leading such a team, a gentleman with whom we worked remarked, 'The team have more consistent ideas about what is wrong with me' (when asked what did we do differently?). His experience had been that the professionals he had worked with in the past had almost competed to convince him that their perception of his experience, and then his needs, was the only valid one. In our work, the key had been to provide the space for him to help us understand his own perceptions, and what might be useful to instigate change in his life.

Interventions in mental health work draw evidence from a number of fields, which include:

- the structure of the delivery framework;
- the most appropriate settings for delivery;
- matching interventions to health experiences and the values of those providing care.

The evidence base is concerned not only with the tasks of intervention but with the context of where, when and by whom. This leads to a number of types of outcome measure:

- service outcomes (use of inpatient facilities, admission rates, cost-effectiveness);
- medical-biological outcomes (symptom reduction, side-effects management, medication usage, rates of relapse);
- social outcomes (housing stability, vocation, finances, inclusion, etc.);
- others which include satisfaction with services; the effectiveness of education; engagement rates; and comparisons to existing service provision.

Within developing services, then, with so many possible outcomes, defining a clear function can be problematic. The function again can be defined from a number

Values	SFT
Respect	Allowing clients time to explore, air their views
	Collaborate and create possibilities
Recognising people as experts in their experiences	As therapists, we may have expert knowledge and skills, but recognise the client's expertise in experience
	The therapist accepts that they can learn from the client
People are more than an illness	The diagnosis is not a focus; the consequences of the experience are what impact on people's lives
	The client is seen as a survivor or victor rather than a victim
	The client has strengths
Being valued for more than your financial worth	Everyone is already doing something of value some of the time
	We all have something to contribute
	The client is seen as resourceful
Inclusion	The client is central to the intervention, and defines where they want to be
	The therapist helps to identify the direction of goals determined by the client
	The client is encouraged to generate solutions, not be 'problem-solved'
	Success is more likely as we enter the client's frame of reference and utilise solution patterns that already exist
Seen as individuals	The solution-focused framework provides a process that is flexible in terms of providing individually tailored interventions, different for each client
	People's uniqueness is celebrated
Capable of reason	The client helps define and map out where they want to be
	The client is encouraged to take positive risks
	The client is the best judge of knowing when they have arrived at where they want to be
Aspirations	Fundamental belief in change, which is constant and inevitable
	People are allowed a preferred future
Beliefs	There is no failure, just different ways of doing things
	If things don't have the desired outcome, the therapist and client accept that they may need to do things differently

(Continued)

	Resistance is the client's unique way of co-operating
	People's experiences are seen as valid and understandable
	The intervention is about facilitating change, rather than defining problems and weaknesses
Flexibility	Meetings are arranged in line with the client's pace of change
	A common language is used, rather than 'professionally' led wording
Risk management	Clients are actively involved in risk management strategies
	Coping strategies are shared and collaborative
Opportunity	Positive images of the future are constructed, and attained in small steps. The therapist encourages the client to take opportunities to move towards their goals
	The opportunity is taken to make small changes, affecting wider systems

Figure 7.3   *A values framework*

of differing perspectives – commissioners and purchasers of care may be concerned with service outcomes that relieve pressures on whole systems; managers may look for the positive impacts of using team approaches; people who receive services are likely to expect more positive experiences of care than they have experienced in the past. Practitioners need to be reassured that their interventions actually make a difference. Function may be difficult to define globally, but it gives the opportunity to look at local priorities and link up with them in providing a service that is meaningful to the society in which it is placed.

In England, the structure needs to absorb the directives of the Care Programme Approach (CPA) and care co-ordination, and local clinical case management procedures. Involving the client in the process of treatment, in terms of decision making, care planning, recognising strengths and potential, and evaluation, is essential whatever the professions involved. Although specific functions can be assigned to various team members (prescribing, explicit assessments, family interventions, care co-ordination, etc.) the core business of day-to-day work will be shared by everyone in the team. In reference to this core business Lachance and Santos (1995) state that 'Staff members must consider themselves generalists and possess certain attitudes, such as flexibility, openness to new ideas, and a distaste for territoriality' (p. 42).

Territories cease to be of importance if we can realign the focus of care to the needs of the person or family we are concerned with. Solution-focused therapy does not align itself to any particular profession or territory; it is a construct of values which transcends such boundaries to explore a range of needs which is holistic and wide-ranging. The needs of those who experience mental illness are not just entrenched in symptomology; they are the same as for other members of society – to have a meaningful occupation, reward for our efforts, vocation, housing stability, leisure, education, relationships and so on. Solution-focused therapy may certainly explore mechanisms for coping with the consequences of symptoms, but also encompasses issues that impact on people's whole life experiences.

Delivery and power

Mental health care has struggled with the notion of translating research into practice ever since it began to focus on treatment rather than segregation. As psychiatry's function moves towards one of management and understanding (with a more conscious emphasis away from control and disempowerment), there are increasing pressures to justify methods of intervention. Growing public expenditure, raised expectations of those using services, and 'recovery' replacing 'maintenance' in the language concerned with potential, pressures those delivering on care to be more explicit and certain about what might lead to positive outcomes. Purchasers and commissioners cannot sustain services that are not effective. Mental health care, though, is at times fragmented into a range of professions who vie for the right to define what such positive outcomes might be. Various schools of thought and accounting, in explaining the experiences of those who are affected by mental illness, provide a competing set of values with which to define intervention.

A solution-focused framework appears to challenge much of this debate. It is concerned with change (rather than defining problems and weaknesses) and movement along paths of recovery. Outcomes can be measured in distance travelled towards goals, which remain flexible and changing. It is about helping people to cope differently, becoming more self-reliant rather than dependent on aspects of service provision. It is respectful and enabling; it challenges inherited and assumed power imbalances in therapeutic relationships.

The concept of power is often associated with *position*. Professionals may jealously guard their positions of influence and expertise. The person receiving services seeks power, too, but not in the same context. Rather, through active involvement, they seek to negotiate choice in treatment, choice in the decision-making process, choice in the management of their distress. This appears to threaten the professional, resulting in a tug of war where position and power are confused with the right to choose. When respect and trust become integral parts of the construct of the user, information – the linchpin in any empowering activity – can be interchanged and assessed. The user needs some credibility to be built into their construct before they are assured access to the professional cocoon of confidentiality. Access to records and involvement in quality assurance initiatives are contributing to positive constructs for users, although perhaps intrinsic to a professional-led agenda. The agencies that deal with the organisation of services are challenged to 'unlearn' traditional structures of establishment and need to demonstrate a conscious commitment to empowerment.

There seems to arise some paradox whereby professionals and politicians, at least on a surface level, seek to empower the user as a consumer of services. This may be attributed to a changing professional perspective on social representation. There is a continuing move away from the medicalised construct towards a more functional understanding of mental illness. Morant (1995) remarks that 'A functional understanding of mental illness is certainly congruent with present day community care policies in which the role of the professional is to help clients function and maintain themselves in their normal social setting.' Morant goes on to discuss her finding that the sense of fear and threat that is embedded in the lay person's representation is not expressed by mental health professionals. Of course, this is a debatable point, but as professionals start to demonstrate a real sense of 'sameness', stigma is reduced for the user. Many healthcare professionals, though, have one foot in each camp – they preach the 'sameness' of experiencing distress and loss of control to users, but belong to the 'otherness' of society as a whole. This enables the professionals to distance and separate the mentally ill from themselves within the social context. The historical marginalised position of mentally ill individuals remains.

The changing construct of the user is being influenced from at least two primary directions. Firstly, the political machine grants permission for involvement through its policies and direction, and in addition, local initiatives highlight pockets of genuine empowerment. What needs to be evidenced, though, is a bona fide shift in the value systems of mental health care professions and the wider society. This can allow a humanistic construction for the user, which rejects historical beliefs and challenges representations of inferiority, deficiency and weakness. Both professionals and people who receive services need to be clear about the aspects of power that they embrace; to separate the personal and political imperatives to enable change, and dare to contest the status quo. Solution-focused frameworks offer a process of intervention bound together by a value set that reflects what people say is useful to them. The stages of intervention are relatively simple and follow a logical order; the challenge is in embracing the principles that drive the beliefs and values that actually make a difference.

References

Cochrane, R. (1983) *The Social Creation of Mental Illness*. London: Longman.
Foucault, M. (1967) *Madness & Civilisation: a history of insanity in the Age of Reason*. London: Tavistock.

Goffman, E. (1961) *Asylums*. New York: Doubleday.

Lachance, K. and Santos, A. (1995) Modifying the PACT Model: preserving critical elements. *Psychiatric Services*, 46(6).

Morant, N. (1995) What is mental illness – social representations of mental illness among British and French mental health professionals. *Papers on Social Representations*, 4(1): 41–52.

Philo, G. et al. (1993) *Mass Media Representations of Mental Health/Illness*. Report for Health Education Board for Scotland. Glasgow University Media Group.

8

The Solution-Focused Approach in Higher Education

Nigel White

At Leeds Metropolitan University we have a team of 25 counsellors of whom 20 are volunteers. Those of us interested in developing the solution-focused aspects of our work (Lian French, Roger Gilbert, Carol Curtis, Arnfrid Beier and myself) have been working to develop confidence in SFT methods. Initially we had the benefit of Alan Atkinson's supervision and we have been meeting with SFT therapists from other settings for peer supervision. Thus many colleagues, both inside and outside the university, have contributed to the development of our SFT work with students. I have included some of their voices in this chapter.

In the current economic situation there is considerable pressure on students, most of whom hold part-time jobs as well as studying. Most students come with depression, anxiety and stress-related problems and these frequently involve both their relationships with others and issues of their own identity. Many come to the service following difficult events (e.g. parental separation, relationship break-up, death of a loved one, pregnancy) but others come because of past issues that are affecting their present lives (e.g. difficult childhood experiences). Most find their problems are affecting their ability to study. There is a wide range of client expectations, from those who want to 'get it sorted' with no idea of what this might entail, to those who hope for continual support throughout their university years. On average we see each client for six sessions.

In higher education there is a seasonal fluctuation in demand for counselling linked to the academic year, with strong pressure to satisfy an immediate demand at certain times. At these times, if we cannot help in the next few weeks (sometimes even days) then our help will not be needed. This has focused our minds on how to give something useful to the students in the briefest time possible. With the help of the volunteers we have avoided having a waiting list. However, the wish to have counselling seems to be rising steadily among students and it is unclear whether we will be able to meet demand in the future. In a ten-week term even a brief waiting list doesn't make much sense. This situation exerts pressure on us to share out the precious counselling hours in the best way possible. De Shazer's comment of using 'Enough sessions to do the job and not one more' comes to mind.

All students are seen for an initial assessment before referral to a counsellor, if appropriate. As well as providing regular counselling we also run a drop in service which supports those waiting for their counselling to begin, those who have finished and would like irregular support, and other unforeseen needs. In

For the clients	For the listener
• The sessions are more enjoyable	• The sessions are more enjoyable
• Conversations make more sense	• There is a more respectful and optimistic feeling
• Conversations seem more relevant to what they came for help with	• Less likelihood that they will take responsibility for the client's situation
• SFT questions, though startling, are appreciated as their intent is clear	• Greater freedom in asking questions
• Keenness to co-operate with SFT	• Better convergence between therapist and client aims
• More rapid progress is made towards goals	• Instant and continual feedback from client on how useful the conversation is
• There is an absence of defensiveness	• Freedom from the limitations of having to have an explanation in mind
• Involvement in planning therapy methods and goals	• Negotiation of methods and goals
• Clients feel trusted and therefore can discover greater trust in self	• Unreserved trust in the client
• More relaxation since the questions are getting at hidden strengths rather than hidden weaknesses	• More relaxation since the questions are getting at hidden strengths rather than hidden weaknesses

Figure 8.1 *Personal experiences of having a focus on solutions*

terms of popularity with students, most would prefer regular one to one meetings. Drop ins are little used, except at the most pressured times of year. Attempts to run groups have usually failed due to low interest.

Rationale for using SFT

I find, from observation, that people relax and open up more when I show a detailed interest in their abilities and successes than when I show a similar interest in the details of their problems. As a result I have become aware of what the experience is like both for myself and my clients (Figure 8.1).

Maps of human nature, followed in many models of therapy, can be useful for explaining phenomena. But the task of explaining is not really what we are asked to do by those who come for help. We are asked to help people 'go on', at a point where they feel unable to do so on their own. What we need is a method of helping people 'go on', rather than a method of explanation.

SFT is not a map of human nature. It is a map of possible conversations aimed at helping people build their own solutions. This is a more modest aim and it contradicts some of the 'practices of immodesty' that are relatively commonplace in the culture of therapy (White, 1999).

SFT practice

In this chapter I'd like to look at the kinds of conversations we hold with students. This isn't the same as the kinds of conversations we start out meaning to have. These have been well described by Berg (1994), de Shazer (1994), White (1995) and others. Their signposts to useful conversations have been immensely helpful. Like the startling questions we sometimes ask our clients, their startling signposts have helped us swerve away from old habits and do something different.

When riding a bicycle, you see an obstacle on the road ahead, say a stone or a pothole. Are you more or less likely to hit it if you keep your eye on it? For me it is more helpful to look away from the obstacle, and concentrate on the space to the side, where I want to steer. Doing that means I am less likely to hit the obstacle. It's not easy to do this as my anxiety pulls my eye to the danger.

SFT work is like that. There's always a pull to look at the danger. SFT is saying, 'Look at the open road.' How? By having the most solution-saturated conversation that you can manage. Why? Because that way there's a better chance the person will go free. SFT work, in practice, is about finding and losing, finding and losing, finding and losing the solution focus. Or perhaps, as in the case study at the end of the chapter, losing and losing and losing and then finally finding the solution focus.

In any therapy meeting, the person's life is reported in ways that are:

- actively generated by the kind of conversation the two people hold between them;
- actively generative of new possibilities of thinking, feeling and acting in the session and of thinking, feeling and acting outside the session;
- actively shaping of both people's lives.

This throws great importance on to the style of conversation, with the 'truth' of the content becoming less central.

As Walter and Peller (1996, p. 18) have said, 'Problem-solving therapies and goal-as-end-point therapies are usually built on a language-as-representation assumption. The therapists think of the shyness and the weight loss as real events for which resources must be developed to change the objectively real events.' 'The language of conversation, narrative, reflection, and text has become more relevant to our approach than the language of observation, interview, information and feedback' (1996, p. 11).

Thus the conversation becomes a main focus and such questions as the following become a principal guide in the work.

- What are the most useful conversations we can manage to have between us? What sorts of conversations will suit you and me, right now?
- How fertile with new possibilities can our conversations be?

Figure 8.2   *Gestalt picture*

For my colleague Lian, the type of conversation she has with 19–22-year-old students is different because of their time of life. She is aware that part of what many students want to tell her is that they are experiencing pain. This may be a first time experience for the student and it may feel like a problem. The student can feel over-whelmed with feelings which demand attention. Lian, to whom pain is not neces-sarily a problem in itself, has found that acknowledging the pain is a form of compliment. She will 'compliment the emotions' and work with them in an SFT way. This may involve looking at past successes or it may involve giving the feel-ings direct attention. She is aware that for students this is the time of life when they are building their own independent resources while feeling unsure whether their resources are adequate for the challenge. She feels as if their expectations are push-ing her into the role of a parent or tutor, which can restrict her scope to do SFT.

She also feels that students can have an unfounded optimism about the future that covers their uncertainty. In asking them to think about goals she is aware that she is asking them to plan in a way which they may not be used to doing. Because of this she is careful to compliment them on their ability to create plans for the future.

My other colleague, Carol, follows her instincts about whether to use SFT or not. If it seems that clients are involved in a process of discovering something about themselves she will use other exploratory strategies.

We have found that some students take to SFT conversations very readily whereas some do not. Some people need help if they are not to spend the session doing more of the same sort of talk that has not been helping up to now. With these people the sensation of what it is like to do SFT work is one of continually feeling pulled towards conversations that the person has had before, either with themselves or with others, and continually seeking for ways to switch the conversation away from a problem focus towards what works.

This has been described by Annie Nehmad (1998) with reference to the Gestalt picture in Figure 8.2. She points out that the territory explored by the solution-focused therapist is the inverse to that explored by the problem-focused therapist, and that a similar thoroughness and rigour should apply in both models. Both are exploring along the same boundary in the client's life. In SFT, this will lead us to ask questions about exactly what went well, whereas a problem-focused therapist will ask questions about exactly what went wrong.

The continual effort to stand back from the hypnotic problem-saturated dialogue and ask one more question, from a place that reminds both people, once again, of the possibility of the preferred future, is what characterises SFT work. My colleague, Roger, believes that there are occasions when people need to tell him about a bad experience or feeling in order to get it off their chest or to feel he has heard them, but that the skill is not to let them go on too long or you end up in their mind set.

For a long time we have been struggling with the question of what to do when SFT does not work. When this happens we examine the work closely in peer supervision to identify what *is* already working. Frequently a therapist presents a case they feel is 'not working' and the others point out and draw out features which show that it is working. The therapist goes back to the case with a new respect for the client's ability to make changes and for his or her own ability to foster solutions. Another frequent outcome of supervision, for me, has been to learn that I need to go back to the beginning and ask the first questions (for example the miracle question) over again. This happened in the case study presented later in this chapter.

When Roger's mind goes blank he sometimes invents a scaling question or repeats the miracle question to get things going again. He has found that his clients learn the questions by repetition and will begin using them for themselves. On one occasion he had a client, John, who could not get past his initial issues. On about the fourth session Roger asked John to tell him about his brother. The conversation felt very different as John told Roger a fascinating story about his brother. By the next session John had started socialising again and said he felt a lot better. After this experience, when Roger is not sure what to do next, he asks clients to tell him about someone to whom they are close, and in particular what they like about that person.

Another thing Roger does is to ask them about something they enjoy doing or have enjoyed in the past. He believes that if something is not the problem it may well be part of the solution. It may also give material for metaphors on some other occasion.

Roger gives an example of this. 'I had an incredible experience of this last year. I had a client who was very nervous and down and one of the issues he had was about doing a presentation for his course. To try and develop some confidence I asked about times in his life when he had felt confident. He told me that he used to feel confident when he starred as the lead in musicals at school. I then asked him what he used to do when he was on stage – learning lines, looking at the audience and projecting his personality. Next time he came to see me he had done his presentation, applied all his stagecraft and his tutor had picked him out for special praise!'

One student Carol saw (Jane) began at three on her scale and went backwards from there, returning for several sessions saying she was worse. She spent the sessions saying that the problem was everyone else's fault. Carol found that they could not maintain solution talk. Eventually Carol became concerned for Jane's safety and decided to do something different. She said, 'I owe you an apology because I haven't heard what you've been trying to tell me and I didn't realise how bad you felt.' The effect was immediate. Jane cried, which she had not done before, and described how she felt 'down a pit with a monster'. Carol listened to these feelings, focusing for the first time on Jane herself, and Jane drew a picture of the pit. Soon it became possible for Carol to ask questions such as, 'What's stopping you falling all the way to the bottom of the pit?' and later, 'What would it take to rescue you from the monster?'

Arnfrid sees two strands in SFT work. The first is to listen and receive, allowing the client to get the problem off their chest. The second is to move on from there, using solution-focused questions, so that something different can begin to find a place in the person's attention and in the person's life. It did seem that Carol's client, Jane, was very different in the sessions once she had managed to contact the thing she was struggling with. Carol found that subsequently she was able to recognise her own needs and think about meeting them by caring for herself. She did not blame others any more.

Culture, race and gender issues

At the university we have a diverse client group as regards culture, race and gender and we try to reflect this diversity in our counselling team. We try to cater for students' preferences for a counsellor of a particular culture, race or gender where the student indicates that there are sensitive issues.

The assumptions behind SFT are a great help when listening to people from groups other than my own. The assumptions that I do not have a more valid view of the world than the other person, that there is nothing of my view of the world that I have to 'get across' to the other person, that the content of what the client is saying is theirs to evaluate, are all helpful. White's ideas have been particularly valuable here as the endeavour to de-centre myself and put the person who is seeking help at the centre of the discussion has led me to find ways of being more sensitive to worldviews, and ways of speaking and being, other than my own. This position is important in any culturally sensitive therapeutic work. The SFT stance has helped me to put it into practice more easily, with more humour and open acknowledgement of my ignorance. There seems to be an easy fit between SFT and the position of 'not knowing', of being puzzled and 'one step behind'. Sometimes this may be a deliberate strategy to lead clients to put themselves in the expert position, but most times it is the simple truth, and it is a relief to work with a model that allows me to be open about this. This is nowhere more the case than in cross-cultural work where the degree of my ignorance is greater than usual.

Integrating SFT

We are all continually integrating SFT with other approaches. Sometimes this feels creative and appropriate and sometimes it feels as if we are dropping back to default models because we cannot come up with an SFT way of responding to a particular situation. We find that, as we become more skilled and confident with SFT, we can have more solution-focused conversations with more clients. However, it seems both helpful and easy to slip in and out of other strategies alongside SFT. The basic maxim of 'do what works' encourages both client and therapist and also makes it possible to negotiate these shifts openly.

Some examples of when we find ourselves integrating other approaches.

- Students whose problem seems to have resulted from striving, which puts emphasis on external performance (e.g. fitting in with other's expectations) at the expense of an awareness of their internal world (e.g. pain indicating that something needs to change). An SFT approach, if it is not careful, can reinforce this striving. A deeper rapport needs to be developed first. Since this may involve a deeper level of trust than the person has ever had with another human being, it may require a lot of listening. Later, there can be a return to SFT.
- Giving information (for example on depression, panic attacks or bereavement reactions), either in the session or in the form of leaflets for the students to take away. We see this as an extension of the 'normalising' strategy and consistent with SF principles.
- Students with study skills issues. We sometimes use a teaching stance to propose a set of strategies for the student to go away and experiment with. The next session can then be about evaluating the suitability of the strategies for that particular person, according to their findings, and adapting them. SFT is re-established as the student begins to shape the strategies and personalise them.
- People who seem to be without the resources to come up with solutions of their own. One of our colleagues in the supervision group, Kate Pearlman-Shaw, finds herself suggesting some strategies in a more traditionally

cognitive-behavioural therapy style. SFT can continue through the interest in and validation of coping strategies, until the person begins to come up with solutions of their own. In our experience the state of 'people being unable to come up with solutions of their own' is best not taken as a 'truth' about that person, but as a conversational position subject to change.

• People with problems which seem to shift from session to session, or within the session, so that a focus for the work is being continually undermined and neither client nor therapist knows where they are. With these people, who may take a few sessions to reveal this presentation, I use a cognitive analytic therapy model, at least initially, to help us both get a map of the terrain. Later SFT can resume.

Personal reflections

In our power-eager culture, it is a challenge for us to find ways of relating to each other which are founded on equality. The quest is particularly poignant with those who need help since, by the act of seeking, they are making themselves vulnerable. I feel ethically drawn to use the most economical intervention needed by the client to achieve their goals. For me there is a personal need to see how kind, how respectful and light of touch conversations can be. How affirming a conversation? How appreciative? What kind of conversation will most likely result in clients surprising themselves into an unaccustomed act of kindness towards themselves?

It is only in the present moment that we have choice. If a person is going to choose to do things differently, it has to be by a choice in the present moment. What kind of conversation will make it easiest for the client to choose to do something different right now? By focusing on solutions and the future we make it possible for the person, *at this very instant now*, to look beyond habitual defeats.

> Now with personal problems and obsessions, to let go of them is just that much. It is not a matter of analysing and endlessly making more of a problem about them, but of practising that state of leaving things alone, letting go of them. At first, you let go but then you pick them up again because the habit of grasping is so strong. But at least you have the idea. (Sumedho, 1992, p. 35)

I once saw a person who had become depressed over many years of caring for others' needs. I asked her the miracle question and she struggled to find a reply. After the session she went shopping and, without thinking, smiled at a shopkeeper. The unusual sensation of the smile on her face reminded her in an instant of what life could be like. She remembered that she could be joyful.

Case study

My conversations with James have veered between SFT and other approaches: they have also included emotions. He is a 23-year-old student who had two years' counselling at his previous university. He is doing postgraduate study and came to us for help with his 'fear of panic'. He lives with his girlfriend, Teresa, who has been supportive. His answer to the miracle question was that, instead of thinking continually of how to avoid panic, he would do ordinary mundane things. I had to ask a lot of questions to get more detail. He said he would have a lie-in and go to university in his own time rather than having to go early in order to be accompanied by Teresa; he would be able to eat anything he wanted, would be able to use lifts, and would feel calm.

At the end of the first session he asked if he could contact me between sessions as he had done with his previous counsellor. I explained that I was not available in this way. He seemed anxious about this.

In the second session we continued doing SFT/narrative work. He has a high awareness of himself and we were able to develop a history of 'persistence', a scale of control and a graded list of experiences which he felt would increase his 'belief in himself'. He explained that other areas of his life, such as moving to a new city to begin a new and difficult university course, were 'no problem'. I was very struck by this and remarked on how ingenious his strategies were if they removed anxiety from so many areas of his life.

In the third session he was saying that he could manage the anxiety and he would like to 'get rid of it'. He reported that he had trained harder in the gym, which he was pleased with, but he also said that the counselling was not helping as it was making him more aware, and this was increasing his anxiety. I agreed we would review the work next time and take a fresh approach. I was thrown by him saying that increased awareness was making things worse. In fact there had been changes for the better and his confidence that he could tackle the anxiety had improved. With hindsight it would have been possible to stick with complimenting the changes he had already made.

At the start of the next session I wanted to clarify what his goal was. He described how he uses panic as a way of avoiding more difficult feelings like sadness. He said his aim was now, 'To be able to experience emotions in a balanced way.' I did not pick up on this and, still feeling thrown, suggested that he tell me more about himself. He told me that the panic 'is aimed towards getting help' which was impossible in his 'tough guy' family where he would be rejected if he was upset. He has memories of being shamed when afraid and upset. He left home with a feeling of relief at 17 and studied at two institutions. The anxiety has been with him all his life, but it got worse until he was 'on the point of a breakdown' when he went for counselling at 21. He never told his parents about it. The panic attacks reach a peak where they become sadness and this is overwhelming.

James helped me understand that he is caught between either employing his strategies of avoidance, which function to prevent him being overwhelmed but leave him afraid, or stopping using his strategies, which leads quickly to him experiencing overwhelming feelings. He has become very skilled at using his strategies, but is fed up with the shadow of fear cast by the feelings he cannot face up to.

James said he was less anxious during these weeks and he put this down to our new approach which was 'taking positive steps'. (I take this, with hindsight, to indicate that I had been going too fast initially. I had moved too quickly to focusing on changes, whereas he had not felt heard.) Two changes then happened: one was that James felt able to have a fortnight gap between sessions, and he began cancelling sessions. (Though cancellations are hard to tolerate in our service, because of the demand for counselling, I took this to be a sign that he was able to be less dependent on me.) The second change was that he began asking about positive things he could do. We planned several strategies together, trialling them in the sessions. Our discussions of how he wanted to outwit anxiety became very detailed. We talked about trying different ways of thinking, he asked me to make him a meditation tape, and he talked of 'facing up to it' by not using his avoidance strategies. He was highly motivated to 'do something', but in the next session he always reported that he could not bring himself to try any of the things he had planned as they felt too frightening.

Several sessions passed and my attempts to return to SFT grew less frequent as I became more discouraged. While sitting with James I was aware of the over-whelming fear, which at times paralysed me too, and also of his desperate wish to do something, or for me to do something. It felt as if we were both failing.

Following discussion with colleagues, I asked him the miracle question again. His answers were similar to before. His goal was still, 'To experience emotions in a balanced way', but this time I remembered to ask, 'When is a little bit of this happening already?' His answers led us to the discovery that he has made progress, not by muscling up to the anxiety in a macho way, but by small step-by-step changes. He called this 'pushing down the barriers slowly'. After this point in our work we were careful to approach change more gently. Our latest idea for homework was, 'Notice the sensation of any emotions that you are experiencing already.'

In session 12 James told me that he was 3 or 4 on a scale where 10 is 'feeling emotions in a balanced way'. His anxiety is less frequent and its intensity is less. He is no longer checking his food; he has a varied diet and was gradually increasing his ability to tolerate stimulants like chocolate. He had become familiar with a raised heartbeat through training in the gym. He had given up some control of the mobile phone, which Teresa carries as he trusts her to charge it. He is starting to feel more, and be more aware of the world around him; he called this 'less self-obsessed'. He was becoming more friendly and getting involved in groups. He was going out and doing more. He had joined a meditation group where he was becoming familiar with a relaxed state. He was less drained as there is less of 'a hurricane' going on inside him: this means he has more energy for other things. He is managing a postgraduate course which all students find hard going and he has seen less of me than he thought he would need to in order to survive.

The richness of this latest account of his changes, and the appearance of positive terminology to describe things happening in his life, contribute to making me feel confident that we are now going in the right direction. In our last meeting (the 13th) he reported his latest changes and his ideas for taking them further. He said he was feeling the anxiety more, but this was tolerable. He agreed that my role had now changed as he no longer needed me to provide direction. He felt comfortable arranging a five-week break.

In our work together we searched for a solution focus. We sometimes found ourselves going up blind alleys, e.g. 'facing up to it', and I was thrown by what appeared to be a setback. The feeling of failure came close to blinding us both to the resourceful ways that James had already been moving beyond the limits of his coping strategies, towards his preferred future. However, once we were able to 'name and thicken the sub-plot' (White, 1995) there was a new energy in the work and it seemed to become less complicated, more straightforward. It felt as if James was well on the way to becoming free.

References

Berg, I.K. (1994) *Family-based Services: a solution-focused approach*. New York: W.W. Norton.

de Shazer, S. (1994) *Words Were Originally Magic*. New York: W.W. Norton.

Nehmad, A. (1998) CAT theory – have we integrated enough? Paper presented to the Association of Cognitive Analytic Therapy annual conference. (unpublished).

Sumedho, Ajahn (1992) *The Four Noble Truths*. Hemel Hempstead: Amaravati Publications.

Ueland, B. (1993) *Strength to Your Sword Arm: selected writings*. Duluth, MN: Holy Cow Press.

Walter, J. and Peller, J. (1996) Rethinking our assumptions: assuming anew in a postmodern world. In S. Miller, M. Hubble and B. Duncan (eds), *Handbook of Solution-Focused Brief Therapy*. San Francisco: Jossey-Bass.

White, M. (1995) *Re-authoring lives: interviews and essays*. Adelaide: Dulwich Centre Publications.

White, M. (1999) Reflecting team work as definitional ceremony revisited. *Narrative Journal Gecko*, 2: 55–83.

9

Solution-Focused Therapy in Schools

Harvey Ratner

The emphasis in this chapter will be on how solution-focused therapy can be used as a form of counselling in a school context. Consideration will be given to how the approach can be adapted, for example, to classroom teaching, but in general the focus will be on one to one counselling with individual students.

The Brief Therapy Practice is a training, consultation and therapy service in London. In September 1997 we were invited to engage in a project to examine the usefulness of the solution-focused approach with students in a mixed comprehensive school of 950 students in central London. The project was to run initially for 15 weeks. It would then be reviewed and continued only if it were felt to be an effective intervention. At the time of writing, the 'project' is now in its sixth year and is a well-established and known resource within the school (it has previously been described in George, Iveson and Ratner, 1999). Although the work remains essentially that of one to one counselling, many sessions are conducted with either staff or parents (occasionally both) present. The therapist has presented the approach on in-service teacher training days, and has also run an anger management group for year 9 boys (aged 14) on solution-focused lines.

An informal follow-up of students seen in the first year of the project was conducted in the second year with members of staff in order to establish a form of quality control. Thirteen students who had been counselled at least six months previously were discussed. Staff concluded that there had been either complete or partial improvement in 69 per cent of the cases. The average number of sessions was four. Although many of the students had been excluded at different times prior to being seen, and in some cases were considered to be at risk of permanent exclusion, none had subsequently been permanently excluded.

Counselling in schools: special features

Most of the referrals relate to students who are at risk of permanent exclusion due to behavioural problems. The young person is, of course, given the *choice* of whether to attend for counselling, but he or she is aware that *not* to attend could be read as further evidence of intransigence and would tell against them. The majority of students should therefore be regarded as being 'involuntary' clients. A small group, hearing about the therapist from friends who have been clients, may specifically request a meeting. For the rest, the therapy is an imposition and their initial attitude is reluctance to talk. They show a marked readiness to attribute blame for their problems to others: typically, they suggest that teachers have unfairly accused them of starting a fight when it was the other student's 'fault'; other reasons given for bad behaviour include the charge that the work is too hard or too boring.

It is in many ways obvious why a school should be interested in a brief therapy approach. As young people are not so inclined to seek out counselling, a short-term and practical approach is the best fit for them, and this particularly suits schools, which are such extraordinarily busy places. In solution-focused brief therapy, 'each session is viewed as potentially the last' (de Shazer, 1991, p. 57). It is possible that the ethos of education makes a solution-focused approach especially appropriate. While there are inevitably some teachers who are cynical in their views about what certain students may be able to achieve, it is this writer's experience that the majority are genuinely interested in and hopeful about their students, and the positive nature of a solution-focused approach fits their outlook.

There is a considerable advantage for the counsellor of young people with school-related problems to be able to have close contact with staff. Just as staff wish to know how the work is progressing, so the counsellor wants feedback as to the effectiveness of his or her sessions. Occasionally a student will report positive progress while the school is taking a different view. It is, of course, not appropriate for the counsellor to take sides. From the counsellor's point of view the school, as referrer, is also their client and so their opinion is extremely important. Where the school continues to be unhappy about a particular student, the counsellor needs to check with the young person what they believe *they* need to do to show to their teachers that things have improved. It is not necessary to get embroiled in a 'truth game' regarding what 'really' happened that led to the school believing things had not improved. In general, the issue is put back to the young person. Their feeling of injustice must be acknowledged, and they can be asked how they cope with the situation. The best thing for the counsellor, being in a not-knowing position, is to accept the student's view but stick with a focus on 'what needs to be different so that others will stop complaining about you'. Only very occasionally is it necessary to request a three-way meeting to try to iron out a seemingly intractable disagreement between a teacher and a student.

When I first began to work at the school I was given a lesson-length (50 minutes) to see a student. Over time this has decreased considerably as the caseload has expanded! Now I feel that 25 minutes is sufficient for a first session and 15 minutes for a follow-up meeting. There are times when this feels inadequate, particularly when I am seeing the student with their parent(s). On the other hand, when things are going well for the young person, the follow-up session need last only five minutes.

Case example

The following is an extract from early on in a first meeting with Patrick (not his real name), a 14-year-old young man in year 10 who has been referred due to increasing incidents in which he has lost his temper and become violent in class.

> *Therapist:* So, talking about here, you started to say earlier that it's not like big problems as you see it, but sort of flashes you feel bad about afterwards. You feel sorry for them afterwards.
>
> *Patrick:* Yeah. I don't know what's wrong with me. One minute I'll be fine... I'll give you an example. Art room about two weeks ago.

At this point, he gives an example of an incident in the classroom that led to him shouting and swearing at the teacher.

> *Patrick:* It was like being totally off my head. I just started shouting, shouting really loud. I've done it before. I threw a chair across the class. It's... I don't know what I'm doing.
>
> *Therapist:* Hmm.
>
> *Patrick:* It just happens, a rush, I just get this rush through my body...

The therapist decides that this could be an appropriate time to begin a search for exceptions: times when Patrick *had* control.

> *Therapist:* I see. When was the last time you can remember controlling it?
>
> *Patrick:* [*takes a deep breath*] Oh, a few times. In the art room one time, everyone was going off with the paint and I was a bit annoyed with that, and someone kept on nicking our paint and then I just calmed down and left it. It annoyed me a bit, but ... it's not serious things, just small things that get me annoyed.
>
> *Therapist:* Yeah. So let me just get this right. I was asking you about a time when you controlled it, so in Art you started to get ...
>
> *Patrick:* Yeah, I started getting angry and then felt it coming on ...
>
> *Therapist:* What did you do to stop yourself?
>
> *Patrick:* Usually when I have a fight, yeah, which I don't often have, I usually get butterflies in my stomach and then I get really angry, and I switch completely. It's like that, yeah, but it's like if someone would make me laugh then it would be fine, it would be gone like before I know it, if I just don't think about it, if I don't think about what's happened, that's fine, I can leave it alone. But if I keep on thinking about it it builds up, what should I have done in that circumstance, it just builds up.
>
> *Therapist:* I'm really interested. You're saying there have been times when you've felt it coming on and you've been able to stop it by maybe someone telling you a joke?
>
> *Patrick:* Yeah ... cheering me up ...
>
> *Therapist:* 'Cheering me up'. But if someone hasn't done that, how have you stopped yourself?
>
> *Patrick:* I just prefer people not speaking to me. I try to get on with my work, just clear it out of my head.
>
> *Therapist:* So you feel it coming on, and what do you say to yourself?
>
> *Patrick:* I say 'I'm not gonna switch, I'm not gonna switch'. But if someone was to say something to me as I was about to, I would be straight off, just like that. The worst thing is when I just turn around and I just switch, and I don't like that when that happens ... it's not so bad when I'm shouting, but it's when the violence comes into it, that's what I don't like.
>
> *Therapist:* Sure. Were you violent on that occasion, the paint ...
>
> *Patrick:* No.
>
> *Therapist:* You shouted, you swore ...
>
> *Patrick:* I was shouting, pointing, swearing.
>
> *Therapist:* At her?
>
> *Patrick:* Yeah.
>
> *Therapist:* Yeah, so how did it end?
>
> *Patrick:* She knows about me. It was, 'have a breather outside'. I had a breather outside, and then I just realised what I'd done. It was her idea I get counselling as well.

I was saying it to my mum before, but she thought it was nothing, she never thought it was really that bad until, like, in the class before, I threw a chair, and that was the worst thing I'd ever done ... it took about five or six people to hold me back.

Therapist: Gosh! So how did you get from shouting to being calm enough to walk out?

Patrick: She said to me, 'Maybe you should take a breather outside'. Dunno. I suppose I thought it was best.

Therapist: So something inside was still able to get control?

Patrick: Yeah. [thoughtful]

Therapist: Does that make sense?

Patrick: I hadn't noticed that before ... that's right.

Therapist: You're saying that in the other incident you actually had other people to hold you. She didn't have to hold you ...

Patrick: I just done it on my own accord, yeah.

Therapist: She just had to say something little like 'go for a walk, go for a breather' and you did!

Patrick: Yeah. But I was still angry at the time.

Therapist: So as you walked out, you were still angry ...

Patrick: I did control myself a bit there, didn't I?

Therapist: How do you explain that?

Patrick: I don't know. I just ... I haven't really noticed that before.

Therapist: So something might have been a bit different on that occasion?

Patrick: [nods]

Therapist: And you said that when you spoke to your mum about it she was thinking it wasn't an issue.

Patrick: Yeah, well she did, but she never thought it wasn't really that big [sic]. I was thinking maybe I should get a child psychiatrist or whatever ...

Therapist: You thought that ... ?

Patrick: Yeah.

Therapist: Really?

Patrick: Hmm. I know I had a problem. And she goes, 'We're gonna have to speak to the people at school and maybe they can get you one'. And she thought it would cost money and everything like that. We're not well off. After that happened, Miss said, 'Maybe we should get a counsellor'.

As can be seen, the discussion had now moved away from the specifics of what Patrick had done to deal with his temper to references to what people thought would be avenues to pursue to help him with the temper. This was therefore a useful point to start a discussion regarding his and others' hopes for the future, and the therapist moved on to ask him the miracle question, and later in the session to use a scale question to assess the degree of progress Patrick felt he'd made towards the preferred future. The exceptions questions (i.e. questions that search for times when problems happen less – in this case when control *is* exerted), it can be seen, helped Patrick to see that control was possible for him and therefore that his wish (and that of others) to have more control in future was perfectly possible.

The question of motivation

One of the commonest complaints regarding young people, especially adolescents, whether in school or elsewhere, concerns their level of 'motivation'.

Adults want them to be motivated towards goals that we, as adults, deem as being 'good' for them, such as getting on with school work. There could be countless reasons why any one young person is appearing to be resistant to doing what is asked of them, and often it is the hope of adults referring a young person for help that the counsellor will find out what is the 'real' problem. From a solution-focused point of view, it is of course not considered necessary to investigate the cause of problems. The obvious exception to this is when there is thought to be a protection factor for the young person, and the counsellor is bound to follow the child protection guidelines and take whatever steps they can to safeguard the young person's safety (protection is, of course, the major exception to the confidentiality young people are told to expect from counsellors).

From a solution-focused perspective, there is no such thing as an unmotivated person. Everyone is motivated towards something, and so one of the tasks of the counsellor is to understand what that something is. There are, in general, two categories of situation that cause most concern with young people. One is when the young person states that behaviour which troubles others is something they actively wish to continue. The second is when they express lack of interest in activities that adults want them to do.

In the first case, what often emerges is that the behaviour that is considered unacceptable is seen by the young person as a way to achieve other acceptable ways of behaving. For example, a young woman who is cutting herself and says she wants to continue to do this may say that her aim is to relieve herself of stress, for example at home. The counsellor can then examine with her other ways of relieving stress, both potential new ways and also other ways she may have already found useful at different times. It is of course generally futile to try to stop someone from engaging in compulsive behaviours like cutting; it is usually easier to start something different than to stop a behaviour or thought process that has become entrenched over time. Another example could be the adolescent who is indulging in risky behaviour (such as substance abuse) in order to impress their peer group. The counsellor would, as in the example of cutting, show respect to the client by not criticising what they are doing – which is not the same thing as agreeing or colluding with the inappropriate behaviour – and would focus on what the young person is trying to achieve by winning acceptance of the peer group and, again, look for other ways of achieving the same end. The principle at work here is to try to distinguish initially between means (cutting, substance abuse, etc.) and ends (freedom from pain and stress, acceptance by peers, etc.).

Regarding the second category it is helpful to bear in mind that 'what we come to call resistance may sometimes reflect the client's attempt to salvage a small portion of self-respect' (Duncan et al., 1997). Given that the majority of students are being sent because adults feel unhappy with them, it is perhaps understandable that they might present initially as uninterested or even resentful. For this reason it is hardly surprising that there is a growing interest in *peer* counselling in many schools (Hillel and Smith, 2001).

There are, however, situations where the student won't acknowledge the problem as the school sees it. It is sometimes necessary to ask the student what they understand would be the consequences if there were to be no change from the school's point of view, and to respectfully enquire as to their opinion about that: for example if the school were to permanently exclude them. In this writer's experience, even the most resentful young person will be able to identify what they would rather see happen. The very fact that they are there with you, even if it feels initially like a one-sided 'conversation', is indication enough that they are unhappy about things and so there is scope for manoeuvre. The adolescent who loudly denounces the injustice of the system whereby they are always blamed for what they didn't do can be sympathised with (which isn't the same as agreeing with them!) and can then be asked how they would like to see things. This would be another example of applying the 'distinguish means from ends' principle, because the outcome of a 'fairer' school will usually be a fairer student, interested in getting a little bit more work done, etc. Of course, this process of questioning does not magically eliminate the sense of grievance. However, once there is a sense of possibility for the future, the question of how the student is currently able to cope with the situation can be addressed.

Solution-focused therapy in teaching

There are obviously considerable limits to how far a therapy approach can be adapted to the setting of the classroom where there is the job of teaching to be done. In some respects teachers already incorporate many aspects of solution-focused thinking into their work, for example in highlighting what students do well and giving praise wherever possible. Solution-focused questions can be adapted to help students with their learning: 'how will you know when you are a reader?' (Rhodes and Ajmal, 1995). With behaviour problems it is inevitable that once a student has been identified as a 'problem' then teachers will begin to lose trust in them. 'Teachers always think you're doing something when you're not', as one aggrieved young man put it. Had one of his teachers been present at that moment, they no doubt could have given many reasons as to why this was the case. The lack of trust can, inevitably, lead to a situation of 'damning with faint praise' where the teacher might say that, for example, they do praise the young person, when in fact what they said was something like, 'That was very good; how come you can't do that more often?' (A student once told me that he'd learned that a question like that was a 'figure of speech': it was not a question to be answered!)

If the situation is not so critical and the teacher is asking for help with a particular student, then a focus on exceptions is probably the single most useful intervention. This means that the teacher is invited to consider those situations when the student is behaving better or working harder and is then asked to evaluate what was different at those times, with particular reference to what *they* may have done to influence the student. In more trying circumstances they should also be asked about how they cope with the student such that they are able to continue to teach the class.

In the context of meetings about students, where several professionals may have differing views about the situation, a way of developing a common aim is to begin by asking if it is right that everyone is present because they feel that there is some hope for the student in question. 'Can we agree that we are all here because we want Jim to be settled and learning in school?' (Harker, 2001). As long as this is answered in the positive, the meeting can then discuss 'What is it that each one of us sees that tells us there is potential?' There will be a pooling of ideas about what seems to work best with that student, and then there can be a discussion regarding what would be signs of improvement: what is wanted rather than not wanted.

Unfortunately, many referrals for help come on the back of 'I've tried everything'. Exceptions questions are seen, in such cases, as almost insulting, implying that maybe things aren't as bad as all that. Coping questions are therefore of crucial relevance here. If the discussion is to result in the counsellor seeing the young person concerned, then extra questions regarding the teacher's view of what would be the smallest signs of progress, as well as their confidence that change of any sort is possible, will help give the work a positive aspect.

Many solution-focused techniques can be adapted to the day to day management of students with behavioural difficulties (Metcalf, 1999). Commendations are usually appreciated by students and by their parents. A teaching assistant or mentor may be able to spend five minutes at the end of the day in 'positive' thinking with the student, reviewing constructive developments. Counsellors only have occasional contact with students, and while they can ask for feedback on positive developments between sessions, inevitably they are going to hear a lot about setbacks; teaching staff, on the other hand, are able to pick up and respond quickly to even the smallest signs of improvement.

A word of caution. Even the teacher who is most sympathetic to the solution-focused approach can be suspicious of having it 'done to them'. After one joint meeting with a student a member of staff commented 'That was a good meeting'. Almost instinctively I asked her, 'What tells you it was a good meeting?' 'Don't you keep doing that brief therapy on me!' she retorted. We both laughed. But I couldn't resist adding, 'Yes, but what *does* tell you?' 'It was the way he came up with ideas at the end. It shows he's not stupid, he *can* do it', came the reply.

Work with younger children

The main focus of this chapter has been on work with adolescents. In general, all the techniques described here can be adapted with sensitivity to work with younger children, as well as older children with learning difficulties.

Concrete descriptions are a feature of all solution-focused conversations, whether with adults or children. This enables children to follow the discussion between adults as easily as possible and facilitates their involvement ... this ... is particularly valuable when the therapist is trying to reach a common understanding of concepts like 'showing more respect', 'behaving' or 'acting your age', which often mean more to adults than to children. (Lethem, 1994, pp. 45–46)

Scale questions can become drawings of ladders or mountainsides; miracles can become magic wands, and role-play can become a very simple way of getting round the problem of asking too many questions and using too many words. A five-year-old boy in his first year talked about how, on a good day, he would walk rather than run around the classroom. He was asked if he was a good walker, to which he replied he was. 'Can you show me how you walk around the room?' At this he obliged with a serious and careful turn about the room, to be met, of course, by the admiring therapist's compliment: 'Yes, you *are* a good walker. Well done!' (My colleague Chris Iveson was the therapist in this example.) It should be noted that a counsellor can compliment a child in this way, but not, in most cases, the teacher. Teachers are right when they complain about having to praise pupils for doing what all the others are doing already. 'To praise little Jonny for finally doing what all the other kids already do is unavoidably to give Jonny the impression he's damaged' (O'Hanlon and Wilk, 1987, p. 166). The ordinary behaviour should be acknowledged but praise reserved for what seems significantly different for that child.

Teachers can use the techniques of solution-focused therapy with the whole classroom, for example employing a miracle-type question to help the class decide what is their ideal classroom environment, and then to use a scale (drawn on the blackboard) to look at progress made and small stepts still to be taken.

'What can we do about students who ... ?': questions teachers ask about students

Students who have unrealistic goals
A simple example might be the student who is determined to take a particular subject they cannot be expected to do well in, and yet they seem determined to do it, even though they are doing badly. At one level, there is of course only so much anyone can do; trying to save them from themselves will only make matters worse. Questions that can be useful here include asking hypothetical future-focused questions, so that the student might deal better with failure if it comes. For example, 'Of course we hope things go well for you, and you have given some examples of what will be signs of that happening. But, let's say it doesn't go how you would like it to. How do you think you will cope with things then? Do you think you might like some help? What would be your way of asking for help? How would I know that you wanted help?'

Students who say 'that's how I am, I can't/won't change'
It is best in these situations to adopt a 'both/and' perspective. Rather than trying to argue them out of it, the student's view should, initially, be accepted. Then

they can be asked about how they can be themselves *and* still be able to do what is good for them and for the class. For example, a student who insists that they will always fight back if someone 'cusses' them can be complimented on being someone who believes in standing up for themselves (note: only this is accepted, *not* the aggression!), and then be asked how they can do this in a way that will be good for them and not lead to them being excluded.

Students who say that last week was better only because so-and-so wasn't 'bugging' them
As usual, it is better to avoid the temptation to argue with this. A more productive line to take is to accept their view of it and follow it through. 'OK, so that was different. Let's just look at what you were able to get on with *last* week. Now, if you were able to get on with more of that *this* week, how would I know? And if you felt you were being "bugged" again, what would be a good way to cope with it so that you still were able to do the best you could do?'

How can we use your approach when we have so little time?
Teachers are obviously right in thinking that others, such as counsellors, mentors and learning support assistants, have more individual time in which to explore solution-focused questions such as future-focused questions and scales. Furthermore, they are likely to be spending much of the time that might be available in 'management' issues related to what the student has done wrong, trying to resolve disputes, confronting the umpteenth incident of lateness or lost books or forgotten homework, etc., etc. But while rules must be confirmed and supported, nevertheless there is little point, as everyone knows, in turning the meeting into a lecture. The student will simply switch off. Young people are generally hopeless at pretending to be listening when they're not; adults can, if they're watching and are not too preoccupied with getting their warnings across, tell this very quickly. The admonitions can usually be very brief, and there is little point in listening to the student's litany of excuses. There is instead an opening for a five-minute conversation around the two essential principles of solution-focused therapy:

• how they managed to do things or cope with things better in the past;
• how things could be different in future and how things could be coped with differently.

Culture, race and gender

The project is situated within a school that has an extremely varied ethnic intake, including refugees from Bosnia, Kosovo and Somalia and children born in Turkey, Nigeria and Zaire. English, therefore, is frequently the young person's second language. There are large numbers of black or Asian British students, and the majority of students are within the Muslim community. Apart from the fact that the therapist is middle-aged and middle-class, he is also white and Jewish! This means that in order to be respectful of his clients he has to be open about his lack of knowledge of the culture and traditions that they come from, and must ask them to explain how their ideas for the future (for example) will fit in with their community's expectations. In this way solution-focused therapy is highly appropriate for working with clients from different backgrounds, as the approach emphasises a not-knowing, non-expert stance on the part of the worker. A useful approach is to talk with the young person about the views that are held by others in their cultural peer group and thereby elicit their ways of dealing with a particular situation. 'If I was a Bengali woman, what would I be asking you now?' It has even been found beneficial to invite the client to bring along a friend for joint discussion.

Another consideration for the therapist is whether racism is a factor in the student's problems in the school, both in relation to teaching staff and in relation to other ethnic groups. Knowing when to enquire about this is a very delicate matter. The counsellor would want the student to feel able to share particular fears with him or her, but the student will probably need to know what the counsellor is going to do with the information before they will disclose anything.

One option for the counsellor is to raise issues with school staff. As an outsider to the school system the counsellor's leverage is very limited, but sometimes they pick up concerns that the school is not aware of, and the counsellor can act as a go-between and facilitate better communication and understanding. An example of this was when the school was considering excluding a pupil and the counsellor suggested a lenient approach based on what he had heard about the anxiety the boy's family was experiencing regarding the fate of relatives in Kosovo.

Acknowledgements

I am deeply grateful to staff at South Camden Community School for enabling me to work with their students. Of the many names I could mention, pride of place goes to Carolyn Kain, Head of the Learning Development Department, who recently took retirement (may you have many happy and healthy years in Portugal, Carolyn!) and Chris Gibson, Excellence in Cities Manager.

References

de Shazer, S. (1991) *Putting Difference to Work*. New York: W.W. Norton.
Duncan, B., Hubble, M. and Miller, S.D. (1997) *Psychotherapy with Impossible Cases: the efficient treatment of therapy veterans*. New York: W.W. Norton.
George, E., Iveson, C. and Ratner, H. (1999) *Problem to Solution: brief therapy with individuals and families*. London: BT Press.
Harker, M. (2001) How to build solutions at meetings. In Y. Ajmal and I. Rees (eds), *Solutions in Schools: creative applications of solution-focused thinking with young people and adults*. London: BT Press.

Hillel, Y. and Smith, E. (2001) Empowering students to empower others. In Y. Ajmal and I. Rees (eds), ibid.

Lethem, J. (1994) *Moved to Tears, Moved to Action: solution focused brief therapy with women and children*. London: BT Press.

Metcalf, L. (1999) *Teaching towards Solutions*. New York: Centre for Applied Research in Education/Simon & Schuster.

O'Hanlon, B. and Beadle, S. (1996) *A Field Guide to Possibility Land*. London: BT Press.

O'Hanlon, B. and Wilk, J. (1987) *Shifting Contexts: the generation of effective psychotherapy*. New York: Guilford Press.

Rhodes, J. and Ajmal, Y. (1995) *Solution Focused Thinking in Schools: behaviour, reading and organisation*. London: BT Press.

10

Solution-Focused Practice in Social Work

John Wheeler

I work as a social worker in a child and adolescent mental health service in a hospital setting. Children and young people are referred with behaviour problems; non-school attendance; soiling; anxiety; depression and eating disorders. The parents have either asked for help or been persuaded to attend by social workers who have concerns over their parenting or by school staff who are dissatisfied with the child's behaviour. Solution-focused practice can often be useful regardless of whether people have sought help or been sent.

I usually invite service users to decide how often to meet. Many find brief contact to be sufficient. I see most families for around five meetings over a four-month period and about 10 per cent for longer.

My post is funded and line-managed by the local authority. The agency's main purpose is to assess and treat troubled or troubling children and adolescents, and includes screening for children with intrinsic difficulties such as attention deficit disorder, and specialist child protection assessments.

Rationale for using solution-focused practice

Social workers are typically expected to know how to bring about change with families who have run into difficulties. Although I had already incorporated other therapeutic approaches into my practice, I was still coming across situations where I was unable to help families achieve the changes they were looking for.

When I discovered solution-focused practice I was struck by the potential difference between problem talk and solution talk. I expected that an emphasis on service users' strengths could greatly enhance collaboration and transform outcomes throughout my service. Early discussions taught me that colleagues needed time to see what solution-focused practice had to offer, so I concentrated on developing my own competence, then gradually promoted the approach through writing and training.

Parents who had lost confidence in their parenting, or lost sight of their child's qualities, responded well. I was so struck by the contribution to my practice with one particular family that I published an account (1995a) of the involvement and the issues raised. Confident in the relevance to social work, I then introduced solution-focused practice to social care staff across a range of specialties. Currently I am providing more extensive training for childcare social workers.

At first I worried about incompatibilities with risk assessment responsibilities, but soon I found the approach was actually an asset. In one family I explored my concerns by saying 'I'm worried about your son's safety. On a scale of zero to ten, where ten means he's totally safe, how safe would you say he is?' They replied 'six', and when I asked what they were doing to maintain this, I heard information which substantially increased my confidence in their parenting. Along with colleagues (Wheeler, Bone and Smith, 1998), I subsequently devised an approach to child protection risk assessment which incorporated solution-focused ideas.

Solution-focused practice

Solution-focused practice can be adapted to many settings. It can be used in office-based interviews; home visits to families; on car journeys and in snatched conversations in corridors. In this chapter I will illustrate how much the approach is currently being used in social work, and how it relates to social work values and legislation.

How is the solution-focused approach used in social work practice?

The approach is currently taught on many social work courses. Established practitioners are seeking training and forming support groups to maintain their practice. The approach has yet to feature widely in social work practice, however. Possibly the term 'therapy' has alienated social workers and managers, who worry that the approach is irrelevant to the demands of social work and the complex lives of many of the people with whom they work. However, a number of social workers in the UK have reported on the relevance of solution-focused practice to their work.

George, Iveson and Ratner (1990) pioneered solution-focused brief therapy in a mental health setting. Pollard (1993) described her use of the model in the Probation Service. Marsh, a social worker in adult mental health, and colleagues, used the approach in a mental health day hospital (Wilgosh et al., 1994). Gilbey and Turner (1994) used the model with groups in a mental health service. I have written accounts of the usefulness of the approach in a child mental health setting (1995b; 2001). Bond (1998) gives an account of Murphy's use of the approach in her training of staff working with children and families. Walsh (1997) and Mylan and Lethem (1999) have described how the approach can be used in child protection. McCarthy (1998) and Shennan (1999), both experienced child protection workers, also recommend the approach, McCarthy describing it as 'the best model I have found so far for facilitating a productive working partnership' (p. 11). Turnell and Edwards (1999) have written about the use of the approach in the most taxing of child protection situations.

There are signs that the approach is being included in the theory base of social work. Although Adams, Dominelli and Payne's listing of practice models (1998) did not include it, other writers are noticing what the approach has to offer. Payne's overview (1997, p. 177) acknowledges the contribution of solution-focused practice to enhancing service users' self-esteem, self-understanding and empowerment. Milner and O'Byrne (1998, p. 161) are impressed by its 'emphasis on listening to the service user's story and focusing on exceptions, which is both anti-oppressive and empowering, seeking solutions within the user's life rather than in the worker's head. Additionally, the way in which service users' situations are framed to empha-sise gains reduces risk in practice and increases creativity.'

Two of the current perspectives in social work are postmodernity and social constructionism, as outlined by Parton and Marshall (1998). Parton has long argued that social work services need to find more collaborative ways of practis-ing if they are to achieve their objectives of empowerment for those who are struggling, and safety for those who are at risk (1997). Solution-focused practice is a practical articulation of the shift in thinking which Parton and Marshall see as necessary. The jointly authored publication by Parton and O'Byrne (2000) stands as a useful example of the fit between Parton's theoretical analysis and O'Byrne's valuing of solution-focused practice.

How does the approach relate to social work values?

In the early days of social work, Biestek's criteria for professional behaviour included being non-judgmental and respecting user self-determination and confi-dentiality (1961). More recently, the British Association of Social Workers (BASW) *Code of Ethics* requires that social workers will:

> Respect their clients as individuals and will seek to ensure that their dignity, indivi-duality, rights and responsibility shall be safeguarded. (BASW, 1987)

The Central Council for Education and Training in Social Work (CCETSW) in particular through *Paper 30* (1990), prioritised anti-oppressive practice as an over-arching feature of social work values. Shardlow (1998) believes the most promi-nent features of this are empowerment, consumerism and the challenging of structures of oppression (1998, p. 31). Solution-focused practice transforms the power relationship between helpers and helped in ways consistent with Shardlow, Biestek and the BASW's *Code of Ethics*.

Solution-focused practice is based on the assumption that service users are experts on their own lives. When someone is asked to rate progress on a scale of zero to ten, it is taken for granted that their reply has value and significance. Solution-focused questions, by assuming that progress will happen, also convey a regard for service users as people who can make a difference to their own lives, however demoralised they themselves might be feeling.

Empowerment is a key objective in a solution-focused approach. When a service user is asked how they have managed to survive so far, or how they have managed to achieve some progress, despite the complexities of their struggle, the worker conveys an assumption that they have been doing something which has counted and made a difference.

Solution-focused practice also offers social workers an opportunity to work in collaboration with service users to rise above the structures in society which have contributed to their marginalisation and degradation. So, when the service user is asked to describe their preferred future, or define goals for change, the worker displays a willingness to accept their plans for their life, instead of imposing an external view of how they should be living.

Assessments can also be more closely connected to social work values when inspired by a solution-focused approach. Social work has always endeavoured to draw on service users' strengths. Solution-focused questioning increases the likelihood that assessments will include the particular complexities of service users' situations and the resources they can contribute to their amelioration.

Solution-focused practice also relates well to notions of consumerism. I often ask 'On a scale of zero to ten, how useful would you say today's meeting has been?' or 'Is there something I could do which might be helpful?' Such questions emphasise the extent to which social work can be experienced as a service made available to members of the public at times of crisis.

How does the approach relate to legislation?

The state is a significant stakeholder in terms of determining what social workers should be doing, and how they should do it. Over recent years a number of themes consistent with solution-focused practice have repeatedly appeared in a range of documents.

- The Community Care Act (DHSS, 1989a), states a commitment to 'a policy of community care which enables ... people to achieve their full potential' (1.1), an intention to 'give people a greater individual say in how they live their lives and the services they need to help them to do so' (1.8) and recommends that 'assessments should focus positively on what the individual can and cannot do' (3.2.3).
- The Children Act (DHSS, 1989b) promoted working in partnership with parents, providing support to enable children to stay with their families, and listening to the wishes of children and young people.
- In the annual report of the Chief Inspector of the Social Services Inspectorate for 1997/1998 (DOH, 1998a), a chapter is devoted to increasing user involvement and independence.
- Messages from research (Dartington Social Research Unit, 1995) prompted a reorientation of services towards family support and away from child protection. When the Social Services Inspectorate subsequently inspected the delivery of family support services (DOH, 1999a) it judged that families still needed to have more say in how they were helped and recommended that 'the

SSD has an organisational culture which is open and committed to learning and in which staff can acquire new knowledge and skills, methods of helping and models of service' (Standard 7, criterion 1).

- Concerns over social exclusion (DOH, 1998b, 2.3), have led the government to encourage services to work together 'to ensure that service users can increase their life opportunities'.
- The Social Services Inspectorate, commenting on mental health services (DOH, 1999b, Standard 5), recommends that 'Users and carers are actively involved in their own assessment and care planning and consulted in service planning.'
- The National Framework for Assessment of Children in Need and Their Families (DOH, 1999c 1.44, p. 13), recommends that 'working with a child and family's strengths may be an important part of a plan to resolve difficulties'.
- Working in partnership with service users is also strongly promoted in *Working Together to Safeguard Children* (DOH, 1999d).

Culture, race and gender issues

Social work has attempted for some time to address the needs of people who have been marginalised because of difference. Solution-focused practice, through its emphasis on seeking the service users' ideas on how to resolve their difficulties, offers a glimpse of the unique context in which service users find themselves, and elicits ways forward which are consistent with that context. Anti-oppressive training, and the more recent emphasis on social inclusion, have alerted social workers to the limitations of their own knowledge and assumptions. As Burnham and Harris (1996) pointed out, the assumption that people from one particular group are the same can itself lead to oppressive practice.

As a male working with female service users, I can never expect to fully understand, for example, the dilemmas experienced by women living with domestic violence. Through using a solution-focused approach I have witnessed women designing unique strategies and plans which have eventually taken them into a future without violence, even though some of the steps along the way made little sense to me at the time.

I sometimes work with Orthodox Jewish families. Here again, solution-focused practice has brought into the work a richer cultural knowledge than I could ever expect to acquire on my own. One Jewish parent pointed out to me in a first meeting that whatever I might assume from how they presented, they were not a typical Orthodox family. Thankfully, solution-focused questions grounded our work in ideas and beliefs which were consistent with their expression of Orthodox Judaism. Sometimes, however, complications have arisen in the application of the approach. When working with Jewish parents on one occasion, I used a scaling question to elicit the mother's view on the behaviour of her son, as she was the parent who spent most time with him. There was no reply, and it was only after her husband had answered the question that she provided her number. Later it occurred to me that her culture probably did not allow her to express a view on this topic until her husband had stated his.

Integrating solution-focused practice

Prior to using solution-focused ideas I drew on systemic thinking to inform my work with families and person-centred counselling when seeing individuals. I still value these models when I believe they can help. Whilst solution-focused practice has become a major influence, I still use the values of person-centred counselling as a guide on how to use the approach, and systemic thinking to make sense of the changes which the approach brings about. Solution-focused questions also often elicit information about service users which enhances the values of person-centred counselling, in particular respect and positive regard. Since systemic thinking has come to value the 'non-expert' position, as advocated by Hoffman (1993), there is also an easier fit between this approach and solution-focused practice. More recently I have incorporated narrative therapy into my practice. Currently, when solution-focused questions appear to jar, I either use a person-centred approach to hear more of the service user's concerns, or use externalisation from narrative therapy to elicit a different stance towards the problems.

Some people are concerned that solution-focused practice pays insufficient attention to feelings. But feelings, actions and thoughts are inextricably interconnected. A change in thinking often changes feelings. A change in behaviour often changes feelings. For example, I once asked a tearful parent what she normally did when she felt the way she did. As she explained what she usually did her tears stopped and she became more animated. Social workers are often the first people to hear accounts of abuse, injustice or trauma. Out of respect, it is very important to hear accounts which have previously been silenced. Merely listening, however, can leave people trapped in their dreadful past. Solution-focused questions such as, 'How did you get through?' alert people to their strengths. It is these strengths which will ensure that their future will not dominated by their past.

Other people worry that solution-focused practice is only a quick fix. For me the strength of the approach is that the strategies which emerge are uniquely tailored to the service user's context, as are the goals for change, and thus more likely to last.

Solution-focused practice can also appear to some as unduly goal-driven. For some clients their context cannot be changed, for example a carer looking after a parent with dementia. A question such as, 'What are your hopes for these last few years of your mother's life?' can usefully take the carer beyond the monotony and despondency which might otherwise overwhelm them.

Personal reflections

Throughout over 20 years of practice as a social worker I have looked for approaches which could be tailored to the uniqueness of people and which could address the complexity of their struggles and ensure that my practice is relevant to the policy directives that shape my professional responsibilities. When I was introduced to solution-focused practice it appeared that this was what I had been looking for. Since using the approach for a number of years I have seldom felt let down and often take delight in my work, fascinated by service users' resourcefulness, inspired by their determination to win through, despite extraordinary adversity.

Ford (1996), in a survey of drug and alcohol services, found that frontline staff reported that the approach had made a difference not only to service users, but also to themselves. Sundmann (1997) researched the impact of solution-focused training on a team of social workers in Finland. The study found that the social workers using the approach made more positive statements about service users, were more goal-focused and worked more collaboratively. They also spoke of enjoying their work more. The affirming and rich view of people found in solution-focused practice can help a social work service avoid becoming a mirror of the demoralisation experienced by many of its service users.

Case studies

To illustrate the variety of situations in which a solution-focused approach can be used, three scenarios are outlined.

1 Ms Evans has approached a duty officer to ask for her mother to be admitted to residential care.
2 Mrs Chan is struggling with her son's behaviour and has telephoned the out of hours service for help.
3 Mr Singh has asked for support from the worker in the day centre he attends.

The process of a solution-focused involvement in each scenario shows how the techniques can be used at each particular stage.

Defining goals for change
With careful timing, service users can be asked questions to clarify goals for change.

Ms Evans: You'll have to put my mother in a home.
Duty officer: How would that help you at the moment?
Ms Evans: I could stop worrying. I'm sick with worry at the moment.
Duty officer: So you need us to come up with something that would help you feel your mother is safe?

Mrs Chan: [telephoning emergency worker] You'll have to do something, my son won't take any notice of me.
Emergency worker: You need to have more control over him?
Mrs Chan: Yes.

Mr Singh: [in day centre] Can I have a word with you?

Day centre worker: What do you need from our talk?

Mr Singh: I'm feeling really low, I don't know what to do.

Day centre worker: So we need to talk for a while, so it's a bit clearer?

Pre-session change and scaling

Often there has been some progress even before the service user and social worker have spoken to each other.

Worker: On a scale of zero to ten, where ten represents all the changes you are hoping to see, where were things when you decided to ask for help, where are they now?

Ms Evans: Well, they were at zero when I decided to call in to see you, but it's at three now. I'm hoping it's not just up to me to worry about my mother.

Mrs Chan: It was at minus 200 when I was looking for your number. Now it's at one. He's calmed down a bit whilst I've been on the phone.

Mr Singh: It was at two when I decided to speak to you. I already had some ideas. Now it's about three. I'm not quite so low now we're talking.

When progress has occurred, there is scope for curiosity about how this came to be.

Further use of scaling

Scaling questions can be used in a variety of ways.

Duty officer: If ten represents your mother being totally safe, what number could you tolerate?

Ms Evans: Seven, I suppose. I always knew things would be riskier as she got older. It was her leaving the gas on which gave me such a fright.

Duty officer: So what would help to put it at four?

Ms Evans: Someone else calling in to check on her. I can't call in as much as I did.

Emergency worker: If ten represents complete control, what number are you aiming for?

Mrs Chan: Six would do. I know all kids are naughty sometimes.

Emergency worker: Has he been at six before?

Mrs Chan: Yes, before his dad' left.

Day centre worker: Say ten represented you being completely clear about what to do. How high does it have to be for you to make a decision?

Mr Singh: Oh, six would do. Sometimes you just have to make decisions and hope for the best.

Compliments

Compliments are another way of helping people remember their resources.

Duty officer: You must have been working hard, Ms Evans, to keep your mother safe.

Ms Evans: Of course. I'm her daughter. Mind you, I wish my brothers would pull their weight a bit.

Emergency worker: I can see, Mrs Chan, you care about your son, and want to keep him out of trouble.

Mrs Chan: Well yes, his father was a rogue when he was young. I don't want him to turn out like him.

> *Day centre worker*:   I can tell, Mr Singh, that you try to make wise decisions.
> *Mr Singh*:   Oh yes. Two heads are better than one.

The miracle question

The miracle question can help to generate problem-free talk, as the following replies illustrate.

> *Ms Evans*:   I'd wake up and find I'd had a good night's sleep.
> *Worker*:   And what would happen next?
> *Ms Evans*:   I'd be happier about facing the day.
> *Worker*:   Who would be the first to notice this?
> *Ms Evans*:   My mother, probably. I'd call round, feeling relaxed and happy. We'd have a cup of tea, talk about the people we know, have a laugh.

This has put Ms Evans in touch with how she interacts with her mother and the choices open to her. Strained relations between the two may have exacerbated her mother's confusion.

> *Mrs Chan*:   I'd go to wake him and he'd be pleasant. Say hello, Mam. Then he'd get up and get dressed. That would be a miracle.

This suggests that the beginning of the day is important. A greeting could send beneficial ripples throughout the day.

> *Mr Singh*:   I'd notice the sun shining and hear the birds singing. I'd know that I could do all the things that have to be done.
> *Worker*:   When was the last time you heard the birds singing?
> *Mr Singh*:   Last year, before my wife died.
> *Worker*:   Had you thought it would take time to get over losing your wife?
> *Mr Singh*:   Of course. We were very close.

Here, Mr Singh is reminding himself that his low mood is located in time and circumstances.

Drawing a first meeting to a close

By the end of a first session people can be in a variety of positions.

> *Worker*:   I hope you've found this talk useful, Mr Singh. Maybe over the next week you could see if you notice some of those things you used to enjoy – sunshine, birds, flowers and so on.

Here, a solution-focused task has been offered. Sometimes this alerts people to experiences they hadn't recently noticed, initiating a positive cycle of improvement.

> *Worker*:   OK then, Mrs Chan. You've got some ideas about how the day could start differently in the family. Do you think you might experiment with some ways of bringing that about?

Here, Mrs Chan is being invited to consider other steps she might take.

> *Ms Evans*:   I'm not so sure about my mother going into a home just yet. I think I need to check things out with my brothers first.

Here, Ms Evans is ready to explore other possibilities.

Next meeting and beyond

> *Allocated worker*:   Hello Mrs Chan, I hear that things were one when you spoke to my colleague. Where are they now?
> *Ms Chan*:   Back to minus ten, I'd say.
> *Worker*:   How have you stopped it being minus twenty?
> *Ms Chan*:   Well, I have told him I'm sick of being treated like dirt and rationed out his pocket money.

Here, although Mrs Chan has lost some confidence, she has still been active in dealing with her son, as her reply illustrates.

> *Worker*:   Hello again, Mr Singh. Last time we spoke things were at three. Where are they now?
> *Mr Singh*:   About four.
> *Worker*:   What's helped to bring that about?
> *Mr Singh*:   Well, my grandchildren came round. I'd forgotten what lovely children they are. My granddaughter looks so like my wife. She has her smile. Somehow that cheered me up. I started wondering about the future. My wife was a wonderful cook. Maybe my granddaughter will be too. She had made some cakes for me.

Here, Mr Singh is feeling a little better, and is recalling other aspects of his life which are important to him.

> *Worker*:   Now it's risen to four, what would five look like? What might help to bring that about?
> *Mr Singh*:   I could visit my grandchildren. I haven't done that for a long time.

Here, a scaling question has elicited other steps Mr Singh might take.

> *Allocated worker*:   Hello Ms Evans. I hear you've had a lot of worry about your mother and you viewed her safety to be at three when you spoke to my colleague.
> *Ms Evans*:   That's right. Actually I'd say it's at six now.
> *Worker*:   How come?
> *Ms Evans*:   Well I invited my brothers round. I said, look I can't carry on with all this responsibility for Mother. None of us really want her in a home. She'd be so unhappy, she's so independent. They agreed, and actually she's going to have a short holiday with one of them soon.

Here, Ms Evans has tried out other possibilities and is pleased with the outcome.

Endings

Once service users' strengths have come to the fore it's important to ensure that they take credit for all they've done to bring the change about.

> *Ms Evans*:   Thank you so much for helping me sort things out for my mother.
> *Worker*:   It had been a big worry for you for a time, hadn't it? But, looking back, what do you think it says about you, that you sorted things out as you did?
> *Mrs Evans*:   I've always been a good organiser. I suppose I'd forgotten that when I was getting so worried about my mother.

Sometimes it is useful to ask about relapse plans.

> *Worker*:   I know you are much happier with your son's behaviour, Mrs Chan. But say he started to slip back, what would you do?

> *Mrs Chan*:   I'd probably pull back on the pocket money again. Give him something to work for. Also I thought I might tell his dad what's been happening. I didn't need to in the end, but it's something else I could do if I needed to.

When social workers have long-term contact they are in a good position to draw on service users' self-knowledge if difficulties return.

> *Worker*:   I'm sorry to hear you are feeling down again, Mr Singh. What are your thoughts on this?
> *Mr Singh*:   Well, I wasn't really surprised. My wife's birthday came round. Even though I've been enjoying life more, I still miss her. I think I always will.

Conclusions

When I first shared solution-focused brief therapy with social work colleagues in 1993, most were interested but many said they were not sure whether they could incorporate the approach into their own practice. Nowadays social workers who come to my workshops are saying, 'Tell us what it is so we can get on and try it out.' Within social work in the UK, solution-focused practice is coming to be known as an approach which gets results, both good outcomes for service users and a sense of achievement for those working with them. Given the good fit with social work values and current legislation, and adaptations of the approach to social work practice by Berg and Kelly (2000) and Turnell and Edwards (1999) and others, I am confident that the solution-focused approach will become a major influence on social work practice in the UK in the foreseeable future.

References

Adams, R., Dominelli, L. and Payne, M. (eds) (1998) *Social Work: themes, issues and critical debates*. London: Macmillan.

BASW (1987) *A Code of Ethics for Social Work*. Birmingham: British Association of Social Workers.

Berg, I.K. and Kelly, S. (2000) *Building Solutions in Child Protective Services*. New York: W.W. Norton.

Biestek, F.P. (1961) *The Casework Relationship*. London: Allen & Unwin.

Bond, H. (1998) Back in the driver's seat. *Community Care*, 19–25 November, pp. 32–33.

Burnham, J. and Harris, Q. (1996) Emerging ethnicity: a tale of three cultures. In K. Dwivedi and V. Vanna (eds), *Meeting the Needs of Ethnic Minority Children: a handbook for professionals*. London: Jessica Kingsley.

CCETSW (1990) *Paper 30: Requirements and Regulations for the Diploma in Social Work*. London: CCETSW.

Dartington Social Research Unit (1995) *Child Protection: messages from research*. London: HMSO.

DHSS (1989a) *Caring for People: community care in the next decade and beyond*. London: HMSO.

DHSS (1989b) *The Children Act*. London: HMSO.

DOH (1998a) Social Services Inspectorate, *Social Services Facing the Future: the seventh annual report of the Chief Inspector Social Services Inspectorate*. London: HMSO.

DOH (1998b) *Modernising Social Services*. London: HMSO.

DOH (1999a) Social Services Inspectorate, *Getting Family Support Right: inspection of the delivery of family support services*. London: HMSO.

DOH (1999b) *Still Building Bridges: the report of a national inspection of arrangements for the integration of care programme approach with care management*. London: HMSO.

DOH (1999c) *National Framework for Assessment*. London: HMSO.

DOH (1999d) *Working Together to Safeguard Children*. London: HMSO.

Ford, A. (1996) An examination of solution-focused brief therapy with substance misusers. MA dissertation, Durham University, UK.

George, E., Iveson, C. and Ratner, H. (1990) *Problem to Solution: brief therapy with individuals and families*. London: BT Press.

Gilbey, G. and Turner, J. (1994) Miracles en masse. *Community Care*, 10 March, p. 30.

Hoffman, L. (1993) *Exchanging Voices: a collaborative approach to family therapy*. London: Karnac Books.

McCarthy, J. (1998) Solution-focused practice in a social services department. *Context*, 35 (February): 11–12.

Milner, J. and O'Byrne, P. (1998) *Assessment in Social Work*. Basingstoke: Macmillan.

Mylan, T. and Lethem, J. (1999) *Searching for Strengths in Child Protection Assessment: from guidelines to practice*. London: BT Press.

Parton, N. (ed.) (1997) *Child Protection and Family Support: tensions, contradictions and possibilities*. London: Routledge.

Parton, N. and Marshall, W. (1998) Postmodernism and discourse approaches to social work. In R. Adams, L. Dominelli and M. Payne (eds), *Social Work: themes, issues and critical debates*. London: Macmillan.

Parton, N. and O'Byrne, P. (2000) *Constructive Social Work*. London: Macmillan.

Payne, M. (1997) *Modern Social Work Theory*. London: Macmillan.

Pollard, C. (1993) Giving hope. *Probation Journal*, 40: 136–139.

Shardlow, S. (1998) Values, ethics and social work. In R. Adams, L. Dominelli and M. Payne (eds), *Social Work: themes, issues and critical debates*. London: Macmillan.

Shennan, G. (1999) Systemic practice within child protection investigation. *Context*, 41: 18–19.

Sundmann, P. (1997) Solution-focused ideas in social work. *Journal of Family Therapy*, 19: 159–172.

Turnell, A. and Edwards, S. (1999) Aspiring to partnership: the signs of safety approach to child protection. *Child Abuse Review*, 6: 179–190.

Walsh T. (ed.) (1997) *Solution Focused Child Protection: towards a positive frame for social work practice*. Dublin: University of Dublin Press.

Wheeler, J. (1995a) Supporting self-growth: the solution-focused approach. *Mental Health Nursing*, 15(2): 24–25.

Wheeler, J. (1995b) Believing in miracles: the implications and possibilities of using solution-focused therapy in a child mental health setting. *Association for Child Psychology and Psychiatry Review and Newsletter*, 17(5): 255–261.

Wheeler, J. (2001) A helping hand: solution-focused brief therapy and child and adolescent mental health. *Clinical Child Psychology & Psychiatry*, 6(2): 293–306.

Wheeler, J., Bone, D. and Smith, J. (1998) Whole-day assessments: a team approach to complex multi-problem families. *Clinical Child Psychology & Psychiatry*, 3(2): 169–181.

Wilgosh, R., Hawkes, D. and Marsh, I. (1994) Solution-focused therapy in promoting mental health. *Mental Health Nursing*, 14(6): 18–21.

11

Using Solution-Focused Therapy with Women

Jane Lethem

My special interest in therapy with women developed largely as a result of meeting many mothers in the course of my work, in the NHS, with children and their families. I am currently based in a child and adolescent mental health service in London. The population it serves is highly diverse socially and ethnically. There are many young solo mothers. Poor housing, poverty or unresolved status as asylum seekers adds to the challenges faced by a significant proportion of our clients.

My connection with the Brief Therapy Practice also brings me into contact with women. Almost all of my clients there have specifically requested to see a woman therapist. Referrals include requests for help with the effects in adult life of child sexual abuse; depression; obsessions and compulsions; concerns about relationships and coping with the effects of marital breakdown.

De Shazer (1985, 1988) has argued against classifying clients according to their problems on the grounds that the similarity between problems is irrelevant to the development of solutions. Similarly, one might avoid categorising clients on the basis of any of the features of their initial presentations: age, ethnicity, life history or gender. Is there any value in considering women clients as a distinct group? Does solution-focused therapy (SFT) have anything special to offer clients who are women? I think the answer to both of these questions is 'yes'.

Rationale for using SFT with women

The basic tenets of SFT, that clients already have strengths and abilities with which to build their own distinctive solutions to their problems, and that problems do not indicate pathology in the person experiencing difficulties, have 'added value' for women. They counteract women's tendency toward self-blame and experience of being blamed, especially when relationships with others are part of the problem. They also challenge the common stereotypes of women with problems, that they are victims or unable to cope (Bailey-Martiniere, 1993). The approach involves clients deciding their own goals for therapy and working out, in collaboration with the therapist, the best ways to move forward. This contrasts, in a liberating way, with therapies that depend for goals upon definitions of mental health constructed by men, with different criteria set for men and women (Broverman et al., 1970).

Within the NHS multidisciplinary team of which I am part, the approach has been viewed as 'user friendly' but there has also been concern about the possibility of overlooking important information, for example indications of abuse or risk. There has sometimes been a suspicion that the emphasis on parents' talents and resources may go hand in hand with an insensitivity to any signs of neglect or abuse on their part, toward their children. Like any other form of therapy, SFT is not a substitute for taking the necessary steps to enable a child to receive protection from abuse or neglect, should these come to light in the course of therapy. Those using the approach are bound by the same ethical considerations as exponents of other therapies. Some social workers and other practitioners are finding aspects of a solution-focused approach helpful in assessment of risk because the approach also highlights potential 'signs of safety' to build on with parents who need to take better care of their children (Turnell and Edwards, 1999; Mylan and Lethem, 1999).

There has also been concern that the 'up tempo' reputation of the approach might indicate that clients who have themselves been abused, or who are contemplating suicide or other forms of self-harm, would be silenced about matters of relevance to their well-being and safety. Colleagues have wanted reassurance that the traditional skills of good listening are also valued by SF therapists. Whilst early writings about solutions concentrated on problem-free talk and solution building and devoted little attention to the most appropriate ways of speaking about the problem(s), there have been attempts to redress the balance. O'Hanlon and Bertolini (1999) encourage their readers to acknowledge problems and distress in an empathic way as well as asking questions or making comments that open up possibilities for improving the situation. I believe it is also helpful to ask clients toward the end of an interview, 'Is there anything else you would like to say' or, 'Is there anything else I haven't given you the chance to say, that you feel it is important for me to understand?' Some clients have found that the lack of potentially intrusive questioning about problems and feelings has enabled them to disclose sensitive information more easily than they had expected.

Women's ways of talking about problems

Research on gender and communication suggests that there are some common differences to be found between female and male styles of conversation, allowing, of course, for individual exceptions, of both genders, to this generalisation (Tannen, 1990). On the whole, from childhood, women have felt familiar with conversations of mutual self-disclosure, about relationships and feelings. They are likely to have had experience of many interactions in which co-operation has been more prominent than competition. When facing challenges, women are more likely to view their circumstances in terms of dilemmas embedded in relationships and to be concerned about the possible emotional consequences of any decisions they may take. This contrasts with men's greater likelihood of focusing on logic and abstraction (Gilligan, 1982).

While SFT's emphasis on problem-free talk and on comparative informality and collaboration between client and therapist seem to place women clients at an advantage, its concrete goals and relative lack of exploration of emotions have led some writers (Burck and Daniel, 1990) to believe that it may constrain them. My view is that SFT has much to offer clients of both genders but that particular aspects of the approach may be of special benefit to women, others to men. From a woman's perspective, part of the benefit lies in the comforting familiarity of the conversational style of SFT, together with the therapist's affirmation of the client's efforts; and part in a gentle and persistent exploration of unfamiliar perspectives on possibilities for the future.

The art of juggling

Women were multi-tasking long before the word was invented. Juggling practical activities and the ever-changing tasks associated with caring for others frequently leaves women feeling that their work is never done or that they are not doing any one task to the standard they would wish. This is a situation rich in possibilities for exhaustion, self-blame and despondency.

Judith, who sought help for the effects of sexual abuse in childhood, explained that it was difficult to find time to 'think things through' because she was struggling to earn a living and care for her mother who needed extra support on account of a degree of physical disability. Judith found herself regularly criticised by members of the extended family about the way she looked after her mother. Her mother too was hard to please. Judith felt resentful of the criticism and self-blaming for not managing to make her mother happier.

Through SFT's attention to small but significant achievements, celebration of skills and identification of partial solutions, Judith's view of herself and her relationship with her mother and other family members shifted toward greater self-respect and determination to carve out some time for her own priorities. She found ways to leave some of the tasks involved in her mother's care to her siblings. By setting limits on her own availability to her family, she allowed herself more time to work on her recovery from the traumatic effects of abuse. She began to re-author a story of her life that acknowledged her endurance and loyalty and in which consideration for her own needs featured alongside those of her mother, in contrast to the story of failure, guilt and frustration which she had brought to therapy.

The perspectives of others

Other perspective questions are a common feature of SFT. For example, 'What will others see you doing when the changes you want happen?' Women are usually highly skilled in viewing the world from the perspectives of others. They often use that knowledge, of what they feel others need or expect, to guide their own behaviour, in an attempt to take responsibility for the well-being of others.

When working with women clients using SFT it is helpful to utilise their existing expertise, in imagining the perspectives of others, while keeping an emphasis on their own wishes and feelings.

When answering the miracle question, women frequently answer with what appears to be someone else's miracle. Sally, who sought help for depression, was worried about her teenage daughter. Her miracle, that she would be a better mother and that her daughter would be less angry, required further exploration. It was helpful to discover what such changes would look like, what Sally would be doing once her daughter was less angry and what that would mean to Sally herself. She was also asked what else she might wish to include in her own personal miracle once what she believed to be her daughter's needs had been fulfilled.

Sally's therapist fed back to her that the interview had revealed many examples of her thoughtfulness as a mother, and signs that some of her daughter's anger was related to her adjustment to growing independence. An attempt was made to put Sally's doubts about her mothering in the context of a tradition of blaming mothers, a tradition that appeared to be convincing Sally that she could never do enough for her daughter. In these ways Sally was given an opportunity to define what a life free of depression would be like: a life that included some goals for herself as an individual as well as a mother.

Empowerment

Clients often come to therapy or counselling burdened by beliefs about how they should be, how they should feel, what they should do about their problems. Some of these 'shoulds' have come directly, through the well-meaning advice of friends, family or other professionals, others through years of taking in more subtle messages about the right way for daughters, mothers, wives, women in general to behave. The case study of Barbara (see p. 124) illustrates that form of pressure. SFT offers a number of ways to help liberate clients from such constraints.

The collaborative attitude of the therapist avoids as much as possible setting the client up with another set of idealised goals, those of living up to the therapist's expectations. As far as possible, the process of therapy is demystified and the client is invited to take the driving seat, with the therapist offering assistance in clarifying where the client wishes to go. A non-judgmental and non-pathologising stance helps to establish a context in which clients, who have internalised the expectations of others, can feel safer to explore their own wishes. Respect for clients' unique solutions to their own troubles is also potentially empowering; in the case of therapy, one size does not fit all.

Issues of difference

No particular attention to issues of difference is recommended in the writings of de Shazer and colleagues who pioneered SFT. However, there are aspects of the somewhat minimalist framework of the approach that allow space for therapists who wish to consider issues of difference and of social justice in their work (Waldegrave, 1985; Lethem, 1994). Clients are given the opportunity to educate the therapist about their perspectives, about life in general, about what they think the therapist should know of their problems and about details of the problem-free futures they would like. As far as possible the therapist 'speaks the language' of the client, clarifying the meaning the client attaches to particular phrases. When this is literally impossible the approach lends itself to working with interpreters more easily than approaches that rely on the use of abstract language, favouring as it does detailed concrete descriptions of activities that are helpful in developing solutions and goals for change.

The therapist attempts to put each problem in context in a non-pathologising way. This usually involves the description of a challenge the client has faced and the strengths shown in the face of adversity. Contextualising can take the form of describing challenging events or circumstances in fairly neutral terms, e.g. as important transitions in the life cycle or as sources of stress. Alternatively, the therapist can choose to name the stresses that are associated with discrimination on grounds of race, gender, age, sexuality, immigration status, socio-economic status, etc. Social injustice involves the kinds of stresses that jeopardise individuals' mental health and welfare and clients can benefit from hearing their therapist acknowledge factors that have been beyond their influence. There are ethical as well as pragmatic reasons for therapists to be willing to speak about these matters. Waldegrave (1985) points out that 'so called non-political ... therapy' is usually a form of relationship that upholds an unjust status quo in which clients are often implicitly blamed for their misfortunes.

When attempting to offer therapy in a way that is inclusive of individuals who are members of any minority or relatively disadvantaged group, and in a way that communicates respect for difference, choice of therapeutic model is but one facet of the service to be offered. It can be illuminating to ask oneself, 'What are the obstacles to women or men making use of this service? Which aspects of it might make members of ethnic minorities feel it is not for them? What kind of welcome would gay clients feel they receive here? Would clients with a disability think our policy of inclusivity was worth the paper it is written on?' Both of the agencies I am associated with have developed initiatives to attempt to tackle issues raised by these questions. In each we are still at the 'work in progress' stage.

Integrating SFT

Prior to my own interest in SFT my main therapeutic influences were cognitive behavioural therapy and systemic family therapy, with a special interest in the problem-focused approach (Watzlawick et al., 1974; Fisch et al., 1982) of the Mental Research Institute (MRI). When I first heard about, read about and observed SFT, it immediately made sense because it incorporated many familiar aspects, e.g. an interactional perspective, concrete goals and scaling questions, and nothing felt incompatible with or in conflict with previous ways of working. While I continue to label the therapy I practise SFT, there are other sources of ideas that have guided my work with women. I am aware that the fact that I sometimes externalise a problem or ask about the history of a wished-for solution illustrates the inspiration of narrative therapy (White and Epston, 1990; White, 1988–89). Just therapy (Waldegrave, 1985), developed by a group of Maori, Pacific Islander and white New Zealander practitioners, has also been an influence in encouraging me to acknowledge the adverse influence of social injustice in clients' lives.

'Is it necessary to be purist about this approach, or can one pick and mix?' asked a workshop participant. I do not expect everyone who learns about SFT to forget everything they have learned about other approaches or to abandon methods they have been using successfully. However, not all therapeutic assumptions and techniques are equally compatible with SFT; it would be difficult to combine with therapies based on the belief that therapy is inevitably a long, slow process in which it is necessary to confront deficits arising from the past as the only way forward. But I am in favour of maintaining a dialogue with therapists of all different orientations, especially when, as in the case of my NHS post, we work in the same service. Questions like 'What is it about this client that gives you hope therapy can help them?' can make sense to therapists of diverse orientations.

There are some issues I would not wish to grapple with without additional forms of help in place, for reasons of safety. For example I believe that SFT questions can enable clients who feel drawn to suicide to consider other possibilities. However, in cases of very high risk, close supervision also needs to be available. Similarly, women with severe effects of disordered eating may need medical attention as well as therapy (McFarland, 1995). In some situations medication, prescribed by a psychiatrist or GP, may facilitate individuals troubled by symptoms associated with diagnoses of psychosis or severe depression to focus more productively on what they wish to get out of therapy.

Newly versed in the art of exception questions, workshop participants sometimes ask, 'When does this approach not work?' or 'When would you not use SFT?' I believe there are few essential exclusion criteria, provided clients' goals present no ethical problems to the therapist. Problem severity alone is no reason to exclude clients from SFT and related approaches. For example, Dolan (1991) and O'Hanlon and Bertolini (1998) have demonstrated that it is possible for clients who have been living with severe effects of child sexual abuse to benefit. I am generally in agreement with O'Hanlon and Weiner-Davis's (1988) maxim that there is no intrinsic value in being in therapy and that the task of the therapist is to assist the client, in moving toward a situation she or he would see as improved, as quickly as possible. Thus I would decline to work using SFT with clients seeking long-term therapy for personal growth or for non-specific 'support'.

Personal reflections

Like most therapists, I suspect, I find that people I have just met socially often ask whether I find hearing about personal problems all day depressing. I usually reply that I do hear some upsetting things but that I also share the process of coping with or overcoming difficulties. I expect, by the end of most working weeks, to 'break even' emotionally. I have found SFT enormously beneficial in the process of keeping the balance between shared grief and shared hope in my own work with clients. The feedback that I have had from supervisees suggests that SF supervision helps them to do the same and to stay aware of resources and strengths in the face of clients whose stressful circumstances threaten to overwhelm.

The habit of solution-focused thinking is hard to shake off and is therefore likely to come to mind when facing personal dilemmas or problems. I have found great relief at times in realising that I have not been doing nothing about an issue but have already taken some steps toward helping myself. Dolan (1998), Weiner-Davis (1992) and Hudson (1996) are women therapists, teachers and writers who have turned their attention to self-help and personal development from a solution-ful perspective.

Case study

The example I have chosen illustrates common issues for women facing decisions concerning relationships. Personal details have been fictionalised to protect the confidentiality of the client.

'I'm becoming obsessed': coping while waiting to make a decision
Barbara, aged 56, referred herself concerning her feelings about a relationship and the fact that she was finding it increasingly difficult to cope. When we met, my first impression was of a vivacious, strikingly dressed woman with an air of confidence. Our mutual greeting gave me the idea that she was someone accustomed to putting other people at their ease. Through problem-free talk, I learned that Barbara, who was Head of the modern languages department in a secondary school would, at the same time of day, usually be making a start on work taken home from school, marking, writing reports, doing paperwork related to organising exchange trips for her students or union business. She told me that she lived alone, had a lot of contact with her adult children and that she had divorced ten years ago: 'we had nothing in common but the children ... and he's gone on being a pretty good father to them'. She said that some evenings she would meet with one of her friends or speak on the phone.

> *Barbara:* You remember asking me about any changes, well I've decided to stop talking to my friends about Mark ... that's ... the relationship ... they're all probably sick of hearing me go on about him, even though they try their best to help. Also I'm getting sick of hearing myself.
> *Therapist:* So are you hoping we can speak about this in a different way? ...
> *[Barbara nods.]*
> *Therapist:* What other differences have there been?
> *Barbara:* I've been rehearsing ... I used to play in a lot of concerts ... then I got too busy. ... Anyway a friend persuaded me to join a band. ... We're giving a concert just after the end of term.

> Therapist: ... What do we need to focus on, in this meeting, to make coming here worth while?
> Barbara: Some way of getting rid of Mark ... I'm becoming obsessed ...

Barbara explained that she had become involved somewhat against her better judgement with a younger man she had met through her union activities. It had taken her by surprise that he should be interested in her sexually and that he admired her independence and assertiveness in a way her husband and other men of her own age had not. The relationship had not been as brief as she had initially anticipated and she felt herself becoming more and more attached to him, before discovering that he was not simply 'divorced' as he had told her, but living with another woman. She had lost trust in him but felt unable to let go.

> Barbara: If I get a minute to myself during the day I start to think about him but it's not so bad then because I know he's at work, not with her. Sometimes we speak on the phone and then I feel better for a while...I know I shouldn't...I never expected that I'd be in love with someone again ... it's not something I was looking for ... by the end of an evening alone by the phone, I can be frantic ... going over every minute of our time together, wondering whether he'll phone...wondering what he ... they ... are doing, wanting to phone...he gets angry if I do ... and yet he says he still cares ... that we're kindred spirits in a way he's never known before ...
> Therapist: It sounds almost overwhelming at times.
> Barbara: It is ... I can't believe I got myself into this ... it's not like me, it's crazy, I get myself so worked up ... I'm desperate. I don't trust myself to drive in the evenings ...
> Therapist: So have you feared for your own safety at times?

An exploration of the extent of Barbara's thoughts of suicide and relationship with alcohol followed in which a number of ways she coped and kept herself from harm were revealed.

> Therapist: What else is helping you cope right now?
> Barbara: Anything that makes me feel normal...work, spending time with my daughter, taking my mind off it ... planning for my son's visit ... yesterday it was doing the crossword, for some reason I managed to concentrate and almost finish it and I thought 'This is more like me.'

As the conversation continued, other details of coping emerged, including Barbara's interest in music and politics. There were glimmers too of humour and enthusiasm. When I asked Barbara the miracle question she initially said, 'to be free of this obsession' and then went on to say that she supposed she should cut off from Mark completely, as all her friends had advised her and as her son and daughter certainly would if they knew the whole story. She said that she had tried to do so but had been unable to keep to her resolution when he got in touch with her and at times the notion of the two of them as kindred spirits filled her with hope. Her feelings for him were sometimes so intense that she wondered whether she should confront him with the possibility of leaving his partner but feared hurt and humiliation if rejected. Part of 'this obsession' involved a self-interrogation about the dilemma she felt she was facing.

Therapist: On a scale of zero to ten, where zero is the most obsessed you have felt and ten is free of the obsession, where would you say you are now?

Barbara: Three.

Therapist: What's helped you to get from zero to three?

Barbara: Work ... keeps me grounded ... and friends. When I get glimpses of normality it makes me more hopeful ... also when I remember life before I met Mark. I'd been on my own for some time ... I like living alone in some ways, so at least I'm not afraid of that.

After a break 'to collect my thoughts' I gave the following feedback:

'Early in our conversation you spoke of the possibility of becoming boring because of the way your feelings about Mark have affected you. I want to say how interesting I've found meeting you and hearing about your life. While you are clearly distressed and in turmoil at times and worried about your thoughts being dominated by obsessing about Mark, the number of things that interest you, your work, your family, music, politics also came across very clearly, together with a sense that communicating and sharing your enthusiasms comes naturally to you ... far from boring.'

'I see that at times you blame yourself for your feelings about Mark, not only because he turned out to be involved with another woman but because of your age, and his. People can still be pretty narrow-minded about what kind of relationships women should have and I wonder whether that kind of criticism can make someone in your situation belittle their feelings at times or not feel entitled to them ... I think that loving someone and then losing them, or deciding to break away from them or finding out that things are not quite as they seemed ... all these are very real and very painful at any stage in life.'

'I've heard you be very generous in your consideration for your friends, your family, Mark and his dilemma in all this. I didn't hear you blaming the other woman, as others might be tempted to do, given the anguish knowing about her relationship with Mark has caused you. I both admire this and find myself wondering whether this capacity to empathise with all these other perspectives makes it particularly difficult to make a decision about what you would like to do about the situation.

'From what I've heard, I think you see two main choices – cutting off contact or giving Mark an ultimatum...there may be options that haven't become clear yet. I guess you've received advice from well-meaning friends and that so far you have not wanted to take that advice. I don't propose to advise you which path to choose, instead I'd like to advise you to think about which aspects of your life you would want to continue whichever path you choose...what you could be doing in the here and now that would be good for you, whatever the outcome with Mark. I believe you are already doing a number of things to help yourself cope with the obsessive thoughts about Mark...and I think it will be important to continue those. Sometimes when big decisions loom, it feels as if the rest of life is on hold. If you also spend some time identifying things you would want in your life whatever happens then it can help with that sense of being in limbo.'

Subsequent sessions developed the themes of coping with obsessive thoughts and paying attention to aspects of life to nurture, whether in or out of the relationship with Mark. Scaling questions were used not only to monitor Barbara's sense of her own progress but also to clarify options and anticipate outcomes realistically. For example, on a zero to ten scale, how much do you want to be in a relationship where you and Mark are committed? On another zero to ten scale, how confident are you that such an outcome is possible? How come your confidence is at that level? What has helped you to reach that level of confidence? What would one point further up the scale look like, what would you be doing then?

When she had reached a level of coping with the obsessions that allowed her to feel sufficiently 'like herself' (seven on a zero to ten scale) Barbara decided to stop therapy. She asked for the door to be kept open in case she felt the need of future help. Barbara continued to have infrequent contact with Mark and to devote energy to 'having a life' at the same time as living with some uncertainty about the future of the relationship.

References

Bailey-Martiniere, L. (1993) Solution-oriented psychotherapy – the 'difference' for female clients. *News of the Difference*, 2(2): 10–12.

Broverman, I.K., Broverman, D.M., Clarkson, F.E., Rosenkrantz, P.S. and Vogel, S.R (1970) Sex-role stereotype and clinical judgements of mental health. *Journal of Consulting and Clinical Psychology*, 34(1): 1–7.

Burck, C. and Daniel, G. (1990) Feminism and strategic therapy: contradiction or complementarity. In R. Joseph Perlberg and A.C. Miller (eds), *Gender and Power in Families*. London and New York: Tavistock/Routledge.

de Shazer, S. (1985) *Keys to Solutions in Brief Therapy*. New York: W.W. Norton.

de Shazer, S. (1988) *Clues: investigating solutions in brief therapy*. New York: W.W. Norton.

Dolan, Y. (1991) *Resolving Sexual Abuse*. New York: W.W. Norton.

Dolan, Y. (1998) *One Small Step*. Watsonville, CA: Papier-Mâché Press.

Fisch, R., Weakland, J. and Segal, L. (1982) *The Tactics of Change: doing therapy briefly*. San Francisco: Jossey-Bass.

Gilligan, C. (1982) *In a Different Voice*. Cambridge, MA: Harvard University Press.

Hudson, P. (1996) *The Solution-oriented Woman: creating the life you want*. New York: W.W. Norton.

Lethem, J. (1994) *Moved to Tears, Moved to Action: solution focused brief therapy with women and children*. London: BT Press.

McFarland, B. (1995) *Brief Therapy and Eating Disorders*. San Francisco: Jossey-Bass.

Mylan, T. and Lethem, J. (1999) *Searching for Strengths in Child Protection Assessment: from guidelines to practice*. London: BT Press.

O'Hanlon, W. and Bertolini, R. (1998) *Even from a Broken Web: brief respectful solution-oriented therapy for sexual abuse and trauma*. New York: Wiley.

O'Hanlon, W. and Bertolini, R. (eds) (1999) *Evolving Possibilities: selected papers*. New York: Bruner Mazell.

O'Hanlon, W. and Weiner-Davis, M. (1988) *In Search of Solutions: a new direction in psychotherapy*. New York: W.W. Norton.

Tannen, D. (1990) *You Just Don't Understand: women and men in conversation*. London: Virago Press.

Turnell, A. and Edwards, S. (1999) *Signs of Safety: a solution and safety oriented approach to child protection case work*. New York: W.W. Norton.

Waldegrave, C. (1985) Mono-cultural, mono-class and so called non-political family therapy. *Australia and New Zealand Journal of Family Therapy*, 6(4): 197–200.

Watzlawick, P., Weakland, J. and Fisch, R. (1974) *Change: principles of problem formation and problem resolution*. New York: W.W. Norton.

Weiner-Davis, M. (1992) *Divorcebusting*. New York: Simon & Schuster.

White, M. (1988–89) The externalising of the problem and re-authoring of lives and relationships. *Dulwich Centre Newsletter*, summer. Reprinted in M. White (1989) *Selected Papers*. Adelaide: Dulwich Centre Publications.

White, M. and Epston, D. (1990) *Narrative Means to Therapeutic Ends*. New York: W.W. Norton.

12

A Solution-Focused Approach to Sexual Trauma

Melissa Darmody

Sexual trauma, including abuse suffered in childhood and violations experienced as adults, fits the criteria outlined in the American Psychiatric Association's *Diagnostic and Statistical Manual* (APA, 1994) as an event that can lead to post-traumatic stress disorder (PTSD). The symptoms of PTSD can include intrusive memories, persistent avoidance of stimuli associated with the trauma, numbing, dissociation, heightened anxiety or arousal, and disruption to normal life functioning such as sleeping, eating, sexual functioning and socialisation. I perceive these responses as a normal reaction or response to a life-threatening or perceived life-threatening event.

Initial research into PTSD was based on the reaction of Vietnam veterans to their experiences in war situations (Horowitz, 1976). As a result of this early pioneering work it became generally accepted that the best way for survivors of abuse and trauma to recover from intrusive flashbacks and other distressing symptoms was for them to re-experience the original trauma via a flooding of memories in a safe therapeutic environment. These traditional models of working are described by O'Hanlon and Bertolino (1998) as the *unexperienced experience model*. This model develops the idea that when people experience sexual trauma they will often dissociate in order to cope. Therefore traditional models are based on the belief that due to the dissociation the trauma survivor never connected with the past experience. The therapist must help these clients regress to the traumatic time and re-experience the event to be able to move on from it. Often this belief that experiencing the event again for the client to 'move on' can lead to therapy being a traumatic event in its own right. So much so that clients often drop out of therapy, or their self-destructive behaviours might increase during the therapeutic intervention. While these 're-experience' approaches still remain popular, a broad range of therapeutic interventions for helping abuse survivors and sufferers of PTSD have been developed. These range from client-centred and psychodynamic approaches to focused bodywork and breathing techniques. More recently the development of Eye Movement Desensitisation and Reprocessing (EMDR), a therapeutic intervention that asks the client to hold a past image in their mind while they engage in rapid eye movement by following the therapist's finger, has shown some optimistic results (Shapiro, 1989a, 1989b).

This chapter offers an alternative style: a collaborative approach to working with survivors of sexual trauma that allows the therapist and client to integrate aspects of the various models of therapy available in a way that is respectful and helpful for the client. An important objective of this new collaborative way of working is to allow the therapeutic work to be led by the client's goals for therapy, while simultaneously encouraging them to develop a new, secure, fulfilling life that becomes more than the experience of the abuse (Darmody, 1998). The therapeutic process tries to establish clients as heroes in their lives; encouraging them to see their strengths and abilities in coping and moving beyond their past trauma to establish hope.

Solution-focused brief therapy (SFBT) can provide a helpful structure when trying to establish client-developed expectations. The model not only provides techniques which can be used in the therapeutic process, but more importantly, outlines different assumptions about how people change. It can also help the therapist to make useful interventions in the therapeutic process (de Shazer, 1985, 1991; de Shazer et al., 1986). These assumptions can create a radical shift in the therapist's view of the client, enabling him/her to be seen as an individual who possesses resources to draw upon in solving personal issues. This new viewpoint shapes the therapist's belief that the client is the authority on how to cope with and move beyond the traumatic life events (Sharry et al., 2001a).

Rationale and practice of solution-focused therapy

Some therapists have difficulty seeing how they could use SFBT when working with survivors of sexual violence. They feel that only regular sessions of therapy over a long period will help people who have experienced sexual violence to progress to a more fulfilling life. However, the term 'brief' can be misleading and may create the impression that the SFBT model is a 'quick fix' or 'surface' therapy. According to Garfield and Bergin (1994) most counselling is brief, with the majority of counselling contracts being for four to eight sessions. Solution-focused brief therapy is no 'briefer' than other therapy models. What distinguishes the solution-focused therapist is not so much the brevity of the work as a mind set towards the client characterised by the features shown in Figure 12.1.

Long term ————▶ As long as it is helpful

This is a challenge to the belief that only long-term counselling can be therapeutic for people who have experienced sexual violence. The alternative pragmatic view is that counselling need not be either long or short term, but need only last for as long as the client feels it is helpful. Some clients might find a long-term, weekly counselling relationship beneficial, but others might not find this useful. They may prefer to use counselling for a limited number of sessions to deal with a specific relevant issue, for example when he or she needs to test for a sexually transmitted disease following a rape. The client may not wish, at this time, to extend the counselling. A solution-focused position respects the client's perception of change and the support he or she needs. If they feel their wishes were

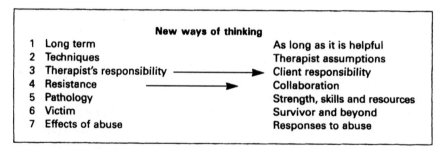

Figure 12.1 *Shift in Thinking*

respected and that the service responded to their agenda they may choose to return for further sessions as and when they need them.

Case example

A young woman comes to a therapist following a recent rape.

> *Therapist*: How do you think I can be helpful?
>
> *Client*: Well, I'm very concerned that I got something from the attack, you know, a disease or something.
>
> *Therapist*: Right, you are concerned about any disease that may have been transmitted during the attack. What do you think we might be able to do to help ease that concern?
>
> *Client*: I'm not sure, I'm just very scared I'm going to die of something now. I really need to know if I have something.
>
> *Therapist*: Well, I can give you the telephone numbers of a place you can go to have a confidential test for sexually transmitted diseases. I can also offer you some appointments here, at the centre, to support you while you are waiting for results of the tests. Would any of these things be helpful?
>
> *Client*: Well, I would like the number for the tests. It would be good to find out for sure – that would really ease my mind. Thanks.
>
> *Therapist*: Is there anything else you think I might be able to do that would be helpful?
>
> *Client*: No, for now I'm just really worried about the disease thing.
>
> *Therapist*: Well, OK, I just want you to know that you are welcome to get back in touch with us at any point, if you feel talking things through would be helpful.
>
> *Client*: OK, Thanks.

This case highlights the importance of the therapist respecting the client's wish for a short intervention at that moment. The client's main objective is to gain the telephone number of a sexually transmitted disease testing centre and she does not want to engage, for the moment, in long-term counselling or support. The therapist respects this and welcomes her back if she feels she would like counselling and support.

Techniques ⟶ Therapist assumptions

A concern some people voice about using SFBT is that it is a technique-driven therapy in which the therapeutic relationship is unimportant. For me the unique contribution of SFBT is not the variety of techniques it employs, but the assumptions it makes about the clients and the therapeutic process. For example, the solution-focused therapist assumes and is curious about what has gone right in someone's life and what their hopes for the future are. For people who have experienced sexual violence, the therapist will want to know how they have managed to cope and what they have achieved, despite the traumatic events they have suffered. The therapist allows the client to decide how important and helpful it might be to explore their past. If, for example, a client states that it would be beneficial for her or him to talk in detail about the abuse they suffered, I would respectfully ask them how this might be useful to them. Clients often answer that if they could face the past and talk about what happened, that would release them from the hold it has upon their lives. I would help them to explore how their lives would change as a result of this release. Once clients have set clear, positive and manageable goals we can explore how they might achieve them, which may or may not involve talking about the events of sexual violence.

Case example

> Therapist: How do you think coming to counselling can be helpful?
> Client: Well, my life is falling apart, everything seems to be going wrong and I can't get a handle on it.
> Therapist: Do you have any ideas about how this might help you get a handle on your life?
> Client: Yes, I think I need to admit what happened to me, what happened to me when I was young, a little girl, I have been keeping things inside for so long I sometimes think my mind will explode with all the thoughts.
> Therapist: So you think admitting to someone about what happened would help. How do you think things would change if you were able to talk about those events?
> Client: Well, I think my mind would stop spinning and I would be able to see a little clearer; also I think that if I was clearer in my own head I would not do my boyfriend's head in. We are always at odds about things, but I know it is because of all these thoughts in my head about the past and what happened with my father.
> Therapist: OK, so you feel that talking about those events might clear your head and that would help with your boyfriend. How do you imagine it would make things different with him?
> Client: Well, I would stop blaming him all the time for things, like I'm always thinking he is a cheat and a liar, I don't trust men, but he is good and has not treated me badly, but I always expect him to, so this causes a fight. I just need to start believing he is a good man, as opposed to the bad men I have met, and I need to realise the difference.
> Therapist: So you think that talking about what happened and clearing your head would help you be clear about your boyfriend being good?
> Client: Yeah, I think so.

In this case study, the therapist allows the client to decide where to begin the counselling. The client has an idea that she needs to talk about the past, and the therapist respects this belief, while at the same time exploring how the client feels that talking about the past will change her current life. The client is able to develop these ideas further, and concludes that her mind would stop racing and her relationship with her boyfriend would improve. The therapist would help the client to explore visible signs, which would suggest to her that things were improving with her boyfriend.

Therapist's responsibility ————▶ Client responsibility

I once showed to a group of trainees a videotape of Steve de Shazer, a founder of SFBT, working with a young drug addict. One of the participants remarked that Steve looked as if he 'couldn't care less' whether the client chose to give up drugs or not (de Shazer, 1998). The trainee meant this as a compliment! In the session it is clear that de Shazer is not trying to *force* a drug-free lifestyle on the client, but is trying to create an environment in which the client can reflect upon what *she would like to do*. The therapist does not impose his or her worldview upon the client. Rather, it is the client's responsibility to state what she wants from therapy and to decide the format and frequency of the sessions.

Case example

> *Therapist:* How might I be helpful?
> *Client:* I don't know, it is not my idea to be here, my husband keeps pestering me to get help, but I don't know how this could possibly help.
> *Therapist:* So it was your husband's idea for you to be here.
> *Client:* Yeah, he is pressuring me and I just want him to back off, so I said I would come.
> *Therapist:* Right, so how do you imagine you could get him to back off?
> *Client:* There are several things he is going on and on about, like my drinking getting out of control and the fights we have … he always blames me, that it's my fault, because of my past. He thinks I need to get my head sorted out because of my past.
> *Therapist:* What do you think?
> *Client:* [*Pause*] I just want him to back off.
> *Therapist:* So what would you need to do to get him to back off?
> *Client:* Stop fighting with him all the time, starting things with him, like I don't trust him.
> *Therapist:* So if you want him off your back the best way to do that is to stop fighting with him. How do you think I might be able to help with this?
> *Client:* I guess if I gain more control over my temper. If I could find some way to control that I'd be happy.

The therapist does not get involved with the family argument but stays focused on what the client wants. Her partner labels the issue as a drinking issue. The therapist gives the client the responsibility to decide the goal, which is to control her temper.

Resistance ————▶ Collaboration

The SFBT model sees 'resistance' as an unhelpful label therapists give clients when they do not conform to the therapist's own belief system. The alternative view is that it is a form of communication from the client requesting that the therapist change the way in which he or she is seeking the client's co-operation. The therapist needs to do something different (de Shazer, 1984). Resistance in the SFBT book is a client strength, namely: the ability to work collaboratively with the therapist and express when the therapeutic process is not working. This shift in thinking can change the therapist's view of the client as 'resistant', 'stuck', or 'in denial' to a person who is collaborating with them effectively. This stance is likely to lead to the therapist enjoying the collaborative nature of the relationship.

Case example

> *Therapist:* I've noticed that in the last session you've been quieter than usual. I don't know if this means the sessions are not being helpful.
>
> *Client:* Well, I'm finding talking about my uncle very difficult. I'm not really sure it's helping, because I feel dreadful and that's very frustrating. Plus there are other things going on also, like that issue with my mother that I talked about before.
>
> *Therapist:* What do you think would be most helpful to talk about today?
>
> *Client:* Well, my mum. Her attitude towards me and her refusal to acknowledge my little boy really infuriates me.
>
> *Therapist:* So you think it would be more helpful to talk about your mother. What do you suppose would be most helpful to talk about in relation to that?

In this case example, the therapist does not pathologise the client's desire to discuss her mother and does not read it as 'resistance' to talking about the previous topic. It is just that the client feels that it would be more useful to explore the issue of her mother at this particular moment. She may return to the topic of her uncle in the future, but the choice to do so or not is seen as the client's alone. The therapist does not label this non-return as pathological.

Pathology ⟶ Strength, skills and resources

The SFBT model's strongest reframe is the idea that it is more useful to actively look for, and enquire about, the client's perceived strengths, skills and resources. Pathologising or labelling clients is replaced with the therapist's respectful curiosity about the client's ability to cope with traumatic events and their strengths in finding a more fulfilling life for themselves. This reframe can be energising for the therapists, who begin to see their clients as resourceful individuals struggling for change.

Case example

> *Client:* I've been having a hard time recently; I'm very low and crying all the time. I just can't stop.
>
> *Therapist:* It sounds like things have been pretty rough for you lately. How have you been managing to cope with it being so difficult?
>
> *Client:* Well, I don't know, sometimes it does not feel like I'm coping, but I guess I just have to get on with it. I've got three kids, you know, and when you have kids you have to get on with it.
>
> *Therapist:* So you're the kind of person who, even when it is really bad, can continue to take care of your kids and get on with the day. That must be really hard to do sometimes, how do you manage to pull it off?
>
> *Client:* I never really thought about it, but I just say to myself in the mornings, you know if I'm lying in bed not wanting to get up, 'Come on! Get up! The kids are waiting!' It is really important for me to be a good mum, a better mum than mine. I guess that's the biggest thing that keeps me going.

> *Therapist:* So you are the type of person, that even when it is really difficult, you are able to get up and keep going for your kids to have a better life … . That's really impressive.
>
> *Client:* Really? You think so? I never really thought about it like that.

In this section the therapist focuses on what the client is able to do, rather than on her difficulty in getting out of her bed and her crying. The therapist helps the client to recognise that her desire to provide a better life for her children is a personal strength.

Victim ────────▶ Survivor and beyond

In the field of working with sexual violence it has become commonplace to refer to people who have experienced these events as 'survivors' rather than 'victims'. A sense of empowerment is fostered by the recognition that whilst being a victim of a crime, they are individuals who have survived a violent event. Dolan (1991) goes further by stressing the importance of living beyond 'survivor-hood'. She argues that although being a survivor is a badge of courage, people who have experienced sexual violence should at some point be able to live fulfilled lives without having their identity defined by their experience of sexual violence. Indeed, all of us should try to move beyond labels such as 'mentally ill', 'divorced', 'single parent', 'learning disabled', etc., to a point where we can live a fulfilled life without the limitations such narrow definitions imply. Though we are all the product of our accumulated experience, as a society we tend to label people on the basis of only one or two (usually negative!) life experiences, instead of seeing within each person a multitude of experiences. Solution-focused brief therapy incorporates a person's whole life experience into their definition of themselves, as opposed to a single negative event. Clients thus begin to see themselves as good parents, successful professionals, keen gardeners, or great cooks, instead of victims of violence.

Case example

> *Client:* Sometimes I feel like such a freak, like everyone only sees the 'rape case' and not me. I mean since the whole thing came out in the media, I think that everyone only sees me as 'that girl'. So I just keep quiet and try not to draw attention to myself.
>
> *Therapist:* That must be very difficult if you feel that people only see you one way. What are the parts of you that they are missing? How would you like them to see you?
>
> *Client:* There are so many things that I was good at before all of this – my music, my friends, I was out every night. I was doing well in school and really getting excited about the new course. Things were coming together for me. I think people thought that girl really has it together and I felt that way. And all of that has vanished.
>
> *Therapist:* So people would have seen you as a good student with a bright career ahead, a good friend and musician. Someone on her way.
>
> *Client:* Yeah!

> Therapist: How do you think you can start living your life again in a way that highlights these sides of you?
>
> Client: I don't know [Pause] I guess I haven't played my music or seen friends in so long. [Pause] I would need to start doing the things that meant something to me and showing people that I am more than just 'that girl', that I'm someone who has other things going on in her life, not just the rape case. I guess I need to prove that to myself first before anyone else. I need to start thinking about me as more than 'that girl' and remember all the things I was good at.

In this case, the client's self-image starts to shift, so that she no longer defines herself on the basis of one event, but remembers or notices other aspects of her life that she wants to develop further. This session could develop ideas of how she might begin to live in ways that are more meaningful to her.

Effects of abuse ⎯⎯⎯⎯⟶ Responses to abuse

Wade (1997) argues for shifting away from language that describes how people were affected by past events to language that redefines how an individual reacted. Professionals working with people who have experienced sexual violence often ask, 'How did that experience affect you?' This implies that the event had an influence on that person which was out of their control, and which *continues* to affect the person in their present life. Wade recommends framing this type of enquiry in the following way: 'How did you respond to those experiences?' This slight shift in terminology gives the client the idea that they responded to an event in a particular way and could choose, if necessary, to respond in an alternative way.

Case example

> Therapist: How do you think I might be able to be helpful?
>
> Client: I'm all screwed up because of my past. My father [pause] my father abused me when I was six and I think that was the root of the problems I'm having today.
>
> Therapist: So that event was very damaging in your life. It changed things. How did you respond to that event?
>
> Client: When I was a kid I didn't tell anyone. I kept it a secret, but I stopped eating, and since then I have not really eaten properly, that is why I've wound up here, because everyone is now worried about my eating.
>
> Therapist: I see, so you responded to what your father did by not eating. How was that helpful at the time?
>
> Client: I guess I was trying to get someone to notice something, I guess, it was so long ago, but when I think back now, that's what I think, that I stopped eating so someone would notice and say something, because I could not talk about what was really happening.
>
> Therapist: So in the past this was a way to get help, the not eating. [Pause] And is the not eating a helpful way to respond now?
>
> Client: No, not now, not back then either, but I could not think of any other way out. But now the not eating is causing more harm than good. I'm in hospital and I can't even be with my family.
>
> Therapist: Do you think together, we could find a way for you to respond to what happened in a way that was better for you now?
>
> Client: We could try. I'm willing to try anything.

The case illustrates the shift whereby clients perceive their response to sexually violent events as being in their own power. This change in thinking can lead the client into believing that she can choose to respond in a different way.

Conclusion

In working with people who have experienced sexual violence SFBT respects the clients' beliefs as to what might be helpful for them. It gives therapists a different way of thinking about their work, enabling them to work collaboratively with clients in developing therapy goals. It highlights clients' strengths, skills and resources. These shifts in thinking can help clients see themselves as more than just the result of a single event in their lives and help them develop more control and direction in the task of building the lives they want to have. It also encourages therapists to find energy in their work by seeing their clients as people, not problems.

References

APA: American Psychiatric Association (1994) *Diagnostic and Statistical Manual of Mental Disorder* (4th edn). Washington, DC: American Psychiatric Press.

Darmody, M. (1998) Working with child sexual abuse from a brief therapy perspective. *Eisteach: Journal of the Irish Association of Counselling and Therapy*, 2(7): 17–20.

de Shazer, S. (1984) The death of resistance. *Family Process*, 23: 11–21.

de Shazer, S. (1985) *Keys to Solutions in Brief Therapy*. New York: W.W. Norton.

de Shazer, S. (1991) *Putting Difference to Work*. New York: W.W. Norton.

de Shazer, S. (1998) *The Right Path or the Other Path (videotape)*. Milwaukee, WI: Brief Therapy Family Center.

de Shazer, S., Berg, I., Lipchik, E., Nunnally, E., Molnar, A. Gingerich, W. and Weiner-Davis, M. (1986) Brief therapy: focused solution development. *Family Process*, 25: 207–221.

Dolan, Y. (1991) *Resolving Sexual Abuse: solution-focused therapy and Ericksonian hypnosis for adult survivors*. New York: W.W. Norton.

Garfield, S. and Bergin, A. (1994) *Handbook of Psychotherapy and Behavioral Change*. New York: Wiley.

Horowitz, M.J. (1976) *Stress Response Syndromes*. New York: Aronsen.

O'Hanlon, W.H. and Bertolino, B. (1998) *Even from a Broken Web: brief, respectful solution-oriented therapy for sexual abuse and trauma*. New York: Wiley.

Shapiro, F. (1989a) Efficacy of the eye movement desensitization procedure in the treatment of traumatic memories. *Journal of Traumatic Stress*, 11: 25–44.

Shapiro, F. (1989b) Eye movement desensitization: a new treatment for post-traumatic stress disorder. *Journal of Behavior Therapy and Experimental Psychiatry*, 20: 211–217.

Sharry, J., Madden, B. and Darmody, M. (2001a) *Becoming a Solution Detective: a strengths-based guide to brief therapy*. London: BT Press.

Sharry, J., Madden, B., Darmody, M. and Miller, S. (2001b) Application of client-directed outcome-informed clinical work. *Journal of Systemic Therapies*, 20: 68–76.

Wade, A. (1997) Small acts of living: everyday resistance to violence and other forms of oppression. *Contemporary Family Therapy*, 19: 23–39.

13

Solution-Focused Therapy and Substance Misuse

Paul Hanton

At the time of writing I work as the manager of a drug and alcohol project for under-18s, part of a larger generic service in a post-industrial town in the North of England. As well as managing the project, I practise as a solution-focused therapist, and I also see adult clients at the generic agency base.

Drug and alcohol misusers present some very real challenges, not least the fact that they generally present at crisis point, and often after some years of misuse. That being said, the vast majority of clients have very similar aims and goals: those of reduction and/or abstinence.

There are mandated clients at the agency on treatment and testing orders whom I choose not to see because I disagree ethically with the government stance on enforced treatment. If a person is made subject to a treatment and testing order, attendance with the therapist can be taken into account in sentencing decisions, and non-attendance may be seen as non-compliance with an order, which could result in a custodial sentence. I am not prepared to be part of a process that could jail someone as a direct result of not coming to see me. If someone is on a treatment and testing order and therapy is not a part of that order and he or she chooses to see me, I will of course see them.

All services at the generic agency and in the project I manage are free. In fact as some young clients have to travel in to see us, we even reimburse their fares.

The core framework of the agency is cognitive-behavioural therapy. Clients are assessed using Prochaska and DiClemente's model of change (1983). In the project there is a person-centred counsellor, a cognitive-behaviourally trained worker, one worker about to embark on SFBT training, myself (SFBT) as well as non-counselling staff. All practitioners in the project have a basic two-day training in SFBT provided by the Brief Therapy Centre in London.

I came to the present project after working almost exclusively in London for the previous 11 years. In my last project SFBT was the core model, chosen on the basis that substance misusers are often chaotic; can sometimes only attend one or two appointments; have definite goals, and should be able to receive the maximum benefit from the minimal input. Clients were offered a maximum of eight sessions. I would, for the most part, agree with this rationale, though chaos is relative, and what may seem chaotic to me may be normal to some.

When I moved to my present post I brought SFBT with some level of enthusiasm. It would be fair to say that this enthusiasm was dampened somewhat by endless conversations in my new agency about transference, counter-transference, projection, and so on. SFBT was seen by most of my colleagues (this was in the late 1990s) as at best a set of techniques, and at worst 'shallow', 'lacking a theoretical base', or as 'another American import'. These views have changed dramatically, due in part to my delivering in-house training which led to a SFBT reflecting team meeting once a month; and partly to the fact that clients have been very positive about the approach (as evidenced in the low rate of non-attendance).

In this chapter I would like to describe how SFBT is suitable for work with substance misusers, particularly alcohol users, and is compatible with Prochaska and DiClemente's model of change as used by many drug and alcohol services today. Although clients are initially assessed using the Prochaska and DiClemente framework prior to seeing a therapist, I never read assessments before seeing a client (except if I am informed there is a significant risk issue). This position seems to me to be consistent with the postmodern, social constructionist framework of SFBT. When I see a client, often a month after assessment, there may have been pre-session changes; there will certainly be some change in substance consumption and/or the client's general situation. Therefore to read an assessment carried out by another practitioner at some point in the past serves no purpose than to tell me how things were at that time, as perceived by my colleague. As an SFBT practitioner I am more interested in what has happened since the assessment, what is happening now, and what the future focus might be.

When working with young people, especially those that misuse substances, time is often perceived very differently than when working with adults. Young people may live for the moment with little sense of the long-term future. I was told once, 'It must be hard when you get old like you, you must be about 30, I don't ever want to be that old' (I was 36). In these instances I may give SFBT an immediate future focus: 'So if things were to move one point up the scale by the weekend, what would be happening?' 'How would your teachers know tomorrow that you hadn't got stoned before school?'

This framework of immediacy often means that young clients do not attend appointments, as they have something else (better) to do, or they turn up late, or even on the wrong day. Whilst it may not be possible to give the client a structured session in this scenario, SFBT allows us to do something, and something is better than nothing. I have carried out some of my most successful interventions in the ten minutes that it takes a client to have a coffee and a cigarette.

When a client presents to the young people's project or the adult service, they often present with a rigid agenda or goal: 'I want to get off drugs/alcohol.' I tend to challenge gently and pay more need to the here and now by saying, 'That is a great goal, how can we use this hour towards that goal?' or, 'What might happen in the next hour that would tell you that you are moving towards that goal?' I may enquire further by asking questions such as the following.

- How will you do that?
- What are the small steps that can be taken?

- When you are not dependent on drugs/alcohol, what will you be doing that's different?
- How will your life look when you no longer need drugs/alcohol?

The wonderful (miracle) question is essential here as it affords the client the chance to look beyond the stated goal, to create a future memory of how life will/could be different. According to Berg and Miller (1992), 'Goals must be stated in positive, proactive language about what the client will do, instead of about what she will *not* do' (p. 38; italics mine).

In my experience many clients who attend a first session have already undergone pre-session change. For example they may have reduced consumption; started an action plan or gathered a supportive group of people around them. This pre-session change needs to be recognised and applauded. One client told me that in the two weeks before coming to her first session she had managed to reduce from six bags of heroin daily (injecting) to half a bag per day (92 per cent reduction), and that she wanted support to 'finish the job' On further enquiry it transpired that she had set herself the goal of returning to college in September (my counselling session with her was in May). She had obtained a course prospectus and was intending to submit her application that week. My role at this point was to be concrete about what needed to be achieved, and contract for a number of sessions (in this case eight) to cover the period between the initial session and the time she went to college. The client wanted to focus on ways to 'come off' which were different from ones she had tried in the past.

Language is important with all clients; with drug and alcohol users especially so. When clients state that they want to be 'clean' does this mean they view themselves as 'dirty', as some people do? Rather than adopt such terms I would reflect back to them that they want to be drug free. I would help them to look at those parts of their life that are not part of the 'dirtiness'. These may relate to their family, their friends, hobbies, successes, strengths and resources. One middle-aged client stated that he could not cope with his drinking any more and that his life was nothing but drinking. This client had a dog that he loved dearly. He had recently built a kennel for the dog. When asked how he had managed to do that, his mood lifted and he spoke in great detail about how he had started it, the steps he went through, and his pride upon completion.

I asked him how could a 'waste of space' (his words) achieve such a thing if all his life was consumed with drinking? Over the next few months we worked on setting small tasks each week, building in more and more until his entire week was devoted to keeping busy apart from Saturday afternoons, which he wanted to keep for drinking. In explaining SFBT to clients I tell them that I believe them when they say they want to achieve something, and that we will work together to maximise their resources. I also explain that I will not attempt to analyse them; that they are the experts on themselves and I am interested to learn from them what works. Importantly, I often tell clients that the fact that they have come to that first session shows they have already achieved something, and that the time spent in therapy is not as important as the time they spend in their lives, coping, managing and growing outside of therapy (Budman and Gurman, 1998).

The opening therapeutic moves are crucial in that they start the process of being future oriented and encourage the client to think of small, manageable tasks rather than the big 'getting off' goal. 'What are you hoping to get out of this session/what would you like to achieve today/how will you know if today's session has been useful?' – these questions steer the client toward a positive use of the time. When clients say they want to get off drugs the therapist's role is to be realistic by gently asking, 'Do you think we will achieve that in the next hour? How will this session help you towards getting off drugs? If this session has helped you to start getting off, how will you know by the end of it?'

In the first session, I use scaling, often following the wonderful (miracle) question. Most clients pick up the use of scales quickly and it often becomes a point of shared meaning and sometimes humour. A client when asked on a third session if things had got better, replied without prompting, 'My drinking has improved about 20 per cent, things with my partner are at nine out of ten (they were five only two weeks previously), and I'm ten out of ten sure I can crack this now.' There was much laughter between us and praise from me at the client's achievements, with of course, a follow-up question as to what had been different; how had the client achieved this and so on.

Task setting with drug and alcohol users needs to be realistic and achievable. Twenty years of heroin use at £100 per day is unlikely to reduce by 50 per cent before the next session and if clients try and fail, there is yet another layer of failure heaped upon them. It is more effective to set small tasks. In some cases SFBT may not be so brief. One client who was drinking a bottle of whisky and ten small bottles of barley wine a day came for counselling for nearly two years, with the sessions remaining solution-focused.

Often the tasks set are unrelated to the substance use. For example, a client was complaining that because he was 'always' out of it, he never tidied his house and that he was sick of living in a pigsty. He went on to say that his life was a pigsty. The last time he had cleaned his house was because his mum was visiting and she didn't know he was a heavy cannabis user. This client's between-session task was to invite his mum over for Sunday lunch for the next four weeks, mainly to help him with his garden, which she was keen to do. For the next four weeks the client had every Sunday cannabis free, kept the house tidy (and his mealtimes were better) and was very upbeat. At the next session he told me that he and his mum were going plant shopping on the Saturday next week, so he would have Saturday and Sunday cannabis free.

As I mentioned earlier, I believe that SFBT is compatible with Prochaska and DiClemente's model of change (1983). I will look at the various stages of this model and how it fits with SFBT.

Contemplation

A client presenting must already be thinking about change, or why would they present? The SFB therapist needs to elicit the future focus. Asking the wonderful question helps the client to create a future (memory) that is not only drug free but also includes doing/being something else. 'So when you have stopped using drugs, what will you be doing instead?'

Preparation

Coming off drugs/alcohol is psychologically difficult, and often physically unpleasant. My role here is to enquire 'how, when and what?' 'How will you cope with physical withdrawals?' 'What will be the signs that will tell you that you are getting better?' 'When will you need some support, who will provide that?' 'What needs to happen to make this successful?' There is often a history of failed attempts at coming off: 'What will you be doing differently this time that makes this more likely to be successful for you?' Between-session tasks here may include disposing of all the alcohol in the house, eliciting support from family with meals, buying over the counter medication to deal with withdrawal pains and booking in some complementary therapy sessions.

Action

Clients in the 'action' stage are starting to stabilise, reduce, or stop. The therapist's role here is to find out what's working, what skills the client is utilising and what resources, internal and/or external, are to hand. It is also useful here to elicit from the client if others have noticed this change, 'So now you are not drunk at 5 p.m., has anyone else noticed that/has anybody commented?' This can also be broadened out so the client can see that their changes have impact on other areas of their life: 'Have your children noticed any differences now that you are not hungover on Saturday mornings?' Praise is also important, as is encouragement. 'What did you do that helped you to not drink in the mornings?'

Maintenance

A client that is maintaining change is sometimes at risk of complacency, and is often very vulnerable. Using drugs and/or alcohol is a full-time job, from finding the money to fund the substance use, to hiding the criminality that is drug use, or being secretive about alcohol use. When all that is gone a client will need to fill that void, so task setting and small goals are essential here, as is 'noticing difference'. One client told me that he would know things were going well if he could manage breakfast; in fact having poached egg on toast was part of his wonderful (miracle) day. We spent some time talking about food, and on his next visit he told me excitedly how good poached egg on toast tasted, now he was no longer drinking. He also commented to his partner over breakfast that 'the miracle was starting to happen'.

A client who has been using drugs/alcohol for some time often feels that they need to make up for lost time when drug free and can create ambitious plans that are not easily achievable. It is the therapist's role here to break down those plans into more manageable steps.

(Re)lapse

Substance misusers often lapse, after some time in positive change, then they may use again. Often the traditional view is that a client needs to start all over again. That may be the view held by many drug workers, especially in the disease model, but as a social constructionist I do not hold with this: it is not my role to change the focus from the positive to the negative, quite the reverse. I will often measure the time in relapse against the time in positive change, illustrating to the client that they have been, for the most part, successful. One way of doing this has been to get a calculator and add up the number of hours the client has been drug/alcohol free in the last week/month/year and write it on a piece of paper, and then add up the number of hours the client has been under the influence, and write this down. This is not to negate the feelings of despair or shame the client may feel, having relapsed, but to put it into perspective. I might remind the client of the strategies and skills that they had employed before, the things that they had done that were successful.

In terms of culture, race, sexuality and other equality issues SFBT can be used, I would suggest, with one or two provisos. Firstly the 'miracle' question. I never (unless the client uses the word) use the word miracle. I prefer to say '... and when you are asleep something wonderful happens'. The word 'miracle' has so many cultural and religious connotations that it will exclude and alienate some clients from their SFBT therapist. To a Muslim or devout Catholic it would be heretical to suggest a miracle when only Allah/God can do this; to a Buddhist miracles simply do not happen. To some drug and alcohol users the 'miracle' would be that society accepts them, that the police stop prosecuting them, and that their six-month wait to see the consultant was only one week. The other reason that I use 'wonderful' rather than 'miracle' is that the word 'miracle' can sometimes be viewed as divine, certainly external, and therefore out of the client's control. 'Wonderful' presents, in my view, a softer, more pleasant view. As an aside I have found that the word 'wonderful' seems to sit better with young people.

My other proviso is that practitioners of SFBT, especially new ones, must not force the client along. It is important to remained solution-focused of course, but not at the expense of acknowledging difference and diversity. It is not as simple as reduction of alcohol or drugs being the only solution, questions must be asked (at the very least in the practitioner's head) about the client's place/role/function in society. For example, it may be harder for a female heroin user to regulate and reduce her consumption when her boyfriend/partner has control of the heroin; for an Asian living in a predominantly white area to elicit peer support, or for a gay man to stop drinking when the only local gay meeting place is a pub.

On reflection, the more I learn about solution-focused therapy, the more I question, the more I realise I have much still to learn. Cade and O'Hanlon (1993) argue that whilst the techniques of SFBT are amongst the easiest to learn, 'doing' SFBT well takes a lot longer. It is not simply a set of techniques that make SFBT effective with substance misusers, but the framework of future focus, the ethos of change, the non-acceptance of an expert stance from the therapist, and the belief in the therapist that the client is able to recall past and present skills and resources and utilise them for the future.

Solution-focused thinking has become a part of my life: I use the model for my own issues, within my family (without being the therapist), at work, and in supervision.

I will end this chapter with a case study of a young man that I had worked with for about two years without being really solution-focused (though I tried). I had for some time mirrored his chaotic lifestyle by responding in almost every session to his current crisis, without really looking forward.

Case study

Darren was 12 when I first met him; he was already drinking heavily, and had started to 'dabble' with heroin. Darren had been referred to the service from social services as he was on the child protection register after being taken to hospital following a serious alcohol and tranquilliser binge. Darren's mum was looking after him and his father was in and out of prison, this time for burglary to fund his heroin habit.

Darren did not really want to engage, though he kept coming, stating that at least I was listening to him and not telling him what to do. I then did not see Darren for about 12 months when he was re-referred and by this time (14 years old) was injecting heroin. Darren desperately wanted to come off heroin, but was finding this difficult when he was increasingly alienating himself from his mum due to stealing from the home, and at the same time coming to terms with his father's 14-year prison sentence for manslaughter. Darren attended a couple of sessions then didn't attend, disappeared from home for two weeks, got caught shoplifting, attended, didn't attend – so the pattern went for about eight months. Then on one occasion Darren told me that he wanted me to help him get into a rehab. After discussing this with Darren, I realised he was clearly not ready for a rehab at this point, his use was chaotic, he had not thought out how he might prepare for the rehab, did not know what a rehab really meant, and had no plans post-rehab. I told Darren that at that point I would not endorse social services' recommendation for a rehab as I did not want to see Darren set up for failure. It is at this point that the relationship, and Darren's focus, changed.

Darren asked me, 'So if I'm not fucking ready now when I am fucking desperate, what have I got to do? Die?'

I replied, using Darren's future-focused question as a 'launch pad', 'I have only said what I think are the reasons why you may not be ready. What do you think would be different if you were ready?'

Darren: Well I suppose if I'd cut down that would prove it wouldn't it?

Me: You don't have to prove anything to me, I am just wondering what else might be happening that would tell you that you were more ready than now.

Darren: Well I would be coming here when I'm supposed to, and not running away from home, and nicking.

Me: So if you were attending appointments, not running away, trying to cut down your gear, and not stealing do you think that you would be ready then?

Darren: I think so. What happens at rehab then?

I will not say that from this point things were plain sailing: far from it. But this was a change point, Darren (and I) became more focused, we looked at what a rehab might entail, went on a joint visit and talked to other residents. Darren became extremely interested in wanting to do a computing course at college on his departure from the rehab. This was even before he went: once he had decided that he had a life after rehab he would not entertain failure at rehab as an option.

Darren attended rehab; he came out drug and alcohol free, though he had a few minor relapses within the first few weeks of 'freedom'. He is currently studying at college on his computing course. About two months before Darren's course started we were still seeing each other monthly as we had contracted a further six sessions to 'ease' Darren into college life. I said to Darren: 'We have been seeing each other a long time now, and it seems to me that you have achieved all that you set out to achieve. When will you know it's time to stop coming, what will be happening that will tell you that you don't need to come here any more?' Darren replied, laughing, 'You really are a mind reader. I was thinking that, I'm all right now, is it OK if I come back once after college has started just to let you know how I'm getting on?' Darren in that last statement told me that he would be 'getting on', and that he was OK now, not the problem-focused response of 'can I come and see you if I'm finding it hard/having difficulties/problems'. Darren had become solution-focused (without him realising at the time, though I told him later), helping me to become solution-focused.

Postscript: Darren is doing well at college and has a part-time job in a restaurant; he emailed me recently to tell me, 'Life is sweet, thanks for everything.'

References

Berg, I.K. and Miller, S.D. (1992) *Working with the Problem Drinker: a solution-focused approach.* New York: W.W. Norton.

Budman, L. and Gurman, A.S. (1988) *Theory and Practice of Brief Therapy.* New York: Guilford Press.

Cade, B. and O'Hanlon, W. (1993) *A Brief Guide to Brief Therapy.* New York: W.W. Norton.

Prochaska, J.O. and DiClemente, C.C. (1983) Stages and processes of self-change of smoking: toward an integrative model of change. *Journal of Consulting and Clinical Psychology,* 51(3): 390–395.

14

A Solution-Focused Approach to 'Psychosis'

Dave Hawkes

All of those who have learned to cope with their voices have discovered the importance of communicating with others about their experiences. Communication is a way of breaking down the barriers of isolation and is essential to the process of integrating voices into everyday life. (Romme and Escher, 1993, p. 145)

Solution-focused therapy can be used successfully regardless of diagnosis. In the past eight years I have worked with 'psychosis' on a day to day basis in my work for the National Health Service. I use solution-focused brief therapy (SFBT) as part of a formal day hospital team; as a visiting community psychiatric nurse working alone, and in a GP surgery 'screening clinic' in a more traditional 'counselling' setting. This means I see clients who are 'sent', who may be inpatients under a section of the Mental Health Act or who have had only one appointment with their GP. I use the model every day with clients who conform to the (arbitrary) label of 'psychosis'.

When I trained in psychiatry what I learned about delusions and auditory hallucinations covered one small part of three years' study, yet formed the majority of work in hospital and community settings in which I worked. I was told these experiences were unreal and had to be denied or ignored, although we had to be sensitive to the person's feelings. It did not take me long to realise what a lot of rhetoric and rubbish this was. (Smith, 1998, p. 6)

It is not easy to find a therapist who works with people presenting 'psychotic symptoms', even though the therapeutic literature suggests that talking therapies can and do help with these problems. In the therapy centres I have had access to in my career as a therapist or as a community nurse trying to get therapy for people, most specialists do not even see anyone who presents with an 'alternative reality' at all. This confines a whole group of intelligent, enthusiastic and motivated people exclusively to the domain of the traditional medical model. Interventions are thus limited to 'distraction', 'reality orientation' and medication. We are consigning all of these people to a form of solitary confinement; to the absence of meaningful conversation. Mental health systems are suffering from a poverty of ideas, interestingly one of the diagnostic factors for psychosis!

This confuses me since most therapeutic models should be able to work with such clients. After all, even Freud's initial caseload was varied, to say the least, and cognitive behavioural therapies have produced research that suggests they are effective with psychotic symptoms. However, on the ground in the NHS it is hard to get anyone to talk to clients with 'psychosis' about anything other than containment, activities or medication.

This reluctance seems to me to be based on the following assumptions:

- these problems are 'harder to solve' than other problems;
- we will make things worse, we will 'collude' with the client's frame;
- talking doesn't help (unless it tells the client to conform to one idea of what is real).

Before we consider the clinical application of SFBT, we need to question these assumptions.

Aren't these difficult cases?

As solution-focused therapists we are familiar with the difficulties of defining meaning in an everyday sense. As Wittgenstein states:

> For a large class of cases – though not for all – in which we employ the word 'meaning' it can be defined thus: the meaning of the word is its use. (1958, p. 42)

It follows that solution-focused therapists should attribute no more concern to working with clients who use words such as 'hallucinations', 'voices' or 'paranoia' than those who use words such as 'anorexia', 'anxiety' or 'divorce'. We still have to find out what the client wants and then see if we can co-operate with it or parts of it. We may not have the power to arrange an audience with the queen, but if we can discover through conversation that the client wants to achieve more in life, there may be other ways to help with this. We will work with the client to find out 'How will we do this?' or 'While you are waiting for this to happen, what will make life a little easier for you?'

I would challenge the traditional view that this group of clients lack insight and are resistant to change. Raphael (1997) found that mental health clients were widely thought of as unreliable, particularly in a research context. While undertaking patient satisfaction research, Raphael investigated the responses and found that only 2 per cent of patients who responded to her survey failed to give 'rational' answers and only 3 per cent handed in 'very incomplete' questionnaires. This group of clients are probably not engaged on an adult level by traditional approaches and this may explain dropout rates from clinics as effectively as any idea that 'psychotic' clients are 'difficult' or 'not committed'. The SFBT approach seeks to gain the co-operation and involvement of the client and is not deterred by the diagnosis or referral letter.

We might collude with the client's frame and make things worse

Trying to define 'psychosis' or 'the client's frame' is difficult enough, without believing that we must not collude with it. Even if we take just one 'psychotic' symptom such as auditory hallucinations as an example, are voices evidence of 'psychosis'? There are two views about auditory hallucinations.

1 Hearing voices indicates illness, particularly schizophrenia. Treatment is needed. This is consistent with much of the research suggesting specific interventions as 'treatments of choice'. This dates to the diagnosis of 'Dementia praecox' identified in (1919) by Kraepelin, who also included '*Hallucinations: auditory*' as a diagnostic factor.

2 Hearing voices is an unusual experience: not necessarily a sign of pathology, but one open to a wide range of interpretations and treatments. The use of voices to diagnose mental illness has been challenged vigorously.

> The reduction of hearing voices to the status of mere pathology is not very fruitful in helping patients to deal with these experiences, it also may be an inaccurate analysis. (Romme and Escher, 1993, p. 245)

Myrtle Heery suggests that 'throughout human history, there have been descriptions of the voice within religion, history, psychology, fiction, and myth' (1993, p. 82). Heery (1989) hypothesises that the psychological literature focuses on the pathology of hearing voices and the religious literature on the divine inspiration or diabolical possession explanation. She suggests however that there is a third, neglected group or category – those who experience inner voices as teachers; as an intrapsychic phenomenon or while meditating. She wishes to 'dispel the common stereotype of the inner voice as the prerogative of saints and psychotics, and thereby encourage research into its liberating effect on our human capacities' (p. 89).

Jaynes (1976) suggests that hearing voices was common to all humanity until around 1300 BC, when the experience was eliminated by the development of 'consciousness' at an individual and societal level. He uses the *Iliad* as an example of a pre-consciously organised society, one where the self does not exist, the mind is not mentioned and responsibility lies with the gods who speak directly to individuals in what could be interpreted in modern culture as hallucinations. So we cannot assume that 'psychotic symptoms' are evidence of 'psychosis'. We cannot be sure whose reality we should follow or what we should 'treat'.

The most common question at workshops when groups are shown solution-focused work with psychosis, is, 'Aren't you just colluding with the client's frame?' The predominant view in mental health is that the aim of therapy should be 'reality orientation'. Watzlawick challenges forms of therapy that impose their version of reality upon clients:

> What is involved here is the apparently obvious assumption that there exists an objective reality of which normal people are more conscious than the so called insane. The idea of such a reality has been philosophically untenable at least since Hume and Kant; in science it has been proven to be equally unsound, since it has been recognised that the goal of science cannot be the discovery of ultimate truth. As far as I know, the belief in a 'real reality' has survived only in psychiatry. (1990, p. 185)

He suggests that the reality psychiatry usually concerns itself with is 'second order' reality. He gives an example of first and second order properties of gold. The first order properties of gold (weight, colour, solidity) can be discussed in terms of scientific 'proof' and in an argument would be easy to 'prove'. However there is a 'second order' property of gold – its value; this is disconnected from gold's physical properties, but attributed to it by a process of consensus, by human beings. The value of gold is not the gold itself. It is attributed to gold by culture, consensus and interaction and may be different from moment to moment, from individual to individual.

'Psychiatric reality', as we might call it, is constructed by attributing meaning, significance or value to labels such as 'insane' 'psychosis' and 'hallucination'. This is Watzlawick's second order reality. Concepts such as 'illness' and 'hallucination' have different meanings to different observers, none more 'true' than another and arguably none more 'provable' than another. None more 'treatable' by a specific intervention than another! Watzlawick suggests that the trap for professionals is when they start to treat labels such as 'psychosis' as if they are 'truth'. As if they are the thing itself rather than a constructed representation of the thing.

Rather than seek 'the truth' of a person's illness the solution-focused therapist concerns him or herself with what the client wants and how he or she is going to get it. What helps and what is possible and realistic for them to do? The therapist to an extent colludes with the client and is proud to do so. SFBT concentrates on what the *goal is* rather than any interpretation of what has gone on or why it has gone on. This focus allows the conversation to move beyond what is real or not, and on to what can be done to make things better and to find out what the client needs to do. For example, the client who believes someone is trying to kill him or her translates into a goal of the client wanting to feel safe again. The belief that aliens are stealing one's thoughts is converted into a goal for the client to concentrate more and be confident about his or her own thinking. Behaviour that would let them know their thoughts were back to normal may include reading more, being able to watch TV and being able to complete the crossword. These are not 'crazy' conversations. Feeling that someone is telling them to do things at night becomes a goal of wanting to be clearer about what they want and to feel more in charge of what they do. What will you be doing when you are safe? What might work to make things even a little bit better?

Rationale for using SFBT

SFBT maximises co-operation since the client is allowed to talk about the issue to someone who first of all listens and tries to work out what he or she wants and secondly helps him or her to work towards getting it. On the way, possible wide-ranging solutions may occur. While waiting to be named the England football manager, for instance, to make life a little better 'Jim' could see his nurse a little bit more; go to football training again and make his bed so that he doesn't get shouted at so much by his mum. As with any other client, the idea of developing detailed, varied solutions – 'multiple endpoints' – is the aim.

These 'multiple endpoints' may be in keeping with a traditional view of 'treatment' or not. For instance, they may include taking medication in the interim, e.g. Jim may concede that medication helps him get on better with Mum and worry less about the England manager's job. If the idea of taking medication comes as a logical part of a client's need to feel safer, sleep better or be more successful then the likelihood of compliance is greater than if they are told to take it 'because it is good for you!'

Obviously the worker will not go along with a goal such as 'stabbing the present England manager' and will instruct the client not to do so and if necessary inform the appropriate authorities. At the same time the worker will explore alternatives to this unacceptable course of action. The solution-focused approach maximises the client–therapist relationship so that clients will tell you such things and at least then the therapist can act upon them. If the worker starts from a stance of 'This is what reality is, what *you* are experiencing is a delusion caused by an illness', it satisfies our control function (we have done our job, our grip on reality is reinforced), but it makes clients more likely to keep things to themselves.

Provided the goal is ethical, legal and moral we will co-operate with it. Therefore tasks such as changing the room around to see if that stops the voices; sleeping more to see if that helps; using headphones and music; talking more to the family; doing relaxation therapy and jogging are all activities the therapist will 'collude' with.

Issues of clinical practice

I follow as much of the basic solution-focused map as possible. However, the clinical application with 'psychosis' requires the worker to do the following.

1 Ensure safety issues and boundaries are identified and discussed before and during therapy.
2 Read the referral letter, as clients usually expect you to have done so. Suspend the information gleaned from it as much as possible, but if it necessitates seeing the client somewhere else or with a colleague, arrange this accordingly.

    The limitations of working with psychosis are not imposed by the model, but by the simple rules which govern any type of therapy. The client and therapist must be safe and able to talk for therapy to go ahead. If this is not the case, it is necessary to stop and ensure one's safety. The client may be offered an opportunity to meet at a later date or in a different place.
3 Stay focused. The worker uses questions to keep the client on track and will try to translate negative or 'strange' answers into the beginnings of new behaviours. There is regular use of scaling and questions such as, 'What else needs to happen that would help you for now?'

4 Be prepared for strange answers to the miracle question. It is important to listen to the ideas you have invited from the client. You may need to slow the pace down and allow the client to talk about strange phenomena before bringing him or her back by asking, 'What would you like to be different, what would help?'

5 Join with clients' puzzlement over how strange things happen. If they begin to suggest alternative 'realistic' explanations for events one needs to show restraint by commenting simply, 'That's interesting, isn't it?' 'It is a puzzle to me too how time travel can be invented although we haven't heard of it yet.' Be puzzled at the logical flaws in arguments clients point out *themselves*. De Shazer (1995) claims that often clients don't take their 'delusional ideas' to their logical conclusions. For example, they report that there are noises and voices coming from a lab in their house but they don't move out, they cope. The worker encourages the clients to deconstruct their own psychotic ideas by leaving them the space to do so; by being puzzled and by reinforcing any 'normal' explanations they propose.

6 The worker might have to do a lot of talking to contain clients who are overexcited or rambling in their conversation. The aim is to bring them back to identifying one small goal and how to achieve it.

7 Feed back any simple tasks that the clients themselves have suggested, particularly any 'experiment' they were willing to try that made sense. Keep any tasks fixed on one small area of change in which the client expressed interest. Ensure it is a task that you feel comfortable co-operating with and that is not to the detriment of anyone else. Accept any suggestions for change that are ethical, e.g. arrange medication if the client wants to try it. If the client asks you to carry out some all-powerful act, such as to read his mind, tell him you can't do it but ask how he thought that would help.

8 I avoid giving tasks that suggest some other party is responsible for reported phenomena, for example when a client feels her partner is sending radio messages through her teeth. It is tempting to agree that the partner must be clever and 'sneaky' to do so. This might help the client to feel that the therapist has really listened, but may also encourage him or her to plot harm against another person.

9 The worker follows up client statements such as, 'I would be out of this unit and off section' by asking, 'What needs to happen to ensure that you get off as soon as possible?' The worker supports the client's plans to remain calm; not give in to the instructions from the voices and to take the necessary medication. The argument that this is collusion, since the client is only co-operating in order to get out, is a naive one. Of course this is the motivation. But as you keep listening for multiple endpoints and the germs of constructive ideas, for example more education sessions, more conversations with the psychiatrist, and you are sure these ideas come from the client and not from you (you are not just giving them a list of tricks to pull to get out), then 'insight based'

change may emerge. If the client puts these ideas into practice, then over time he or she will be released. If the worker is sceptical about the changes the client reports it is possible to check out the evidence and feed it back to the client: 'You said you were attending classes but the staff here report you haven't been for some time. How come? Does going to the class not help, have you any other ideas how you would want to move forward?'

If the client's responses give cause for concern, make a mental note and check back near the end of the session. For example, 'You were thinking of killing yourself, how worried should I be on a scale of zero to ten that you will do it today?' If the answer is ten then the worker needs to look at how this risk can be reduced to a reasonable level. If there is no way to reduce the risk it may be possible to deliver a positive message based on the client's stated intentions. For example, 'You really care about your family, I'm not sure that harming yourself is the only way to protect them and I certainly need to try and keep you safe this evening. I've got some ideas but what would you be prepared to do to keep safe?' Finally you would need to inform the relevant authorities. As a community psychiatric nurse, if I can help the client to agree to a voluntary admission I would then try to make the admission as smooth as possible for him or her. I would always make clear that this is a temporary solution and offer to see the client again on the ward if this would help. Clients who leave distressing sessions early or hold extreme ideas may need the worker to inform the family and relevant agencies of his or her concerns. Where there are agency procedures these should be followed. If there is worrying information in the referral letter which is not mentioned by the client, the worker needs to check it out gently. For example, 'You say you're fine but the referral mentioned that you have been hearing voices, have they gone at the moment? What do you think about this?'

Integrating SFBT

What else has been found to work with 'psychosis' and can SFBT integrate with it?

Medication

The common myth in mental health is that the effective treatment for psychosis is medication. In acute phases this may be true, but generally it is useful to see medication as a necessary evil in order to attain the baseline requirements of safety and communication discussed earlier; to allow talking and relationships to begin. Medication is the means to the end, not the end itself! Warner (1994) in order questions its effectiveness by taking a long-term view of recovery rates from schizophrenia. In an analysis of 85 follow-up studies, he found that recovery rates for patients admitted to hospital since the introduction of psychiatric drugs are not significantly better than for those admitted after the second world war or during the first two decades of the century.

Rappaport (1978) and associates randomly assigned 80 inpatients to chlorpromazine medication treatment or to a placebo treatment. At three-year follow-up the clients who took placebo medication in hospital and were off all medication on discharge showed the greatest clinical improvement and the lowest levels of functional disturbance and pathology. It is questionable if chlorpromazine is as effective an anti-psychotic as modern medications, but Rappaport's assertion that anti-psychotic medication is not the treatment of choice, at least for certain patients in the long term, is a challenging one.

Everitt (1996) justified the search for psychological interventions by claiming that:

> Unpleasant side effects and non-compliance make medication an unpleasant and unsatisfactory intervention for some patients. Anxiety and depression accompany many symptoms with a high risk of suicide in this client group. These factors highlight the importance of establishing reliable treatment alternatives to medication (p. 139)

Using psychological interventions with psychotic symptoms is not new (Ayllon and Azarin, 1968). Family therapy, and particularly the idea that clients in families who express high levels of emotion at home have a higher rate of relapse, has led to the research of Brooker (1990) and to planned programmes for training community psychiatric nurses in psychosocial interventions. Although the relevant studies have won wide acceptance they are small in scale and methodologically flawed.

'First person singular therapy' (Fowler and Morley, 1989) asks clients to reframe voices as coming from them and encourages clients to bring on voices and then banish them. Sartorious et al. (1993) were sceptical of the relevance of insight-oriented therapy in the treatment of schizophrenia. Solution-focused therapists would not be so sure. If a client wants to engage in writing in order to understand his or her past, I would not dismiss it. If it works, do more of it. The therapist needs to be flexible towards the client's proposed solutions so that the client feels he or she has some power and control in their choices. For many people the experience of making a free decision and following it through is evidence that the voices do not run their lives. If clients want to pursue Buddhism orpsychoanalysis as part of a plan to eliminate their voices I would co-operate with them.

Scharfetter (1996) attempts to co-operate with clients in an exploration of their experience of psychosis. He aims to shape his therapeutic interventions to fit the client's subjective experience. Green et al. (1980) suggested that clients use an earplug to reduce the auditory input. He also advocated that the client name objects out loud in order to disrupt the voices. Birchwood (1986) claimed a 46 per cent success rate for a sponge earplug.

Various theories have formulated hypotheses to explain psychotic symptoms. These include the self-generation of voices through a vocal process; mental illness; high levels of expressed emotion in families; anxiety and stress, and faulty cognitive processes. Treatments suggested include:

- family discussions
- distraction
- challenging the voices
- medication
- earplugs
- focusing on the voices
- systematic desensitisation.

Solution-focused therapy does not advocate a specific treatment, but adopts the principle that treatments are helpful if the client says they are!

Despite the positive nature of the above interventions, they do not in themselves give clients what they say they need. Clients report they need a genuine human relationship with a professional who does more than just tell them what reality is, or argue about what is real and what is not (Coleman and Smith, 1997; Hawkes, 1998).

Summary

SFBT arguably provides the necessary environment to allow positive relationships to occur, encompassing the best of all of these approaches to helping with psychosis. De Shazer has advocated interviewing without a hypothesis and supporting clients in their own preferred method of hallucination control. This means that solution-focused brief therapy can do 'all of the above'. The focus on 'what helps and what can make things better', rather than on what is 'real', is more useful and allows clients (in distress about what is real themselves) more respect and control over therapy. Most importantly SFBT provides a framework for therapists to talk to people suffering from 'psychosis' about their experiences and how to help in a field where the label itself has excluded people from therapy for too long.

References

Ayllon, T. and Azarin, N.H. (1968) *The Token Economy.* New York: Appleton Century Crofts.

Birchwood, M. (1986) Control of auditory hallucinations through occlusion of monaural auditory input. *British Journal of Psychiatry*, 149: 104–107.

Brooker, C. (1990) Expressed emotion and psychological intervention: a review. *International Journal of Nursing Studies*, 27(3): 267–276.

Coleman, R. and Smith, M. (1997) *Working with Voices, from Victim to Victor.* London: Handsell Publications (MIND).

de Shazer, S. (1995) *Coming through the Ceiling* (videotape). Milwaukee: Brief Family Therapy Center.

Everitt, J. (1996) Psychological management of psychotic symptoms. *Psychiatric Care*, 3(4): 139–143.

Fowler, D. and Morley, S. (1989) The cognitive behavioural treatment of hallucinations and delusions, a preliminary study. *Behavioural Psychotherapy*, 17: 267–282.

Green, W.P., Glass, A. and O'Callahan, M.A.J. (1980) Some implications of abnormal hemisphere interaction in schizophrenia. Cited in J.H. Gruzelier and P. Florheny (eds), *Hemisphere Asymmetries and Psychopathology.* London: Macmillan.

Hawkes, D. (1998) Hearing some important voices. Internal research for BHB Trust and South Bank University.

Heery, M.W. (1989) Inner voice experiences: an exploratory study of thirty cases. *Journal of Trans Personal Psychology*, 21(1): 82.

Heery, M.W. (1993) Inner voice experiences: a study of 30 cases. Cited in E. Romme and S. Escher (1993) *Accepting Voices*. London: MIND Publications.

Jaynes, J. (1976) *The Origin of Consciousness in the Breakdown of the Bicameral Mind*. Boston, MA: Houghton Mifflin.

Kraeplin, E. (1919) *Dementia Praecox and Paraphrenia*. Edinburgh: Livingstone.

Raphael, W.L. (1997) Psychiatric hospitals viewed by their patients. London: King Edward's Hospital Fund.

Rappaport, I.M., Hopkins, K.K. and Hall, K. (1978) Are there schizophrenics for whom drugs may be unnecessary or contraindicated? *International Pharmacopsychiatry*, 13(10/11): 107.

Romme, E. and Escher, S. (1993) *Accepting Voices*. London: MIND Publications.

Sartorius, N., Girolamo, G. and Andrews, G. (eds) (1993) *Treatment of Mental Disorders: a review of effectiveness*. Washington, DC: American Psychiatric Press.

Scharfetter, C. (1996) *The Self Experience of Schizophrenics* (2nd edn). Zurich: Psychiatric University Hospital.

Smith, M. (1998) The voice of reason. *Mental Health Nursing*, 18(3): 51.

Warner, R. (1994) *Recovery from Schizophrenia: psychiatry and political economy*. London: Routledge.

Watzlawick, P. (1990) *Munchausen's Pigtail or, Psychotherapy and Reality: essays and lectures*. New York: W.W. Norton.

Wittgenstein, L. (1958) *Philosophical Investigations* (3rd edn). Gem Anscombe Translation. New York: Macmillan.

15

Solution-Focused Reflecting Teams

Harry Norman

Bristol Solutions Group is a network of freelance consultants and counsellors interested in taking solution-focused thinking into new and different contexts. We have been called 'the world's first cross-disciplinary solution-focused network and support group' (Jackson and McKergow, 2002). The group's interests include working with organisations and teams, mentoring, coaching, counselling, non-managerial supervision and clinical supervision. Those of the group who are counsellors are mandated to receive clinical supervision. As we are all trainers, we are curious how to mentor and develop our solution-focused skills in ways that are congruent with solutions approaches. One of the group, John Henden, had positive experiences of reflecting teams as part of Bridgwater Community Mental Health team. John briefed us about the model and we started using the approach for our own clinical supervision.

Our meetings became more transparent and egalitarian and we noticed that our creativity, self-confidence and enthusiasm for meeting together increased. After a while I noticed that the group was using the model idiosyncratically – for example, we were opening the reflecting phase by offering compliments to the presenter. We discussed this and decided to add a distinct affirming phase (Figure 15.1).

Subsequently, on reviewing the literature (Andersen, 1987, 1991) I discovered that what I had taken to be the original reflecting team model was in fact a 'creative misunderstanding' (de Shazer, 1991) of the practices of the Bridgwater Community Mental Health team!

SFRT and solution-focused brief therapy

Having named this way of working the 'Solution-Focused Reflecting Team' (SFRT) I pondered whether it was a 'real' solution-focused model. I considered renaming the model 'solution-based' or 'resource-focused' reflecting teams. When we discussed this in the group colleagues pointed out that the term 'solution-focused' is used increasingly as a generic term and that also the structure of SFRT is analogous to a solution-focused brief therapy (SFT) meeting. This is clear when you include the client's contribution as part of the system (Figure 15.2).

We also discussed how 'respect' is communicated in a SFT and a SFRT meeting. In the solution-focused tradition 'respect' is expressed by anticipating that clients have a degree of competence already, and that the role of the practitioner

PHASE	ACTIVITY
PREPARING	The person who wishes to receive help ('the presenter') comes to the meeting with a specific request for help with a practice issue.
PRESENTING	The presenter outlines the situation to the team.
CLARIFYING	The team members ask the presenter questions to understand the situation more clearly.
AFFIRMING	The team members tell the presenter what impresses each of them most about how he or she is handling the situation.
REFLECTING	The team members take it in turn to offer appropriate input. This input often sparks associated ideas from other members of the team.
CLOSING	The presenter responds to what has been said and (usually) sets him or herself a goal based on the reflections.

Figure 15.1   *Solution-focused reflecting team (SFRT) – structure*

includes helping them to find existing behaviours which can be amplified. Thus 'respect' in the SFRT model is represented by the affirming phase.

We discussed the role of suggestions. Usually, a solution-focused practitioner refrains from making suggestions based on his or her thoughts about the content of the client's words, and favours suggestions based on research into how the client copes, or how the client creates possibilities. However, in the SFRT meeting the team is free to offer any reflections to the presenter. As the model is 'neutral' regarding the content of the reflections, this means that the content of the reflections is not always within the solution-focused tradition. One advantage of this is that the model can be used in teams working in other traditions.

The reflecting team

There are very few rules to follow. The rules we have are all about what we shall not do: We shall not reflect on something that belongs to another context ... and we must not give negative connotations. (Andersen, 1991, p. 61)

KEY SOLUTION-FOCUSED ACTIVITY	SFRT ANALOGUE
Clients have ideas how therapy could be useful. They have an idea what they want to say and what they hope to gain from the session	PREPARING
Clients tell their story and explain the help they want	PRESENTING
The counsellor asks questions to develop his, or her, understanding of what is hoped for, who is involved, and what qualities, resources and skills the client brings to the situation	CLARIFYING
During the course of the meeting the counsellor searches for opportunities to compliment the client on personal qualities, resourcefulness and skills	AFFIRMING
The counsellor considers 'the story so far' and explores ways in which the client could make further progress	REFLECTING
The counsellor and the client discuss how the client could make progress after the session	CLOSING

Figure 15.2   *Solution-focused therapy and SFRT – analogues*

In family therapy it is common for the therapist and client group to be seated in a room with a one-way mirror in it. The supervising team sits behind the mirror and directs the therapist by phone or intercom. Thus the therapist and the client sit in a room that literally reflects them (Andersen, 1991). Furman and Ahola (1992) describe how they invited teams to come out from behind the mirror and join in the therapeutic conversation. Bristol Solutions Group has no particular home, nor do we have a one-way mirror for some of us to sit behind, so when we started to meet we sat around a table!

When operating as a reflecting team, the Bridgwater Community Mental Health team shares the responsibility for interviewing the client throughout the team and we followed them in this respect.

Clinical supervision with a solution-focused reflecting team

Solution-focused skills are useful for mentoring or clinical supervision of practitioners using solutions approaches, and they can be used helpfully with practitioners who do not use solutions approaches (Miller, 1991). The focus in the session is to attend to and understand the work the presenter describes and his or her agenda in relation to it. We do not search for parallel processes, unmet needs or unresolved relationships which might figure in other forms of supervision.

Group size

We find that a group of four to eight members works particularly well. Larger groups can adapt the model by giving each member a budget of one or two clarification questions, one affirming statement and one or two reflections.

Time keeping and managing the process

One person, whom we designate the process manager, keeps each session on track by ensuring that the team follows the phases in sequence. This role is rotated if there are a number of presentations. We usually allocate between 20 and 30 minutes for each session. It can be helpful for the process manager to alert the group regularly to how much time is left. We find it helps if we agree a timetable and running order at the beginning of each meeting. We make sure that we have time for a cup of tea together and schedule time at the beginning for feedback from previous meetings and 'parish notices'.

Confidentiality

The team agrees its own understanding about confidentiality.

Seating

Solution-focused reflecting teams seem to do better sitting around a table. This helps with note taking. For instance, if during the presenting or affirming phase a group member has an idea which belongs in the reflection phase, writing it down enables him or her to concentrate on the present moment and to recall it for use at the appropriate time.

Phases

The process manager helps the meeting to stay 'in phase.' This gives the meeting flow – an atmosphere of rapport, ripples of nods and smiles as members recognise their questions and input coming out of others' mouths, and increased creativity. Sometimes members are bursting to say something 'out of phase'. In the past we used to speak freely out of phase. However, we agreed that this disrupted the flow of the meeting and have become more disciplined. Sometimes a group member asks permission of the team to step out of phase for a specific purpose, and this seems to work as we get back into phase quickly once that purpose has been achieved.

Listening to the presentation

We listen carefully to the presentation:

- in order to give positive feedback;
- for exceptions, goals, and preferred futures;

- for the 'facts' as perceived by the presenter;
- for who is a 'customer', and what they are a 'customer' for.

Clarification

The members of the group ask open questions in no particular order. Leading questions are discouraged. For example, questions that often start:

'Have you thought of ...?'
'Have you considered ...?'
'Have you tried ...?'

Leading questions set an inquisitorial tone and shift the enquiry away from the presenter.

Fact finding

Each member asks questions to make sure that he or she clearly understands the situation and the presenter's desired outcome from the meeting. A major part of the team's job is to clarify 'the facts'. In the solution-focused tradition 'facts' are descriptions of specific actions and sequences of actions that could be seen or heard on videotape. These are descriptions of events verifiable by the senses, rather than interpretations of events. We try to distinguish between what the client has disclosed about their internal state, emotions and internal dialogue and what the presenter may have inferred, interpreted or intuited about these. We want to do this because the presenter's inference, interpretation or intuition might be confusing the issue – and us! (O'Hanlon and Wilk, 1987).

Goals

We are *very* interested in the client's goals and the goals that significant others have for the client. We are interested in checking for goal and outcome statements that are 'well formed,' e.g. salient to the client and significant others, positively stated and actionable.

Assets

We are interested in any progress the client and the presenter have made. How optimistic is the presenter? What are the reasons for that optimism? We want to find out about ways in which those involved are doing better than they think they are doing.

Affirming

The members of the team tell the presenter briefly what they are most impressed with about the presentation. Sometimes a team gets bogged down as each person tries to think of new things to appreciate. There is no guideline that says you shouldn't be impressed with the same thing as another team member! The criteria for a 'good' compliment are that it should be sincere and pertinent to the situation under discussion.

We have noticed that team members often talk about two or three items that impress them. However, when each person thinks carefully and affirms only one thing, it makes a bigger impact on the presenter, in fact it seems hypnotic! The consultation break in solution-focused brief therapy and the affirming phase in SFRT are analogous as they both involve compliments and often elicit trance-like behaviours (de Shazer, 1988). The suggestibility quality often leads to the presenter later amplifying compliments offered in the affirming phase. The affirming comments from the team invite the presenter to expand current awareness of his or her own ability.

Positive feedback encourages us to continue to do what we are doing well. As well as raising the presenter's self-esteem it also bonds the group. As the team members make their affirmations, the presenter listens and speaks only to say 'Thank you' after each affirmation.

Reflecting

The members of the group take it in turn to say one thing at a time in response to the presentation. While the team is reflecting the presenter remains silent and listens carefully. Reflecting in this way encourages the team members to listen carefully to each other and build creatively on each other's input. The input offered at this phase could include anything that the members consider relevant: technical input; advice; reflections; metaphors, even poetry. The reflecting phase often has a slow pace to it, with pauses between reflections. Reflections often begin with the words 'I wonder' or 'I was wondering'. During the reflecting phase we are in the habit of saying, 'Pass' when it is our turn to reflect and we have nothing to say. We know we have finished when the timekeeper calls time or we have all said 'Pass .

Occasionally, when the presenter's client for example is at risk, team members make procedural or legal points to help the presenter. This is best done at the beginning of the reflecting phase as it tends to discourage 'flow.'

Closing and review

The presenter responds briefly to what has been said and often reviews the reflections, stating what he or she thinks is most applicable.

A team in action

The case had first been brought to the team a couple of meetings ago when the composition of the team was different. The presenter had prepared notes as well as his casenotes which he consulted during his presentation.

Presenting

The person who would like help speaks to the team.

> Presenter: I'd like to bring you up to date with a case I have brought to you before.
> The client is a minister in a church. He had a miserable childhood during which he

was emotionally neglected. His self-esteem was assaulted throughout that time and he felt absolutely worthless, living in abject poverty for most of his early years. His mother, who was a single parent, became mentally ill and died in a psychiatric hospital. For years he survived – he was a survivor! He had an internal dialogue with himself as part of his survival strategy: 'I can do this, I can master this situation I will try and get through. I don't need to keep on with this menial job, I'll get something better!' He coped this way until he was about 40 and then he went into the ministry.

Everything was fine until some time after he moved to a new parish. One of his parishioners, who ran a youth group, mentioned in passing that it was a great experience for him when he was hugged by a little boy who had appreciated something he had done for him. This was a trigger for the client to fall apart. He couldn't sleep at night, he was all over the place; he was desperately unhappy. All his life came before him and he just viewed it as a total failure. He acknowledged to himself that he had been desperately unhappy all the time. He used words like 'desperate', 'tragic', 'desolate', 'abandonment', 'despair' – very powerful words. He became suicidal, consulting the tide times and planning to go into the sea at high tide and slip away by night. I felt he was seriously at risk.

We worked on various issues, sorting things out as far as his life was concerned; looking at what was working; building on his survivor-hood; his strengths and skills; complimenting him and acknowledging the steps he had taken. Things got quite a lot better, the suicidal thoughts went away and he was having these depressive episodes less frequently.

Since I presented the case at the last meeting I have seen him twice and although he's improving, he says, 'I am feeling much better, although I still have these deep experiences when I keep thinking back to one thing and another.'

One thing I asked him to do was to keep a diary as he had always been aware of his 'internal dialogue'. He finds keeping the diary useful. Every few weeks he sends me pages of it to read. I invited him to do the healing-letter exercise described by Yvonne Dolan (1998) in which you write to an absent person, in this case his father, and then construct a reply, and he has done that. The letters are very powerful. Although he has made a lot of progress he is still having, in his words, 'depth experiences' when he feel desperate, desolate and adrift in life. I am wondering what to do next. Perhaps we should look at other areas where he could continue his improvement and reduce the negative 'depth experiences' he has. He appreciates the need to work in the present and the future and he is good at it!

Process manager: Clarification questions please.

Clarifying

The team asks questions to understand better the situation from the presenter's point of view.

Team member: I got a bit lost in the story. Who did the little boy hug?
Presenter: Someone he met in his new congregation.
Team member: And it was just being told this story that triggered things off?
Presenter: It was just being told that it was great that little Jimmy came along and just hugged him appreciatively for a party they had put on. Just this story was the trigger.
Team member: How does he define his goal or goals?
Presenter: His goals are to live a meaningful and purposeful life for the rest of his life without these despairing night-time experiences. He would rather stay asleep from half past three onwards, when he wakes up and cries desperately. It wakes his wife up and they sit chatting for a couple of hours before they go back to sleep. So that's what he wants – to stay asleep during the night and live a purposeful and meaningful life. He doesn't describe it in any more specific terms than that. Maybe he could.
Team member: May I ask what role does his faith play, if any?

Presenter: He's a bit 'nominal', actually.

Team member: I know that denomination!

[Laughter]

Presenter: He daily questions his faith and some days it is stronger than others and is helpful and other days he curses God for leaving him in this situation. He oscillates.

Process manager: Any more clarifications? No? We move now into the affirming phase.

Team member: I am really impressed by your finding out what works for him, and building on it and the diary and the letters, and making him write. It seems to be very effective and I am impressed by you spotting that it would be.

Team member: I was impressed by your gentle firmness and your level approach. With the client having a lot of ups and downs that would be helpful.

Process manager: I am impressed that you have seen him twice and he has made all this progress and written all this material. There's clearly a lot happening. I also thought you did well to pick up on the internal dialogue and the writing exercise.

Team member: I think I was really impressed with your willingness to listen to his words for how bad it is, his 'despair'. Your willingness to hear those words and to join in acknowledging the level of despair – acknowledging how bad it has been for him. That impressed me and I had a feeling that you feel quite tender towards him.

Team member: I am impressed by your perspective on this, you have got the big picture of these different things that have happened right through his life from the start through to now and into the future. Also which bits are working, with the examples that we have heard, and what there is still to do. The positioning of it is very clear, very clearly laid out so that if you hear some more ideas, or have more ideas, you will be able to fit them into this.

Team member: All the work you are doing so far seems to be smack on the nail.

Process manager: OK. So we move into the reflecting phase.

Reflecting

The team members take it in turn to offer input that seems appropriate to help the presenter. This input often sparks chains of association within the team who offer further input based on each other's contributions.

Team member: I have a reflection – the word 'normalising' springs to mind. Given what he has been through you can say something like 'You may well feel like that'! It fits what our colleague here was saying about acknowledging the client's experience.

Team member: I don't know how this fits, perhaps it doesn't, but as someone who is also an ex-minister who has struggled with faith in the past, then there may well be a struggle with his father figure and God as a father. I see almost two parallel struggles going on, which is why I asked about the faith. Going back to Yvonne Dolan, I know he has written to his earthly father so to speak, it may be worth repeating this process for the spiritual father – who may come down in his own terms.

Team member: When you were talking, I found myself thinking about a half way point in the middle of the night somewhere between having these 'depth experiences' and sleeping all night. I wonder if there's something in between? Maybe there are cognitive interruptions he can do consciously when he wakes up in the middle of the night with other pictures, thoughts or internal dialogue.

Team member: I would be interested in the pattern of his waking. So, yes, I would be teasing out what happens when he first rises to consciousness – almost before he opens his eyes – step by step. Different steps at that point will lead to different thoughts or different patterns of behaviour.

Process manager: Clearly he has had an awful time in many ways. I caught myself wondering to what extent you had pursued, and to what extent it might be worth pursuing, some of the exceptions in amongst all of this dreadfulness, despair and abandonment. Were there times when he has managed to sleep all night?

Team member: Just what I was going to ask. How often does he sleep through the night?

Team member: On a completely different tack. This artistic thing, he gets satisfaction from writing dialogue. That is clearly positive. Is there some way you and he can build on that?

Team member: Perhaps I should have asked a question at the clarifying phase but I don't get the impression of much support or sense of warmth around him. I am wondering which of his duties, whatever they might be, bring him the most joy and what it is about them that brings him the most joy.

Team member: His wife must be amazing, she wakes up with him and listens to him at all hours of the night. I was thinking about a merger of these two points. It isn't as mundane or as simple as 'counting your blessings', but there clearly are some. What does he do that makes people respond so warmly? It's a little bit as if the world is going on and he is just plonked in it. Unhappily plonked there and not inter-acting somehow!

Team member: Some of the days he thinks he is plonked there by God, doesn't he? You say his faith vacillates and that sometimes it is stronger than at other times, so I was interested in him writing to his Heavenly Father and having a dialogue on paper to work out what the things to be joyful about are.

Process manager: I was going to say something very mundane but you never know, it might help. I always find four o'clock in the morning a pretty dreadful time of day myself on the rare occasions when I happen to be there. Does it have to be a cognitive strat-egy that he employs at such times? Could it be making a cup of cocoa or something more behavioural like that? And there might be something in the exceptions that might explore some of these angles, because history is full of people who do things like that. Do things to get back to sleep rather than think things to get back to sleep.

Team member: Yes, what you said sparked something else off in my mind. Isn't four o'clock in the morning the time that sometimes God wakes people up because he wants to say something nice to them? Isn't that the time when it is easiest to be close to God because it is a very quiet time, so it is easier to listen to God?

Team member: Does he have children? Exceptions in that area – good times! This is a very powerful image that has been started off.

Team member: From my own perspective there are some similarities. I was brought up without a father. So some of your client's questions are familiar – the sense of loneliness, the sense of not belonging, of having no father. On the religious side all these things are taken care of in a sense, so what does this Heavenly Father provide that the earthly one did not?

Team member: Yes, pass.

Team member: You said that since you have seen him he's had lots of good times. You are at a great advantage because you have them written down in his diary, so being specific about the good times might be useful when he is feeling full of despair.

Process manager: Ben Furman says, 'It's never too late to have a happy childhood'. I say it's never too late to have a happy retirement!

Team member: I am suddenly feeling a bit cautious about our headlong rush into positive experiences for this man. I had a thought that whatever his scale of progress is on a one to ten scale I don't know where his destination would be. Say it's seven or something like that, in the past he has experienced the pits and I am wondering if it would be useful to get some kind of calibration, some kind of grading. Say he has been at one. What would three, four and five be like? Because maybe up to four he's going to be talking about coping better with despair and the horrible stuff, and then when he gets a bit higher than that, he may start talking about reaching positive things. So I am just thinking it might be an idea to do that. That would also place the more positive things that we hope for, and he hopes for, in some kind of relationship to the despair and the things he is coping with.

Team member: Without wanting to labour the religious point, what signs of healing does he see in his congregation? And what would he recognise as healing in himself?

Team member.   This is a question I might have asked earlier. What stopped him when he was down at the pits and looking up the tide tables?

Team member.   Pass.

Process manager.   Pass.

Team member.   Pass.

Team member.   Pass.

Team member.   Pass.

Team member.   Pass.

Team member.   Is it possible that somewhere in his faith he could get a group of people set up who are sort of rooting for him or praying for him? Is there some sort of facility for that, it might not be local, is there some kind of group somewhere that could pray for him so he could feel that support? Thank you.

Team member.   Yes a sort of prayer partner.

Presenter.   Well thank you, everyone. Thanks, that was very useful. I have made a note of what seemed like the most helpful comments. Some of the things you have said I am already doing. The point about repeating the exercise for God as the father figure, following on from the exercise he did writing to the natural father. I think that would be quite useful, because there is that sort of anger towards God for abandoning him and giving him this sort life as some kind of punishment, as his earthly father did by giving his mother a few pieces of silver and disappearing and leaving her to bring him up on her own. The idea you mentioned about his night times. I think one thing he does when he wakes at an unearthly hour is he lies there, and it's always much worse when you are lying down thinking about your worries than if you stand or sit up. It puts a totally different light on things. I think he does lie there and hope he is going to go back to sleep – to think himself back to sleep. Of course it doesn't work – it rarely does! So what's wrong with going down and making a cup of tea, or going down and doing the crossword, or doing something different? As for the point about creative satisfactions, he has got an artistic side and he is planning to learn bridge and he is going to an art class with his wife, which he finds useful. He says, 'We'll do something together and I'll do something fulfilling outside my work role.' He has got friends in other parts of the country. I think some of them are friends he has made through his ministry in other areas and it would be useful to have a prayer partner in some form praying for him, a situation where he feels supported. To have that support would be good. He can't get that support in his particular fellowship, as he says, 'When you are at the top you are on your own,' but maybe he could make use of other peoples' support if they are slightly removed.

Thanks very much I will keep you posted.

[Six months after the final counselling session, the client wrote expressing gratitude for work that had been done in seven sessions of solution-focused counselling. He referred to the 'enormous changes' he had made in his life and said that he and his wife were now enjoying 'the next chapter in their life together'.]

Conclusion

Initially, I felt some tension between the solution-focused tradition of offering clients rather minimalist assignments as possible ways forward, and the 'free flowing' reflecting phase. However, part of the point of the reflecting phase seems to be that it offers the presenter more choices for possible ways forward. And, on reflection, well thought-out minimalist solution-focused interventions often open up more choices for clients where, previously, they were stuck. For me, solution-focused reflecting teams satisfy some questions such as: 'How should creative input and feedback in a self-managed learning group be structured?' and, 'How can a self-managed learning group lead itself most effectively?'

Solution-focused reflecting teams address a need for a mentoring or clinical supervision model for groups of solution-focused practitioners and groups of eclectic practitioners. They also meet a need for support teams that are convened on an *ad hoc* or occasional basis. Following presentation of the model at three European Brief Therapy Association conferences, practitioners in several countries reported that the model was being used to good effect. The Job Retention Team in Bristol has used the model in vocational rehabilitation groups with mixed groups of practitioners and clients, as has the Unemployment Project and Sick Leave Project in Skoghall, Sweden.

Solution-focused reflecting teams have been used by social workers in child protection, with different members of the team speaking for different interests and priorities. Learning support groups have used them and comparisons have been drawn to action learning. They have also been used and valued by business support groups, who have been impressed with the usefulness of meetings involving people with apparently unrelated skills and business interests.

Solution-focused reflecting teams offer a resource-oriented, transparent and structured format which encourages productive and efficient meetings. They are being used creatively by skilled practitioners and by mutual support groups in an expanding range of contexts.

References

Andersen, T. (1987) The Reflecting Team: dialogue and meta dialogue in clinical work. *Family Process*, 26(4): 415–428.

Andersen, T. (1991) *The Reflecting Team*. New York. W.W. Norton.

de Shazer, S. (1988) Utilization: the foundation of solutions. In S. Lankton and J. Zeig (eds), *Developing Ericksonian Therapy* (pp. 112–124). New York: Brunner Mazel.

de Shazer, S. (1991) *Putting Difference to Work*. New York: W.W. Norton.

Dolan, Y. (1998) *One Small Step*. Watsonville, CA: Papier-Mâché Press.

Furman, B. and Ahola, T. (1992) *Solution Talk*. New York. W.W. Norton.

Jackson, P.Z. and McKergow, M. (2002) *The Solutions Focus*. London: Nicholas Brealey.

Miller, S. (1991) A conversation with Scott Miller at his workshop 'Symptoms of Solutions' in London, 2–3 November.

O'Hanlon, B. and Wilk, J. (1987) *Shifting Contexts*. New York: Guilford Press.

Appendix 1

CONDUCTING A SOLUTION-FOCUSED REFLECTING TEAM MEETING
Check for agreement on confidentiality.
Agree the time available and divide it up.
Nominate a timekeeper/process manager who may also participate in the meeting.

Phase	Who speaks? Who listens?	Activity
PREPARING		Each person prepares in advance and is clear about what they hope to gain from the meeting when they take their turn as the presenter
PRESENTING	Only the presenter speaks The team members listen	The presenter describes the situation they would like some help with
CLARIFYING	The team members ask questions The presenter answers	The team members ask open questions in no particular order **Aims:** To understand the situation and the desired outcome of the meeting from the presenter's point of view To understand the client's goals and check that they benefit the client and significant stakeholders – and that the goals are positively stated and actionable To be clear about recognised and unrecognised assets such as: • what is already impressive • ways in which the presenter and/or the client are doing better than they think • progress with ideas, thoughts and actions recently, or since the last meeting To ask open questions in no particular order – questions that invite clarification (leading questions are discouraged)
AFFIRMING	The team members speak in any order The presenter listens and may only speak to thank the team members	Each member of the team tells the presenter briefly what he or she is most impressed with
REFLECTING	The team members speak in sequence The presenter listens	The team members respond to the presenter's presentation Each member says one thing at a time or passes. This cycle continues until everyone has said all they want to say, or they run out of time
CLOSING	The presenter speaks The team listens	The presenter responds briefly to what was said in the reflecting phase, usually stating what they feel is most applicable

16

Solution-Focused Therapy – The Future

Bill O'Connell

A parable

Once upon a time there lived a band of wandering tribespeople who enjoyed telling short stories. They visited other communities and shared with them tales of ordinary but heroic people who overcame great odds in their lives. Those who heard the stories were called customers, because it was the custom to listen to stories!

Their stories were about how people could create their own futures. They were about people's resources, competencies and solutions. They told their customers that 'there was nothing wrong with them that what's right with them can't fix'. These stories sounded like miracles because the characters in them felt empowered in their lives. By the end of a good evening's storytelling, the listeners noticed how they felt better, happier, calmer and more positive. One of the strange things about the stories was that everyone heard them as if they were their own stories.

After hearing them, many people changed their lives and lived by the new story they had heard about themselves. The storytellers became much sought after by people all over the country and abroad.

In another part of the country were tribes who had ancient traditions of telling long stories about the mysteries of life and human behaviour. Their stories illuminated the secret corners in people's lives and helped them to understand why they had the lives they had. These storytellers saw themselves as experts. Their particular expertise lay in telling stories which explained who failed, why they failed and how they failed in life. Many people found these myths helpful, but others decided that the short stories were more satisfying and deserted to the short-story tellers.

The long-story tellers were understandably unhappy about this. They had trained in the secrets of their art for many years and now they saw their knowledge and status being undermined. They dismissed the short-story tellers as 'fast story drive-thru merchants'. Some however tried to introduce short stories into their repertoire but others stayed faithful to the old stories.

Some of the more enthusiastic short-story tellers got carried away and told their audiences that their stories were the *only* stories. They thought they were much better than the long-story tellers who they felt were out of touch with people. Some of the less wise among them would not speak to the long-story tellers and only had meetings with other short-story tellers, where they reminded each other that they were the best.

After a time someone thought it would be a good idea to write down the best stories in a wise book so that people in other countries could read them. They began to argue among themselves about which stories to include. Some of them wanted to make the short stories even shorter. This group became known as One Feathers. After a while their stories became so short that only they understood what they meant. Some people did not join the One Feathers. They kept telling the old stories because they found that more people understood them. They were known as the No Feathers.

In order to sort out this disagreement the two groups turned to one of the people who had started to tell the very first stories. He was known as Two Feathers and was much revered, though not greatly loved. When Two Feathers was pressed about which stories were the best, he said he was happy for people to tell any stories they found helpful. But he was very clear what were his stories and what were other peoples.' This made some of the One Feathers and the No Feathers angry and they broke away. The No Feathers became friends with the Long Story tribe and eventually began to tell short and long stories. The One Feathers joined up with a group of Minimalists who mimed stories instead of telling them.

Eventually some people came to realise that it didn't matter very much which story people told as long as it was helpful to the listeners. They said it was like the story of *The Wizard of Oz*. There was no wise wizard at the end of the Yellow Brick Road, only the message that we could find our own wisdom, our own courage, our own hearts. We could find the grace and strength and wisdom to live our lives in peace and harmony.

As with all good parables, I will not kill it by trying to explain it!

Does the solution-focused approach have a future?

I believe that the model will still be popular 10, 20 years from now because its values and principles are enduringly human. They resonate in peoples' lives. The core values of respect, choice, collaboration, equality and dignity fit the demands of a multi-cultural, multi-racial society in which difference is celebrated. Acting upon a deep respect for the client's expertise is the antidote to the medicalisation and therapisation of life's problems. Solution-focused ideas have swept all before them because they affirm the humanity of both the helper and the helped. They instil hope instead of cynicism and despair; they stimulate change where there was rigidity and inertia; they liberate the best in people.

As this book demonstrates, the growth of the solution-focused philosophy is not restricted to the world of therapy. It has already proved its usefulness as a bridge across professional boundaries. It helps practitioners to transcend territorial disputes by realigning the focus of care to the needs of the person or family. Across the disciplines there is a discernible convergence of values. In education, social work and mental health for example, we find an increasing emphasis on the expertness of the pupil, client and patient. There is a discourse about genuine partnership with service users, although there is much to be done before the talk is walked.

In psychology we are witnessing the emergence of growth psychology which escapes from a preoccupation with pathology and recognises clients as resourceful problem solvers. It acknowledges that most people cope with what life throws at them without seeking professional help. Linley and Joseph (2002) claim that between 30 and 90 per cent of survivors of traumatic incidents report at least some positive changes in their lives consequent on the trauma.

We need to remember too that solution-focused is not a static theory but a living, moving, breathing movement. What has amazed founders of the approach, such as Steve de Shazer, is its penetration into many areas of public life – business; education; mental health; personal social services; work with offenders; with people with learning disabilities; advice and guidance work; coaching; psychology and psychotherapy, to name only a few. Virtually any field which requires good interpersonal skills can benefit from the solution-focused perspective. I personally have taught the skills to groups as diverse as shop stewards; hospital managers; careers officers; drug workers; classroom assistants; mental health workers; residential social workers and marriage counsellors, with perhaps the most unusual being a group of clairvoyants. (They liked the future-oriented aspects of SFBT!)

This rapid expansion has not been accompanied by an infrastructure to support it. In the United Kingdom it is something of a cottage industry with no central focus. As a result, there are many thousands of people who have been enthused by it, but who have been unable to develop their practice beyond short courses. Perhaps the time is right for a National Association for Solution-Focused Therapists to become the public voice of SFBT, registering and accrediting therapists, supervisors, consultants and trainers. It would develop codes of ethics and practice and operate a transparent complaints system. It would take the lead in dialogue with the government and with other professionals in the field. It would promote the solution-focused cause with public bodies which demand evidence of effectiveness and good practice before they will fund and support the work. I suspect however that the 'professionalisation' of SFBT would not be wholly welcome among solution-focused workers themselves. They tend to enjoy their freedom, although at times it makes them look unaccountable. Many like to think they occupy the radical fringe and do not want to be subject to the constraints imposed by the mainstream. While understanding the wish to retain the innovatory and creative dimensions of the work, it seems to me that there are dangers in allowing so many people to call themselves solution-focused counsellors or trainers who have not undergone any substantial training, and who, in some instances, have no professional bodies to whom they are accountable. Such a position does not make it easy to weed out people who may be exploiting or abusing their clients. Whatever the situation in other countries, time is running out in the UK for solution-focused workers to become organised and professional.

Conclusion

Yvonne Dolan (1998) has an exercise she calls 'A letter from the future'. In this exercise the client writes an imaginative letter from some time in the future – say five or ten years. This letter is to a friend and in it the writer describes what life is like for him or her now. I'd like you to imagine that the following is a letter from the future written by solution-focused therapy.

A letter from the future from solution-focused therapy

21 May 2013

I am writing to you my old therapy friend to let you know what is happening in my life at the moment. I am not as young as I used to be. There was a time when I was the new kid on the block, shouting my mouth off about one thing or another. I was a thorn in the side of the therapy establishment. Maybe I was a bit arrogant then. I thought I had discovered the secret of the universe. When the research results came in it taught me a little humility. It was clear I was being helpful, but maybe some of my friends had exaggerated how helpful!

Time has treated me kindly since then. I still hold the ideals I had in my youth. I still feel intolerant of therapists who undermine clients, who lay burdens upon them, who fail to see the qualities and strengths of the people who come through their doors. I still rage at therapists who take over people's lives and set themselves up as experts. But I have had some of my own rough edges knocked off me. I have learned the importance of always listening to the client. I have learned how important the relationship is and that techniques are never a substitute for human warmth and compassion. I have come to realise that we need to understand the way in which we construct language if I am to be allowed to help clients to make changes.

In my old age I have revisited my family roots and discovered a lot of relatives I did not fully appreciate. Alfred Adler, for a start. He was really the man who gave me the miracle question.

I spend a lot of my time in strange places these days, far removed from the therapy room. I enjoy the company of a wide range of people who talk on the same wavelength. I meet teachers, nurses, shop stewards, careers officers, probation officers, classroom assistants, prison officers and others who seem to know me well. I am amazed at organisations which invite me in to change their problem-focused culture. I like being a tool to help people keep on learning throughout their lives. I stand in awe of the creative ways in which I am being used by practitioners working in very challenging situations – in major traumatic incidents, with children who have been tortured and abused, with people in psychiatric hospitals and prisons. I love the way in which workers skilfully adapt me to the needs of their clients.

I also meet some strange people who claim to be me ... but I hardly recognise them. I think there must be more than one way of being me! I am surprised when

I hear people say how simple I am, as if I am only the sum of my rather elegant techniques. I overheard someone the other day saying that 'solution-focused therapy could be written on the back of a teabag'. I don't know why or how some-one could write on the back of a teabag but in fact I am very complicated, particularly in the way I use language. I only wish people would take me seriously and understand the principles, values and philosophy which underpin me. My practice might be simple (although not always easy) but my thinking is very hard!

Anyway ... I thought you would like to know that ten years on I am still alive and kicking!

References

Dolan, Y. (1998) *One Small Step*. Watsonville, CA: Papier-Mâché Press.
Linley, P.A. and Joseph, S. (2002) Post-traumatic growth. *CPJ Counselling and Psychotherapy Journal*, 13(1): 14–17.

Appendix One: Solution-Focused Agencies

- Training, consultancy and supervision

  Focus on Solutions
  Bill O'Connell
  Tel: 0121 422 2525

- Short courses and presentations by international figures are provided by:
  The Brief Therapy Practice
  Tel: 020 8968 0070

- The University of Birmingham offers an MA in solution-focused brief therapy.
  It is delivered in three- or four-day blocks, some of which are at weekends.
  Parts of the course are delivered via the Internet.

For further details contact:
  The University of Birmingham
  Weoley Park Road
  Selly Oak
  Birmingham
  B29 6LL
  Email: m.a.jordan@bham.ac.uk

Index

Adams, J. F., 14
Adams, R., 108
Adler, A., 2, 171
adolescent residential unit staff, outcome-comparison studies, 16
age, and family power issues, 44
Ahola, T., 158
alcohol, 10, 25
    outcome-effectiveness studies, 20
    see also substance misuse
American Psychiatric Association *Diagnostic Manual (DSM-IV)*, 21, 129
    reframing, 3
Andersen, T., 157
anxiety, 25, 26, 34, 84, 106
    'fear of panic', case study, 91–4
    outcome-effectiveness studies, 18
assertiveness groups, 26
Atkinson, Alan, 84
auditory hallucinations, 148
    therapeutic interventions, 153

behavioural parent training, 48, 49, 50
    combining with solution-focused approach, 52
behavioural problems
    social work, 106, 112, 113, 114, 115–16
    work with families, 41, 45–6
    see also parent training; schools
Beier, A., 84, 89
Berg, I. K., 2, 20, 67, 86, 116, 140
Bergin, A., 130
Bergin, S. L., 13
Bertolini, B., 129
Bertolini, R., 119, 123
'best hopes', 41, 62
between-session tasks, 9
    groupwork, 32
    substance misuse, 141, 142
Beyebach, M., 14, 17
Biestek, F. P., 108
Birchwood, 153
Bond, H., 107
Bowie Child and Family Services, 13
Bridgwater Community Mental Health Team, 156, 158
Brief Family Therapy Centre, Milwaukee (Milwaukee group), 12, 18, 20, 21

Brief Therapy Practice, London, 18, 38, 61, 118, 138
Bristol Solutions Group, 156, 158
British Association of Social Workers *Code of Ethics*, 108
Brooker, C., 153
Bruges alcohol clinic, 20
Buddhism, 143, 153
Burnham, J., 110
Burr, W., 19
business support groups, 166

Cade, B., 144
Care Programme Approach (CPA), 80
Catholics, 143
Central Council for Education and Training in Social Work (CCETSW), 108
Child and Adolescent Mental Health Service, 106, 118
child protection, 20, 99, 107, 119, 166
    risk assessment, 107, 119
children
    outcome-effectiveness studies, 17, 19
    see also families; parent training; schools
Children Act, 109
chlorpromazine, 153
classroom teaching, 100–1
client-centred goals, 7, 50–1, 118
client-directedness, 44
client explanations, 2–3
client groups, 1
client responsibility, 133
client–therapist relationship see therapist–client relationship
clients
    alternative stories, 4–5
    benefits of solution focus, 1, 85
    as experts, 39, 79, 90, 108, 130, 140
    focus on strengths, skills and resources, 2, 51, 52, 118, 130, 134–5
    'internal locus of control' and outcomes, 14
    post-therapy enquiry, 13–14
    as problem solvers, 2, 4
    referral to groupwork, 25–6
    socialisation by professionals, 3
    unawareness of technique, 13, 14

clients *cont.*
  usefulness of solution-focused groupwork, 26
  values, and solution-focused view of, 79–80
Cochrane, R., 74
Cockburn, J. T., 16
Cockburn, O. J., 16
cognitive analytical therapy, 91
cognitive-behavioural therapy (CBT), 27, 33–4,
  90–1, 122, 138, 146
Community Care Act, 109
community vs. institutional approach to mental
  health, 74–5
comparison studies, 12, 13, 15–17
competence seeking, 7–8
  group exercise, 31
'competency talk', 40, 45
compliments, 6–7, 9
  affirming in reflecting teams, 160–1
  parent training groups, 51
  social work, 113–14
  work with families, 39–40
  work in higher education, 87, 92
  work in schools, 102
Consumer Reports study (1995), 17
consumerism, 3, 108, 109
Coping Resources Inventory (CRI), 20–1
couples therapy, 61–73
  'best hopes', 62
  case study, 68–72
  couples as individuals, 67–8
  'hopes fulfilled', 62–4
  motivation, 66–7
  the next small step, 65–6
  outcome-comparison studies, 17
  questions as interventions, 66
  what are you already doing that might
    help?, 65
  when it doesn't work, 72
  working without the problem, 61–2
Cruz, J., 19
culture, race and gender issues
  groupwork, 33
  social work, 110–11
  work in higher education, 89–90
  work in schools, 103–4
  work with substance misuse, 143–4
  see also difference issues
Curtis, C., 84, 87, 89

Darmody, M., 20–1
De Jong, P., 2, 18, 20
de Shazer, S., 2, 8, 18, 21, 38, 39, 61, 66, 84,
  86, 118, 121, 133, 151, 154, 170
definition, 2–5, 21
depression, 5, 25, 34, 84, 91, 106, 118, 121

depression, *cont.*
  medication, 123
  outcome-effectiveness studies, 18
Diagnostic Manual (DSM-IV) see American
  Psychiatric Association
difference issues, 121–2
  see also culture, race and gender issues
'dismantling' studies, 13
Dolan, Y., 123, 124, 135, 162, 171
domestic violence, 51, 110
  couples therapy case example, 68–72
  Plumas project, 20, 51
Dominelli, L., 108
drug misuse *see* substance misuse
Duncan, B. L., 13

Eakes, G., 19
eating disorders, 25, 106, 123
  following sexual trauma, 136
education, 59, 169–70
  see also higher education; schools
Edwards, S., 107, 115
efficacy vs. effectiveness studies, 17
Eisengart, S., 12
empowerment, 2, 44, 82, 108–9, 121, 135
Epston, D., 3
Erickson, M., 2
Escher, S., 146, 148
European Brief Therapy Association (EBTA),
  14, 21, 166
Everitt, J., 153
exception seeking, 7, 52, 65, 108
  process research, 13
  work in schools, 97–8, 101, 102
'expertism' 2
Eye Movement Desensitisation and
  Reprocessing (EMDR), 129

facilitation techniques, parent training groups, 49
  case illustration, 55–9
  finding fit, 54, 57–8
  predicting, 53–4, 55–6
  reviewing 54, 56–7
  summarising and planning, 54–5, 58–9
families, 38–47
  case example, 44–6
  convening, 39
  fluidity and client-directedness, 43–4
  joining, 39–40
  power issues, 44
  process research, 14
  what is the family doing to get what it
    wants?, 42–3
  what does the family want?, 40–2
  see also social work

family therapy tradition, 38, 39, 44, 153, 158
feelings
  behaviour, thought and, 34, 111
  'complimenting the emotions', 87
  'experiencing in a balanced way', 92, 93
  parents' desire for children to talk about, 41
'First Person singular therapy', 153
fluidity, 43–4
follow-up sessions
  groupwork, 32–3, 37
  in schools, 95
Ford, A., 112
Formula First Session Task (FFST), 14
Franklin, C., 19
French, L., 84, 87
Freud, S., 146
Furman, B., 158
future focus, 2, 4, 170
  couples therapy, 61–2
  fluidity in family work, 43
  students with unrealistic goals, 102
  work with substance misuse, 139, 144–5
'future video', 30

Garfield, A. E., 13
Garfield, S., 130
Garner, N. E., 16
gender
  and communication, 119–20
  and family power issues, 44
  see also culture, race and gender issues
George, E., 18, 107
Gilbert, R., 84, 88–9
Gilbey, G., 107
Gingerich, W., 12
Global Assessment of Functioning/Global
    Assessment of Relational Functioning, 21
goals and goal setting, 7, 111, 118, 160
  clarity predictive of successful outcome, 14
  groupwork, 30
  parent training, 50–1
  'psychotic' clients, 149
  school students' unrealistic, 102
  social work, 112–13
  work with families, 40–1, 43, 45–6
  work with substance misuse 139–40
Goffman, E., 74
Green, W. P., 153
groupwork, 25–37
  aims and objectives, 28–9
  case studies, 34–6
  culture, race and gender, 33
  developing solution-focused practice, 27
  first session, 29–32
  group composition, 27

groupwork, cont.
  personal reflections, 37
  pre-first session processes, 27–8
  session 2 and beyond, 32–3
  solution-focused and cognitive-behavioural,
    27, 33–4
  usefulness of, 26
  see also parent training
growth psychology, 170

Harris, Q., 110
Hawkes, D., 5
healing-letter exercise, 162
Heery, M. W., 148
Helping Resources Inventory, 20
Henden, J., 156
Hernandez, L., 13
higher education, 84–94
  case study, 91–4
  culture, race and gender, 89–90
  integrating solution-focused therapy, 90–1
  personal reflections, 91
  rationale for using solution-focused
    therapy, 85
  solution-focused practice, 86–9
  see also students
Hoffman, L., 111
Hopwood, L. E., 18
'how' questions, 7–8
Hubble, M. A., 13
Hudson, P., 124

Iliad, 148
institutional vs. community approach to
    mental health, 74–5
interventions, 5–9
Isebaert, L., 20
Iveson, C., 18, 102, 107

Jaynes, J., 148
Johnson, L. D., 16
Joseph, S., 170
Jurich, J. A., 14
just therapy, 123

Kelly, S., 116
Klingenstierna, C., 20
knowledge, local and universal, 4
Kraepelin, E., 148

labels and labelling, 3, 4, 5, 76, 134, 135,
    146, 149, 154
Lachance, K., 80
LaFountain, R. M., 16
Lambert, M. J., 16

language, 5
  difference issues, 122
  importance with substance misusers, 140
learning support groups, 166
Lee, M. Y., 18
Leeds Metropolitan University, 84
Lethem, J., 101–2, 107
letter from the future, 171–2
Lindforss, L., 15
Linley, P. A., 170
Lipchik, E., 67
Littrell, J. M., 14, 19
Lonnen team, Sweden, 14

McCarthy, J., 107
Macdonald, A. J., 15, 18–19
McKeel, A. J., 13
Magnusson, D., 15
management consultancy, 21
Marsh. I., 107
Marshall, W., 108
medication, 123, 150, 151, 152–3
mental health, 107, 110, 74–83, 169–70
  delivery and power, 81–2
  history and construction, 74–5
  outcome-effectiveness studies, 17–19
  perceptions of experience, 75–6
  relationships and values, 76–81
Mental Health Act, 146
Mental Research Institute, California, 2, 122
'message, the', 9
Miller, S. D., 13, 140
Milner, J., 108
miracle question, 8, 171
  couples therapy, 62–4, 68–70, 72
  groupwork, 30
  just the beginning, 63
  not recalled by clients, 14
  process research, 13
  social work, 114
  standard version, 8, 63
  two for one, 63–4
  'wonderful' question with substance
    misusers, 140, 142, 143
  work with clients suffering with
    psychosis, 151
  work with families, 41–2, 46
  work in higher education, 88, 92, 93
  work in schools, 102
  work with women, 91, 121, 125
Morant, N., 82
motivation, 62, 66–7
  couples, 67
  school students, 98–100
multidisciplinary teams, 25, 78, 119

Muslims, 104, 143
Mylan, T., 107

narrative therapy, 111, 123
National Framework for Assessment of
    Children in Need and Their Families, 110
National Health Service (NHS), 118, 119,
    123, 146
  usefulness of solution-focused groupwork, 26
Nehmad, A., 88
'notice' tasks, 9, 28, 31

O'Byrne, P. 108
O'Hanlon, W., 2, 119, 123, 129, 144
obsessive-compulsive disorder, 25, 118
offenders
  outcome-comparison studies, 15
  outcome-effectiveness studies, 20
OQ–45, 16, 21
origins, 1–2, 38
Orthodox Judaism, 110–11
outcome research
  anti-psychotic medication, 153
  criteria for inclusion, 12
  efficacy vs. effectiveness, 17
  outcome-comparison studies, 15–17
  outcome-effectiveness studies, 17–20
outcomes, differing perspectives in mental
    health services, 78–80

parable, 168–9
Parent Effectiveness Training, 49
parent training, 48–60
  becoming solution focused, 50–1
  case study, 55–9
  combined model, 52–3
  outcome-comparison studies, 16
  overview, 48–9
  Parents Plus Programme, 48, 49–50, 53, 59
  principles, 50
  solution building with parents, 53–5
Parton, N., 108
Payne, M., 108
Pearlman-Shaw, K., 90–1
peer counselling, 99
peer review, 12
peer supervision, 84, 88
Peller, J., 86
person-centred counselling, 111, 138
Piercy, F. P., 14
Plumas domestic violence project, 20, 51
Pollard, C., 107
post-modernity, 108
poststructuralism, 5
post-therapy enquiry, 13–14

post-traumatic stress disorder (PTSD), 25, 129
power
    and delivery, in mental health care, 81–2
    issues in families, 44
praise–ignore formula, 50, 55, 56
pre-session change, 6–7
    parent training groups, 55–6
    process research, 13, 14
    social work, 113
    work with substance misuse, 140
Primary Care Mental Health Team, 25
Probation Service, 107
problem-free talk, 6
    work in higher education, 88–9
    work with women, 120, 124
    see also 'competency talk'
process research, 12–15
Prochaska and DiClemente model of
        change, 138, 139, 141
psychodynamic psychotherapy, outcome-
        comparison studies, 16
psychosis, clients suffering with, 123, 146–55
    clinical practice issues 150–2
    collusion 147–9
    as 'difficult' cases, 147
    integrating solution-focused therapy, 152–4
    rationale for using solution-focused
        therapy 149–50

race see culture, race and gender issues
racism, in schools, 104
Rambo, A., 13
randomised controlled trials, 15, 17, 20
Raphael, W. L., 147
Rappaport, I. M., 153
Ratner, H., 18, 107
reality, first and second order, 148–9
rehabilitation, outcome-comparison studies, 16
rehabilitation groups, 166
relationship difficulties, 18, 25, 48, 84, 118
    case study, 124–7
research, 12–24
    future developments, 20–1
    outcome-comparison, 15–17
    outcome-effectiveness, 17–20
    process, 12–15
    with clients suffereing with psychosis, 147
'resistance', 51, 66, 99, 133–4
Romme, E. 146, 148

Santos, A., 80
Sartorius, N., 153
scaling, 9
    child risk assessment, 107
    couples therapy, 65

scaling, cont.
    groupwork, 32, 36
    process research, 13
    social work, 107, 113, 115
    suicide risk assessment, 152
    work with families, 42–3
    work in higher education, 88, 89
    work in schools, 102
    work with substance misuse, 141
    work with women, 126, 127
Scharfetter, C., 153
schizophrenia, 148, 152, 153
    outcome-effectiveness studies, 19
schools, 52–3, 95–105
    case example, 96–8
    culture, race and gender, 103–4
    motivation, 98–100
    solution-focused therapy in teaching, 100–1
    special features, 95–6
    teachers' questions about students, 102–3
    work with younger children, 101–2
    see also students
self-harm, 99, 119
    see also suicide risk
Seligman, M. E. P., 17
sexual trauma, 118, 120, 123, 129–37
    from effects of abuse to responses to
        abuse, 136–7
    from long term to sufficiently long, 130–1
    from pathology to strengths, skills
        and resources, 134–5
    rationale and practice of solution-focused
        therapy, 130
    from 'resistance' to collaboration, 133–4
    from techniques to therapist assumptions,
        131–2
    from therapist to client responsibility, 133
    from victim to survivor and beyond, 135–6
'shadows', 4–5
Shaha, S., 16
Shardlow, S., 108
Shennan, G., 107
Shilts, L., 13
Smith, M. 146
social constructionism, 108, 143
social exclusion, 75, 110
social injustice, 122
Social Services Inspectorate, 109–10
social work, 106–17, 169–70
    case studies, 112–16
    culture, race and gender, 110–11
    how solution-focused approach is
        used, 107–8
    integrating solution-focused practice, 111
    outcome-comparison studies, 16

social work, *cont.*
  personal reflections, 111–12
  rationale for using solution-focused practice,
    106–7
  solution-focused approach and legislation,
    109–10
  solution-focused approach and values, 108–9
  solution-focused practice, 107
  solution-focused reflecting teams, 166
socio-economic class, 18, 19, 20
solution-focused approach, 1–11
  definition, 2–5
  future for, 168–72
  guidelines, 10–11
  interventions, 5–9
  language, 5
  origins, 1–2, 38
  'professionalisation', 170
solution-focused reflecting teams, 139,
    156–67
  in action, 161–5
  clinical supervision, 158–61
  the reflecting team, 157–8
  and solution-focused therapy, 156–7
STEP programme, 49
stress-related problems, 84
students
  outcome-comparison studies, 16
  outcome-effectiveness studies, 19
  process research, 14
  see also higher education; schools
substance misuse, 4, 48, 99, 112, 133, 138–45
  action, 142
  case study, 144–5
  contemplation, 142
  maintenance, 142–3
  outcome effectiveness studies, 18, 20
  preparation, 142
  (re)lapse, 143–4
  see also alcohol
suicide risk, 119, 123, 125, 152, 162
Sumedho, A., 91
Sundman, P., 112
systemic thinking, 111
  see also family therapy tradition

techniques *see* interventions
therapist-client relationship
  collaborative nature, 2, 120, 129–30, 133–4
  effectiveness and, 12–13
  importance, 6, 150
  joining with families, 39–40
  relating patterns, and outcomes, 14

therapists (helpers)
  assumptions about clients, 62, 66–7, 131–2
  benefits of solution-focused approach, 1, 22,
    85, 112, 124
  guidelines, 10–11
  respectful curiosity, 4, 52, 134
  usefulness of solution-focused groupwork, 26
Thomas, F. N., 16
Thompson, R., 19
treatment and testing orders, 138
Triantafillou, N., 16
Turnell, A., 107, 116
Turner, J., 107

unexperienced experience model, 129
Universidad Pontifica, Salamanca (Salamanca
  group), 14, 17–18

values
  and relationships, in mental health care,
    76–81
  social work, 108–9
Vaughn, K., 19
Vietnam veterans, 129
Vuysse, S., 20

Wade, A., 136
Waldegrave, C., 122
Wallgren, K., 20
Walsh, T., 107
Walter, J., 86
Warner, R., 152
Watzlawick, P., 148–9
Weakland, J., 2
Webster-Stratton, C., 49
Weiner-Davis, M., 123, 124
Wheeler, J., 16
White, M., 3, 86, 89–90
Wittgenstein, L., 147
women, 118–28
  the art of juggling, 120
  case study, 124–7
  empowerment, 121
  integrating solution-focused therapy, 122–3
  issues of difference, 121–2
  personal reflections, 123–4
  the perspective of others, 120–1
  rationale for using solution-focused therapy,
    118–19
  ways of talking about problems, 119–20
  Working Together to Safeguard Children, 110

Zimmerman, T. S., 16–17